THE AMERICAN COLONIAL MIND AND THE CLASSICAL TRADITION

THE AMERICAN COLONIAL MIND AND THE CLASSICAL TRADITION

ESSAYS IN COMPARATIVE CULTURE

RICHARD M. GUMMERE

HARVARD UNIVERSITY PRESS
CAMBRIDGE, MASSACHUSETTS

1963

Publication of this volume has been aided
by a grant from the Ford Foundation.

Distributed in Great Britain by Oxford University Press, London
Library of Congress Catalog Card Number: 63-20767
Printed in the United States of America

TO C. R. G.

The thought of our past years in me doth breed
Perpetual benediction. — WORDSWORTH

PREFACE

THIS book is concerned with a topic that has never been treated as a whole — the impact of Greek and Roman ideas on the lives and thoughts of the men who settled and colonized America from the Jamestown of 1607 to the establishment of the United States in 1789.

For a clear understanding of these personalities and activities, it has seemed best to present their indebtedness in the form of essays, largely biographical, rather than in an impersonal "thesaurus" of parallels or quotations, statistically classified. A selective process, dealing with certain significant individuals and episodes, clarifies the relationship of the colonial mind to the ancient heritage and furnishes enough total unity to reveal a definite cultural stage of Western civilization.

If it is true that history repeats itself, we shall gain by a backward glance at the Wessex of King Alfred, which was civilized by the aid of Latin theology. We may note the efforts of Charlemagne and Alcuin to create a pseudo-Renaissance. The long arm of medieval scholasticism resulted in the sharpening of both sacred and university education. Petrarch and the humanists, Erasmus, and Montaigne set the individual free with the help of the ancient testimony. The Elizabethan dramatists, North in his *Plutarch*, Goethe, Winckelmann, all found a new freedom in the classical tradition. The Golden Age of Burke and Gibbon, the later obligations of Matthew Arnold, T. S. Eliot, and Eugene O'Neill, were explorations in the Hellenic field, where the literature of the Renaissance gave a new life to current interests. These epochs fall into line as parts of a long series of inspirational change, with material fortified by Greece and Rome. The strength of the classics has been not only their essential vitality, but their contribution to contemporary cultures. It is almost a paradox, this variety of influence stemming from the serene continuity of a great heritage.

My objective is to let these architects of the New World speak for themselves, as did the articulate leaders noted above. It is clear that the classics cannot survive if they stand majestically alone, if, as some recent correspondents in the *Times Literary Supplement* (November 9, 1962), analyze the situation, they do not "make clear their living virtues" and "receive contemporary interpretation." Their continuity calls for comparative study, by the layman as well as the scholar, in these days when technical science is dominant and the humanities suffer from a loosely defined status. It is not mere imitation or reflection that counts: it is a process of *refraction* that created this noteworthy trend of ideas in the nearly two centuries of American colonial development.

Our colonial predecessors did not force their study of the ancient sources into group patterns. Instead of theorizing, or seeking a strict and logical arrangement of ideas, they took from the past whatever was relevant to their own concerns and transmuted the material into their own language. The Terentian motto, *Quot homines, tot sententiae*, held good for Americans of the seventeenth and eighteenth centuries. They cut the Gordian knot of complicated theoretical or political arguments and restated the cases to suit their own views. At least until the Revolution they were intensely local. At all times they were pragmatic rather than philosophical. Province differed from province. The Law of Nature was interpreted from many viewpoints; and it was not a clearly accepted principle until the Declaration of Independence spelled it out for the thirteen colonies. We shall see that the democratic element in the *Politics* of Aristotle was anathema to John Winthrop but a panacea to James Otis and Samuel Adams. Plato as a political scientist was not taken seriously by the colonial statesmen, notably so in the case of Jefferson and

John Adams. But to religious leaders, such as Increase Mather, William Penn, and John Witherspoon, he was "an aid to those who would live in the spirit." Some regarded Ovid as a dangerous libertine; but Samuel Sewall, a conscientious *censor morum*, indulged his habit of writing Latin verses after the manner of the exiled Roman poet. The reality of witchcraft was taken literally by the two Mathers; but the Salem trials were denounced by Robert Calef, who objected to the Greek and Roman parallels cited by their supporters. Science, in company with the classics, progressed from the medieval theories of natural philosophy to the practical discoveries of a later John Winthrop and the researches of Logan, Franklin, and Bartram.

With all this variety of opinion, the Greco-Roman testimony served as material for churchmen and deists, Tories and patriots, country squires and city merchants, men of learning and self-educated seekers after the equivalent of college. Their treatment of this heritage was informal. To prove a point in a controversy, the same classical passage frequently served as an argument for each side. Texts were often quoted from memory and occasionally altered to suit the circumstances. The colonists played, so to speak, by ear. They were "amateurs" rather than "professionals"; and their leaders, who were interested in the spirit rather than in the techniques of Greece and Rome, would have understood the recommendation of Howard Mumford Jones in his *Ideas in America*: "Instead of bringing America to Greece and Rome, we should seek to discover what it is that Greece and Rome have to bring to America."

I may illustrate what I mean by mentioning two later Americans whose treatment of the classics reminds us of this pre-Revolutionary attitude. Emerson's method was characteristic. In college he "resolved to make himself acquainted with the Greek language and antiquities and history with long and serious attention and study, *though always with the assistance of circumstances*" (R. L. Rusk, *The Life of Ralph Waldo Emerson*). He was not copying: he was digesting and weighing the evidence, and applying it. James Russell Lowell, in his tribute to Agassiz, recommended a somewhat similar procedure:

> Let me treat him largely. I should fear
> If with prying eye I chanced to err,
> Mistaking catalogue for character.

It is this flexible human approach that I hope these essays may encourage — one that is congenial to the general intelligent reader who sees the connection of the Greco-Roman heritage with his law or politics, his art or science, his economics or philosophy. This interest partly accounts for the current increase of plays, motion pictures, novels, biographies, and translations of ancient masterpieces. Such readers may or may not have studied the original languages; but they are attracted by the ideas which have moved thinking men for centuries. In any case, it is almost axiomatic that the more the scholar makes his findings clear to the layman, the more valuable is his contribution.

There are several temptations which the critic or reader must resist in any survey of early American writings and speeches. In the first place, the evidence furnished by the colonists themselves makes unnecessary all the modern propaganda on "the value of the classics." What the classics did to inspire the American public with intellectual ammunition in the days before the country became a nation might serve as an example of effective realism. The enthusiast for Greek and Latin should also understand that window dressing must be distinguished from fundamental ideas, symbolically or realistically expressed. Slogans, tags, and random uses of mythology are no proofs of classical knowledge, for they were often learned by heart for publicity purposes. Again, a too rhapsodic reliance on "the grandeur and the glory" of Rome and Greece is a handicap to an accurate diagnosis of the true influences. One must, furthermore, allow for pedantry. Cotton Mather, author of the fascinating *Magnalia Christi Americana*, wrote his books and pamphlets with Greek and Latin volumes marked and propped up at his elbow, in contrast to John Dickinson who correlated the old and the new with logical identification. Another inaccurate impression, prevalent today, is the assumption that the colonial writers, especially in the field of political science, derived their ideas only through the medium of standard British and European masters and that ancient authorities received little direct application. The evidence (particularly in Chapters Six, Ten, and Eleven) indicates that ancients and moderns were equally consulted. It is true that Pufendorf, Harrington, Locke, Montesquieu, and others were familiar reading, that busy men sometimes turned to historical summaries like those of Adam Ferguson and the Abbé Mably. But the briefest glance at the activities of colonial leaders, from Nathaniel Ward and the Mathers to Madison and Jefferson, will indicate that they were entirely at home in Latin and in many cases, especially the clergy, in Greek.

There are some outworn arguments which need not be elaborated in these chapters. I hesitate to enter into the centuries-old controversy of the *querelle des anciens et des modernes*. It is out of date, especially since modern criticism has given us sounder definitions of classicism and romanticism, showing that they are associates rather than enemies. Most important of all, I cheerfully leave to the expert and the research historian those problems of American political or religious or literary significance which are raised so often as a result of new discoveries and interpretations. The classicist should not pose as an authority on American history; and the American scholar should welcome reliable evidence based on the background of Greece and Rome. It is not the classicist's function to decide whether the rebel Bacon or Governor Berkeley was right, whether the Constitution is a democratic or an aristocratic creation, or whether Samuel Adams was a statesman or a demagogue. It is idle to compare two such distinctive poets as Edward Taylor and Philip Freneau, the one a mystic and the other (*malgré lui*) a satirist on the order of Juvenal. My objective is to make clear the various ways in

which the colonists used classical sources for illustration of
their own ideas and problems.

Although this phase of the colonial mind has never been
presented synoptically, there are certain branches that have
been treated with skill and distinction, recognition of which
will be recorded in my notes and bibliographies. Educational
statistics and curricula are available. The relation of theology
to academic learning has been clarified. The ancient sources of
the Constitution have been studied. Greek and Latin books in
the libraries of Virginia planters, Philadelphia merchants, or
New England divines are fully listed. Modern studies in the
field of pure literature are appearing in growing numbers. We
have come to see that the classical heritage ranks as a good
third to the Bible and the English Common Law and that the
Celtic or Teutonic element does not play much of a part until
the nineteenth century, except for Jefferson's and John Dickinson's special interest in Germanic origins.

Since this book is intended for the layman as well as the
scholar, translations are supplied, in most cases from the Loeb
Classical Library, except where the meaning is obvious. Notes
are used sparingly, following the advice of Winston Churchill,
who remarked that they should be "life-lines rather than tow-
lines." In addition to the notes and brief bibliographies arranged at the back of the book, fully documented articles by
the author, from which these chapters have grown, are mentioned for the convenience of the scholar. Finally, the reader
may be reminded that, because the characters in these pages
are selected for their significance as humanists rather than for
their prominence in American history, he will miss the names
of Jonathan Edwards, Tom Paine, and some other outstanding
personalities. The main thread here is the colonial reaction to
the classical tradition.

Those who are interested in further reading along these
lines will find helpful the series known as Our Debt to Greece
and Rome (Boston: Marshall-Jones Company, 1922–1926;
New York: Longmans, Green, 1927—). The microfilming
and the gradual publication of the complete writings of John

Adams, Jefferson, Franklin, and Hamilton will delight both the historian and the general reader.

I am grateful for editorial permission to use, in whole or in part, my articles from the following journals: *Proceedings of the American Philosophical Society*, *The American Quarterly*, *Harvard Studies in Classical Philology*, *The Harvard Library Bulletin*, *The Boston Public Library Quarterly*, *Transactions of the Colonial Society of Massachusetts*, *The Classical Journal*, *The Classical Weekly*, *The Essex Institute Historical Collections*, *The Maryland Historical Magazine*, *The Pennsylvania Magazine of History and Biography*, and *The Philological Quarterly*. Special thanks are due to the officials of Widener and Houghton Libraries of Harvard University, the trustees of the Boston Public Library, the Massachusetts Historical Society, the American Antiquarian Society, the Historical Society of Pennsylvania, and especially to the American Philosophical Society, which has generously continued a grant to carry on studies in this field.

Besides certain friends and colleagues who have made helpful suggestions (most of them acknowledged in the bibliographies and notes), I should like to offer special thanks to the following: Howard Mumford Jones, whose comprehensive knowledge of colonial Americana has been generously available at all times; Berthold L. Ullman, who furnished an extensive list of ancient and modern topics and sources, besides encouraging the publication of articles in the field of colonial classics; and Zeph Stewart, who read the manuscript with constructive criticism. To Clive Foss, my research assistant, I am greatly indebted. Last but not least, the patience and understanding of my wife has made any tribute of mine inadequate.

R. M. G.

Cambridge, Mass.
May 1963

CONTENTS

THE AMERICAN
COLONIAL MIND
AND THE
CLASSICAL TRADITION

It was no little rivulet that flowed from Greece into our city, but a mighty river of culture and learning. — CICERO, *De republica*

A really cultivated mind is made up of all the minds of preceding ages. — FONTENELLE, *Digression sur les anciens et les modernes*

I should as soon think of closing all my window-shutters to enable me to see, as of banishing the classics to improve Republican ideas. — JOHN ADAMS TO BENJAMIN RUSH, 1789

THE CLASSICAL BACKGROUND
OF THE COLONIAL MIND

In the period between the first Virginia settlement and the formation of the United States, there was more circulation of ideas, more interaction of conflicting philosophies, than is usual in the history of colonies. There are several historical reasons for this intellectual activity. With but one or two exceptions, the American founders were men with a college education; in most cases their venture was more than merely commercial; and nearly all had in mind some workable ideal. Although trading corporations and stock companies played a part in prompting and organizing colonization, the religious motive was emphasized, and in every charter that was granted the right of the individual to the English Common Law was assumed.

Another ingredient, however, has been only fragmentarily studied. It is well worth while to investigate the extent to which the classical tradition affected the education, the statecraft, the church, the literature, and later the art of the North American colonies from the first settlements to the birth of the nation. This classical tradition penetrated deeply into the speeches and writings, the formal and informal language of provincial Americans. Their intellectual life reflected such a background. If one agrees with Jefferson as witness and with Stuart P. Sherman as critic, it is clear that between 1607 and 1789 this inheritance from Britain and Europe merged into the spirit of the age and became a progressive force rather than a relic of antiquity. According to Sherman: "It is insufficiently recognized that in the third quarter of the eighteenth century America, like England, was at the height of her classical period. I mean the period when statesmen, poets, and painters most deliberately and successfully imitated the examples of the ancients. The public characters of Washington and his friends, like those of Burke and his friends, were in the grand style, were in a style more or less consciously moulded upon that of the great Republicans of England, Rome, and Athens." [1]

From the very beginning, the American settler seems to have combined an ingenuity in solving the problems of taming a wilderness and adapting himself to a pioneering experiment with a persistent retention of the mores and cultural values brought overseas from the mother country. George Mason, in a letter of 1766, "To the Committee of Merchants in London," explaining the attitude of provincial America, borrowed a passage from the *Epistles* of Horace: "In crossing the Atlantic Ocean, we have only changed our climate, not our minds: our natures and dispositions remain unaltered." [2] Even in the case of illiterates (and there were many who had to be content with "making their mark"), this culture was looked upon with respect. History shows that the buckskin-clad explorer or the tree-ringing farmer, after establishing himself in his new surroundings, turned back eastward for the materials of his education. For example, when the new settlement at Lexington, Kentucky, had got under way, one of its first actions was the purchase of standard classical authors and the planning of a seminary. [3] In spite of all the numerous controversies that we note in colonial history — frontier versus seaboard, radical versus conservative — the transatlantic cultural pattern held good.

The prevalence of the homeward-looking motif is exemplified by an old woodcut portraying George Sandys, translator of Ovid's *Metamorphoses* and the first Englishman to do his poetical work on the American continent, lying in meditation on a Virginia beach, holding a volume of the Latin poet. His costume is full-dress Elizabethan. A ship, reminder of the mother country, lies in the offing, with sails unfurled. [4] At this time there were many exchanges back and forth in college attendance between Britain and America. Pulpit duties and responsible positions were offered by the British. Of the forty-five Harvard graduates up to 1650, twenty-eight went "home" to take up work in England, some of them permanently. Attendance at foreign universities, especially from the southern colonies, continued until the Revolution. The theological training of Ernest Muhlenberg, the Pennsylvania-German clergyman, was based on Latin: he took his diploma at the University of Halle and wrote several books on botany in the Latin tongue. Increase Mather held degrees on both sides of the Atlantic, and he was equally at home in pulpit and in council chamber. William Byrd of Westover received nearly all of his education in Holland and England: he was a Virginian in the colonies and an Englishman in London. From John Winthrop, Jr., to Benjamin Franklin, scientific attainments were honored in the Old World no less than in the New. On the whole, in cases where the reason for emigrating to America was a search either for more liberty or for more elbowroom, the geographical change did not mean any alteration in the "imponderables."

With all of this deep-seated loyalty to the home traditions, there was the greatest variety of opinion throughout the colonies themselves. The same classical source was interpreted in different ways at different times. The metaphysical Aristotle, who reigned supreme in the college world of early provincial days, gave way to the political Aristotle, who became the ultimate source for the Constitution. The Law of Nature, illustrated by Cicero, the Stoics, and the Roman legalists, was perhaps the most invoked doctrine of colonial times. At first, especially in New England, it was kept strictly in second place as a handmaiden to seventeenth-century theology and scholastic philosophy, in the form of the Divine Law. But with the increasing interest in classical testimony, it was recognized as an equal partner of the Christian message. The Law of Nature became the chief slogan for local self-government, in the tracts of John Wise, in the writings and speeches of James Otis, and continued with increasing force in the appeals of Samuel Adams and the final statement of the Declaration of Independence. Even John Dickinson, who stressed constitutional legality, praised this Law as an antidote to internal taxation, with plentiful allusions to antiquity. It was the panacea for colonial political troubles and the watchword of the sometimes interrupted but inevitable march toward democracy. Jonathan Mayhew and Samuel Davies preached it from their pulpits; and the Tory Jonathan Boucher filled his collection of sermons with cautionary parallels to cases of Greek and Roman resistance to authority.

In order to understand the colonial attitude toward this classical tradition, we may observe its effect on the non-scholar, the average citizen. Its prevalence both in Old and New England is proved by a protest of the Reverend Thomas Hooker of Connecticut, a most learned and essentially democratic leader in a tract written before emigrating to America: "I have sometimes admired [wondered] . . . why a company of Gentlemen, Yeomen, and poore women, that are scarcely able to know their A.B.C. . . . have a Minister to speake Latine, Greeke, and Hebrew, and to use the Fathers, when it is certaine, they know nothing at all: they goe to hell hood-winckt." [5] This understandable advice, appropriate to the situation of a pioneer pastorate, would have been superfluous in eighteenth-century Charleston. John Rutledge recorded the activities of Mr. Timothy, the editor of the *South Carolina Gazette*, when he was irritated by the new tax: "Mr. T. was so breathless he ran out of English, and imported a font type in the Greek alphabet and used it liberally, with thoughtful translations, so that anyone could know what had happened to the tyrants of Syracuse and Sparta. Mr. Gadsden was also breathless about it, in Latin and Hebrew as well as English." [6] Gadsden himself resigned from the Charleston Library Society because the organization rejected his suggestion of spending 70 percent of its annual appropriation on the purchase of Greek and Latin classics.

Other chapters will deal with individuals and issues on a larger scale. But one catches the spirit of a nation or a community from its everyday affairs and through the by-products of its culture. Perhaps the most pervasive popular vehicle of communication was the almanac. There are no reliable statistics on American literacy before 1870, when the Census first gave the national figures. But the almanac, with its extensive circulation among farmers and tradesmen during the colonial period, indicates a high standard of intelligence.[7] Along with astronomical calculations, the horoscope, zodiac signs, comets, and weather or crop conditions, the editors reserved a certain amount of space for the airing of their own ideas, whether in the form of essays or of original verse, with classical illustrations predominating. The first almanacs appeared in New England. Forty-one out of forty-four issues before 1687 were edited by Harvard graduates as a sort of volunteer assignment. The progress of science from astrology to astronomy, from the cosmology of Aristotle to Kepler, Galileo, Gassendi, and Copernicus, went hand in hand with ancient mythology and history. To what extent the readers coasted over the technical terms to find the positions of the "houses" and the conjunction of the planets we cannot tell; but the interpretation by some "scholler" was less interesting to the fireside gatherings than the prose or verse in which the editor tried his literary wings, with a view to instruction and entertainment. Samuel Danforth, for instance, in the 1648 number hailed the approach of March in a breezy couplet: "Awake, ye Westerne nymphs, arise and sing,/ And with fresh tunes salute your welcome Spring." The 1650 issue, edited by Urian Oakes, later president of Harvard, furnished readers with a brief compendium of history, beginning with the Roman Empire.

This almanac atmosphere is redolent of ancient mythology and folklore. "Pluvius" bestows refreshing showers. The healing Sun, in the guise of Apollo, weds "Faire Tellus" (Earth).

A complete package is offered for May 1656, covering the signs of Taurus, Aries, and Gemini — a progress toward summer weather:

> Now Sol hath 'scaped the Oxes horn,
> The Ram, the winds, the stormes and harms;
> The loving Twins, by Leda born
> Will entertain him in their arms.

With or without acknowledgment, but often with explanatory comment, the editors draw on Ovid, Cato, Vergil, Cicero, Seneca, and particularly the *Astronomica* of Manilius, whose pictorial representation of the zodiac signs by various parts of the human body is customary in colonial almanacs. Cotton Mather in 1683 has recourse to original Latin verse in recommending diligent Bible reading, with a background of classical learning. The significance of comets, Pliny's explanation of rainbows, the mysterious *primum mobile*, and the difficult problem of the eternity of the Universe were boldly discussed by these young purveyors of knowledge. We may select one especially interesting idea, found in Israel Chauncy's 1664 calendar — a motto from the fortieth chapter of Isaiah, with the often quoted story of the Creation in Ovid's *Metamorphoses*: "Though all other animals are prone and fix their gaze upon the earth, He gave to man an uplifted face, and bade him stand erect and turn his eyes to heaven." [8] But contemporary problems are not ignored: the almanac of 1676, in the troubled period of King Philip's War, concludes with the Vergilian cry: *Dabit Deus his quoque finem* (Even to these sufferings God will put an end). This was a pagan litany often used by the early settlers. The infiltration of such academic learning reveals an interest in the classical heritage, often in diluted form but nonetheless effective.

Franklin's pamphlets, with the sources adapted and made his own, especially the proverbs of Aesop and Publilius Syrus, stand out from all other almanacs. In the Middle Colonies the change from general information to controversy and satire was a natural development. Daniel Leeds, who began a series in 1687 which was continued by his sons Titan and Felix, filled his calendars with religious and political quarrels until 1746. Daniel, an ally of the renegade George Keith in a Quaker schism, provoked for his friend the best nickname in colonial history — "Proteus Ecclesiasticus." Even these editors were armed with the satire and sarcasm of Horace and Juvenal; but their best efforts ran second to the inimitable Poor Richard. We must return to New England for a really distinctive dynasty of editors, whose publications reflect the contemporary scene with sympathetic understanding.

The almanacs of the Ames family began with Captain Nathaniel Ames and ran from 1725 to 1775. While the first publications illustrate the pattern of astrology tending toward scientific awareness, with its by-product of instruction plus entertainment, and while those of the Middle Colonies were mostly local in focus, the Ames series became the mouthpiece of provincial patriotism. Just as poetry began with the idealistic meditations of Anne Bradstreet and Edward Taylor, culminating in the classical satire of Freneau and Trumbull, and just as the theses of college seniors became increasingly concerned with public issues rather than with metaphysics, so the pre-Revolutionary almanac became an instrument of patriotic propaganda.

Nathaniel Ames III, in 1767, presented a plea for agriculture as the secret to colonial happiness, reproducing the famous apostrophe of Vergil to the Italian farmer: "Oh! ye husbandmen, how happy would ye be, did ye know your own advantages!" [9] The year 1772 brought forth a trumpet call for freedom, commending and advertising John Dickinson's "Attic eloquence and Roman spirit," with plaudits for *The Letters from a Farmer in Pennsylvania*. The second Ames, who seems to have relied on Dryden's translations, was worried by Land Bank problems and went to Horace for a pessimistic comment on the current slackening of Puritan standards.[10] His son, however, who is reported to have been the composer, in Latin and English, of an inscription for a bust of Pitt in 1766, preached in the style of Samuel Adams: " 'Twas toil that taught the Romans how to conquer: from the Plough they led their legions on to war." With dark warnings about disguised "Caligulas" and other exhortations, he printed his weather calculations and news. In January we find: "Saturn and Venus do joyn here/ With Mars, to meet Heaven's charioteer." In March: "The Ram that bore fair Hellaen once away/ Hath made dark night equal to lightsome day." April brings some Ovidian advice to sailors: "Smooth-faced Thetis bids you hoist your sails."

The Virginia almanac, a late starter, was a sprightlier creation. An "Ode to Tobacco," in the Williamsburg number of 1772, recommends the weed, as did William Byrd fifty years before:

> Mix the cool juices of the Rhenish vine,
> Nor envy Horace his Falernian wine.
> Thy worth in Virgil's sacred page had shone,
> And a fifth Georgic had been all thy own.

Amid pastorals and *vers de société* we find occasional scholarly allusions. A Virginia issue contains, along with the human-body zodiac, a *Spectator*-like essay on pleasure, mentioning Varro's collected definitions or opinions on happiness and referring to Lucian's "catalogue of the Notions of several Philosophers." It turns finally to the superiority of Socrates' definition of the body as dross over the Egyptian theory of bodily preservation.

Echoes of antiquity reveal themselves on unexpected occasions in the workaday lives of the colonists. At a Virginia council meeting in 1625, Mr. Pooley the clergyman and Thomas Pawlett clashed over church policies, tobacco, and tithes. "The lie was passed," and Pawlett "taxed Mr. Pooly with speaking false Latten and teaching false doctrines." The story in Livy, of Tarquin cutting off the tallest poppyheads (in other words, getting rid of the most prominent opponents), is a frequent citation in colonial annals.[11] In 1634 Samuel Mathews, a council member, protested to Governor

Harvey of Virginia against the "calling away of citizens from private labours to any service of the Governor's upon any colour whatsoever." When Harvey disagreed, Mathews "turned his back and with his truncheon lashed off the heads of certain high weeds" — a prophetic action which ended in Harvey's removal. The same figure was used by Captain Phips in New England (1768), when the plan to try Americans in English courts was broached: "Will they not think that those who support the rights of the people are, like Tarquin's poppies, to be cut off for over-topping the rest?" John Adams, in his *Discourses on Davila*, applies it to the "liquidations" of the French Revolution.

Diaries, correspondence, and memoranda reveal spontaneous interest in classical antiquity. Richard Lee II wrote in his journal in Greek, Latin, and Hebrew. His library included Florus, Orosius, Corderius, Homer, Horace, Lucian, Vergil, Ovid, and Cicero. It was said of another Virginian by the mother of his inamorata that "until he understands Latin he will never be able to win a young lady of family and fortune to be his wife." William Byrd proposed to his second spouse in Greek, with the whimsical request that she reply in English, "to Mr. *Ornis*." The Latin of the lawcourts and of tombstone inscriptions[12] was taken for granted, even if the unlettered were mystified. Newspaper articles, full of historical references, were circulated all along the Atlantic seaboard. One wonders how Samuel Adams got across the Latin similes which seemed to stimulate his Liberty Boys. We cannot take literally the humorous saying of Jefferson, that "American farmers are the only farmers who can read Homer," [13] or the repeated superlative of John Adams that all Yankees were Jacobins and their own lawyers. But we can rate the colonial mind high on the basis of mental aptitude.

Two attractive cases of nonacademic amateur interest in ancient literature will further illustrate its prevalence in the colonies. John Saffin of Bristol kept a commonplace book in which he entered some imitative verse, stories from Plutarch, even an echo of Lucretius, and quotations of every descrip-

tion. He had worked his way up from a Plymouth apprenticeship, marrying the daughter of Thomas Willet, the first
mayor of New York. In Boston he became a judge, speaker
of the house, and a councillor. Though he did not enter the
door of learning, he looked wistfully in at the window. We
meet with some typical seventeenth-century doggerel, "Soll
and Luna and the fermament/ Seem to instruct us how we
should lament," which was a brief elegy on the death of
Charles Chauncy, the president of Harvard. A neighbor, the
book collector Samuel Lee, is called a "Scaliger," a "Cicero."
The Roman orator's praise of history as "the messenger of
antiquity" is recorded by Saffin, as it was also by the Mathers
and many others. Francis Quarles, the author of *Emblemes,*
is called upon, without acknowledgment, for several lyric
loans. Besides his extensive reading in translated classics, Saffin
produced a grammatical word play, perhaps original, perhaps
taken in garbled form from some textbook: "Nature *declines*
men through all the cases, *viz.* Nominative by Pride, Genitive
by Luxury, Dative by Bribery, Accusative by Deception,
Vocative by Adulation, Ablative by Extortion." We should
smile at these efforts were it not for the fact that no publication was intended by the recorder, and that the dog-eared
volume represented an attempt to compensate for missed opportunities.

Another interesting case is that of John Smith of Burlington, son-in-law of James Logan. His father was a West Jersey
councillor, and he himself was appointed to that position in
1753. His brother Richard was a delegate to the First Continental Congress, and another brother wrote a history of the
province in 1765. Obviously, his home atmosphere was a
cultivated one; but no one knows about his schooling, presumably a dame school and private tutoring. Like many
Middle Colony men of the period, he entered business at an
early age. In any case, there was no nearby advanced institution to attend, and he was well on in years before the College
of Philadelphia opened its doors. At sixteen he was translating
the *Colloquies* of Corderius and reading French with ease

His library contained English and French translations of Plato, Middleton's Cicero, Seneca, and Epictetus, Gordon's Tacitus, Savage's *Select Collection of Letters of the Ancients,* Dacier's life of Pythagoras, Whiston's *Josephus,* and Kennett's *Antiquities of Rome.* His chief literary accomplishment was a series of essays in the *Pennsylvania Chronicle* over the name of "Atticus," imitative of the *Spectator* and replete with classical allusions. Since they ran in seventy numbers from 1767 to 1770, they evidently possessed a local appeal. A friend and collaborator with Franklin in many projects, he represents the typical cultivated amateur.

The vocabulary of this colonial period reveals many words which are out of use today, and many which are closer to their Latin derivation. Omitting the technical terms of the botanist or astronomer — those that are in most cases the permanent possession of scientists of all eras — as well as certain manufactured slogans, the industrious etymologist can assemble nearly two hundred archaic usages that were normal at the time. We can easily identify *ingenate, incautelous, politure, maculation, irritament, exauctorate.* The King's Charter of 1606, with a glance back into Roman history, gave to Sir Thomas Gates the authority to "deduce a colony into that part of America commonly called Virginia." Other words now in use have changed their meaning. *Notify* meant to make a *thing* public. *Imbecility* cast no slurs on a person's mental powers: it signified weakness of body or of situation. To us *security* implies safety: to the colonist it was the equivalent of freedom from worry. On his voyage home from England in 1755, the Reverend Samuel Davies meditated happily on "*complacential* surveys of Divine things." [14] The meaning is clear; the usage is rare even for those days.

Nathaniel Ward, author of the "Simple Cobbler of Agawam," in his capacity as a skeptical humorist, whimsically piles up astonishing coinages and combinations, pilfering from the lexicon or inventing curiosities of his own: "Polypiety is the greatest impiety in the world"; "Take away the *vericulum* out of the world, and it under-worlds all." A diatribe on women's dress lampoons "nugiperous gentle-dames who deck themselves out in *nudius-tertian* [day-before-yesterday] fashions." Such a desire for display produces "preterpluralities of Taylors in London." An upholder of the middle-ground doctrine, he scores "Seekers, looking for Nuntios from Christ." He laments the misunderstandings between Presbyterians and "Plebsbyterians." Words like *quisquilian* (miscellaneous), *Indenominable quaemalry*, "direful dilacerations," *mundicidious* (world-destroying), appear in the extreme baroque coinage of the seventeenth century. Heretics "interturbe the state with Amalekitish onsets." Misguided persons desire "not satisfaction but satisdiction." "True religion is *Ignis Probationis,* which doth *congregare homogenes et segregare heterogenes.*" Ward admitted, in his *Mercurius Antimechanicus*: "I have been so much habituated and half-natured into these Latins and Greeks, ere I was aware, that I can neither expel them nor spell my own mother-tongue after my old fashion." Cotton Mather's *ignivomous, flammivorous,* and *pamphagous* are understandable enough; but they were eccentricities which the plainer style of the eighteenth century discarded.[15]

Certain commonly used words, however, required a deeper knowledge of their ancient meanings. Joshua Scottow, who published in 1694 a *Narrative of the Planting of the Massachusetts Colony*, complained that New England had gone sour, due to the witchcraft craze and other lapses: "Our sweet scent is gone; we smell rank of hellebore, henbane, and poisonful hemlock, as if we were laid out to be the American Anticyra" (a sort of pagan Bedlam). The reader of Horace or Juvenal would recognize the reference. Many other such words were in general use and were understood by educated Americans: *lustre,* the five-year period in the Roman calendar; *symbolize* (as used by Plautus and Terence), meaning to "pay one's dues"; *Itineration,* meaning travel on official inspections (still in occasional use). John Adams characteristically objected to Hamilton's financial procedures as too much *thesaurization.*[16] One of the best illustrations of this

Latin-in-English habit is found in Madison's letter to Jefferson concerning the choice of a federal capital: "Philadelphia, as least *eccentric* of any place capable of affording due accommodations, was the first proposed." This adjective, needless to say, was purely geographical.

Assumed or imposed names, increasing as pre-Revolutionary tension grew, are beyond counting. Tom Paine signed himself "Atlanticus," implying the universality of his appeal. Joseph Galloway, in his *Letters from Cicero to Catiline the Second* (Charles James Fox), opened each epistle with a sentence taken from the Roman orator's storehouse of invective. Samuel Adams, who assailed Governor Bernard as "Verres, Tyrant of Sicily," ran riot with his *noms de guerre* — Vindex, Valerius Poplicola, Determinatus, Sincerus, Candidus — which were varied from time to time in a pretense at concealing identification. Hamilton styled himself "Manlius" when addressing himself to the nation's first misunderstanding with France, "Phocion" in support of the Jay Treaty, and "Pacificus" in support of neutrality. Notable among several codes was one list of "appellations for certain official characters," [17] concocted by Hamilton and Gouverneur Morris as a cipher for political information. Washington is "Scaevola," John Adams "Brutus," Jefferson "Scipio," Madison "Tarquin," and Randolph "Lysander." Madison was so called because he went over to the camp of Jefferson; and Randolph, like the Spartan, exposed himself to suspicion in his correspondence with the Francophiles.

Classical history supplied sobriquets favorable or unfavorable to an extent that grows almost wearisome. Samuel Adams was to the Tories "that pale lean Cassius," who, as Chastellux remarked, "got at the Tories by way of the Greeks and Romans." George Read was attacked as "Dionysius the tyrant of Delaware." John Winthrop, Jr., was "A Hermes Christianus." These names are variations on a theme that was prevalent in early New England, namely, "typology," in which Old Testament or classical figures were compared with New Testament or modern personalities, to the honor and credit of the latter.[18] Montesquieu christened Penn "un véritable Lycurge,"[19] to which Voltaire retorted that it was unjust to the founder of Pennsylvania to compare him with the Spartan who, he claimed, had ruined Greece. Fabricius the Incorruptible and Cato (both from Addison's play and from Plutarch) appear attached to models of colonial integrity. The French, especially after the *entente* of 1781, were lavish in praise of the American leaders. Louis Philippe, Comte de Ségur, recorded in his *Mémoires* an account of a meeting with Franklin, Deane, and Arthur Lee, describing them as "quelques sages contemporains de Platon, ou des républicains du temps de Caton et Fabius."[20] It is fair to say that Plutarch was to the rebellion what Cicero was to the Declaration, and Aristotle and Polybius to the Constituttion. In the Age of Enlightenment, which lay halfway between the Absolute Way and our modern realistic approach, expressions of this sort were so customary that we must be careful not to confuse embroidery with the underlying pattern. Gouverneur Morris, to whom our national document is indebted for its final revision, saw this point and recommended the avoidance of too much theory in government, which would produce "the same pedantry with our young scholars just fresh from the university, who would fain bring everything to a Roman standard."[21]

Seals and medals in many cases were worded and stamped in this tradition. George Mason designed the original seal of the Old Dominion: "*Virtus*, the Genius of the Commonwealth, treading on Tyranny . . . In the exergon, the word *Virginia* over the head of *Virtus*, and underneath the words *Sic Semper Tyrannis*. On one side of her Ceres, with a cornucopia in one hand and an ear of wheat in the other. On the other side *Aeternitas*, with the globe and the phoenix. In the exergon these words: DEUS NOBIS HAEC OTIA FECIT."[22] When in August 1776 a committee of the Continental Congress was considering a gold medal to commemorate the evacuation of Boston,[23] there were several suggestions. Franklin recommended a depiction of the Egyptians being overwhelmed in the Red Sea. Jefferson fancied a combination of the Children of Israel and the Hengist-Horsa invasion of England. The French artist Du Simitière proposed "Liberty, with her spear and *pileus*, leaning on General Washington." But John Adams characteristically voted for "The Choice of Heracles, as engraved by Gribelin — the hero resting on his club; Virtue pointing to her rugged mountain and persuading him to ascend. Sloth, glancing at her flowery paths of pleasure, wantonly reclining on the ground, displaying the charms both of her eloquence and person, to seduce him into vice." Jefferson had favored a classical motif in 1774, the device of a father presenting the Aesopic bundle of rods to his sons (the thirteen colonies) and the motto *Insuperabiles si Inseparabiles*. The original corporation of the Georgia settlement designed "The genius of Georgia Augusta, with a cap of liberty on her head, a spear in one hand, and the horn of plenty in the other"; and when Oglethorpe's expedition set sail, Charles Wesley gave them a benediction combining a scriptural message with a Horatian background — *Christo duce et auspice Christo*.[24]

Washington, not classically trained but with classical tastes, approximates the pattern of his era.[25] On his retirement from military service, he ordered busts of Alexander, Caesar, and other personages, "not to exceed fifteen inches in height or ten in width," together with "sundry small ornaments for chimney pieces." For his library he sent for busts of Sallust, Terence, Horace, and Erasmus. An invoice from his English dealer included "A Groupe of Aeneas carrying his father out of Troy, neatly finished and bronzed with copper — three pounds, three shillings. Two Groupes of Bacchus and Flora, each two pounds, two shillings," with instructions as to their places on the chimney piece. For his Richmond statue Washington was to be clad in Roman dress, holding a truncheon and crowned with a laurel wreath, but he finally objected to "any servile adherence to the garb of antiquity." [26] The statue was modern except for the standard bundle of thirteen fasces. Pitt's likenesses, on the other hand, were in the complete style of a Roman senator. The objects of art collected or ordered by Jefferson were predominantly classical, from the Farnese Hercules to "Curtius leaping into the Gulph."

We meet with such symbols throughout the colonial era, from Morton of Merrymount with his "Bacchanalia" and "Festivals of the Goddess Flora," through the classical pageant in Boston which Benjamin Tompson headed in a greeting to the new governor, Lord Bellomont, to the celebrations held at the time of the French Revolution and the ratification of the Constitution. The artist John Trumbull painted many men of distinction, both ancient and modern. He portrayed the death of Paulus at Cannae, Brutus condemning his sons, the episode of Lucretia, and the great Belisarius reduced to beggary. Before his professional career began, he had read Eutropius, Nepos, Vergil, Cicero, Horace, Juvenal, the Greek Testament, the *Iliad* and Rollin's *Arts and Sciences of the Ancient Nations.*

These Greco-Roman sources were so deeply imbedded in the common fund of knowledge that it is often hard to trace their origin. For example, does Franklin's *Socratic Dialogue* between Philocles and Horatio (1730) derive directly from Xenophon's *Memorabilia,* which Franklin studied and imitated, or from *The Moralists* in Shaftesbury's *Characteristics?* Does the quotation from Blackstone's *Commentaries* in Hamilton's early essay *The Farmer Refuted,* citing without acknowledgment Cicero's famous definition of the Divine Law, mean that Hamilton was familiar with only one, or with both? At any rate, Benjamin Franklin knew his public. He stated a popular policy when he took over the editorship of the *Courant:* "Gentle readers, we design never to let a paper pass without a Latin motto, which carries a charm in it to the Vulgar, and the Learned admire the pleasure of construing." Sometimes this tendency takes an extreme and often absurd form, as when Francis Pope, who settled on the Potomac in 1663, named his plantation "Rome" and altered "Goose Creek" to "Tiber." [27] The countersign at Fort Cumberland for July 6, 1756, by order of Colonel Washington, was "Xanthippe." John Randolph ran riot from Rollin and Plutarch when he named his horses: "Gracchus was got by Diomed, his dam by Chanticleer, grandam by Old Celer, great-grandson by Mark Anthony, and Vixen by Regulus." Washington's group of slaves reads like a selection from Ovid; and those on the Mepkin plantation of Henry Laurens included Tully, Mentor, Valerius, Claudius, Lavinia, and Melissa.

Whether from memory, from the original texts, or from handbooks and *florilegia*, it was a frequent habit to fortify an idea or an argument with a "snapper" from the Latin. Cotton Mather, praising Sir William Phips, borrowed Lucan's epigram: *Nil actum credens cum quid superesset agendum* (Regarding his mission as unfulfilled if anything were left undone).

We might wish that Benedict Arnold had abided by the spirit of his bookshop signboard at New Haven: *Nec sibi sed toti genitum se credere mundo* (Deeming himself born, not for his own but for the world's service). *Cedant arma togae* (Ballots are better than bullets) is of frequent occurrence, drawn from Cicero's self-laudatory poem. Both almanac writers and statesmen repeated a line from the astronomer Manilius: *Ornari res ipsa negat, contenta doceri* (Do not embellish the truth: let it only enforce its lesson). One military proverb had wide circulation: *Plus animi est inferenti periculum quam propulsanti* (There is more spirit in an attack than in a defense). John Adams drew out from his schoolboy memories a saying of the fabulist Phaedrus, on the problem of taxation and representation: *Quid refert mea/ Cui serviam, clitellas dum portem meas?* (What difference what master I serve, as long as I carry my own saddlebags?).[28]

When Franklin solicited subscriptions for the new hospital in the *Pennsylvania Gazette* of August 1751, he must have been appealing to a well-educated group of citizens. He bracketed the Biblical "I was sick, and ye visited me" with the Ciceronian "Nothing brings Man nearer to God than planning for the health of his fellow-man," and with the haunting couplet, *Post obitum benefacta manent, aeternaque virtus/ Non metuit Stygiis ne rapiatur aquis* (After death, one's good deeds remain; and virtue, forever living, has no fear of being swept away beneath the Stygian waves).[29]

These illustrations from antiquity can be found in all circles, high and low, from a farmer who notes the weather, or a shopkeeper who wishes to impress his clientèle, to the scholar-politician in search of precedents for the founding of a nation. The man in the street who knew some second-hand Roman history caught the atmosphere of the times; and every corner of ancient culture was known and applied by the owners and users of extensive libraries such as Increase and Cotton Mather, James Logan, William Byrd, Jefferson, and John Adams.

From whatever point of view we regard the colonial re-actions to this classical tradition, it is clear that an increasing interest in matters Greek and Latin gathered force and spirit between the years 1607 and 1789. Patrick Henry's speeches are a well-worn story to us, but their effect at the time was impressive. The Congress listened to him, as Charles Thomson tells us, in the spirit of Aeneas' audience at Dido's palace — "All fell silent, and gave him their fixed attention." Edmund Pendleton, describing the Virginia Convention of 1776, may be taken as a faithful witness: "The young boasted that they were treading upon the Republican ground of Greece and Rome," scorning in their enthusiasm the in-adequacies of the old regime. Washington's manifesto in answer to Burgoyne, in August 1777, speaks the same lan-guage: "The associated armies in America act from the noblest motives, liberty. The same principles actuated the arms of Rome in the days of her glory; and the same object was the reward of Roman valour."

The evolution of this feeling, sometimes exaggerated but always with a background of respect for the authority and inspiration of the old materials, has been sufficiently indicated. We may now turn to certain episodes, personalities, and principles which show clearly that in this field the colonists found a clarification of their ideas and a liberating force. The classical tradition produced valid arguments for all sides and an astonishing variety of opinion.

THE VIRGINIA ARGONAUTS

THE "myth," as the Greeks called it, has always been a vital element in any human venture. Throughout history, fancy has often been the precursor of fact. Eleanor of Aquitaine added drama to one of the Crusades by dressing her attendants as Amazons and herself as Penthesilea. Rienzi invoked the tribunician power in order to strengthen his popular appeal. Early Virginia became a fertile field for imaginative symbolism, although the ultimate objective of the early colonists was religious and commercial, as well as the attainment of political supremacy in a new world. The Earthly Paradise they so often wrote about was supported by mythological and historical examples: "There is not a work of more excellent hope under the sun, and farre excelling those noble deeds of Alexander, Hercules, and those heathen monarks, for which they were termed gods among their posterity." [1] William Crashaw, in a sermon preached to the departing voyagers, dwelt on the beneficent possibilities of exploration: "If the ancient Romans converted the ancient Britons to civilitie, let the English here repay the debt." The author of *Nova Britannia* in 1609 and *The New Life of Virginea* in 1612, invoking Scipio, Caesar, and Augustus, urged that the English not be idle or overconfident, as were the Romans when they clipped the wings of the goddess Victoria so that she "might take her flight no more." [2]

This symbolism is exemplified in an author of ancient times who appeared on Tidewater bookshelves with more regularity than any other. A passage from Plutarch's *Theseus* may serve as our text: "May I therefore succeed in purifying Fable, making her submit to Reason and take on the semblance of History! But where she obstinately disdains to make herself credible and refuses to admit any element of probability I shall pray for kindly readers and such as receive with indulgence the tales of antiquity." [3] Most of the American efforts at colonization were based on the fascination for something new. William Hubbard, in his *General History of New England*, strikes the prevalent note: *Est natura hominum novitatis avida* (It is man's nature to strive after novelty).

However we may define the "myth" that tempted so many to come to the New World, it seems to have become a publicity slogan. The adventurers were seeking the *Meta Incognita*, the Unknown Goal — a name which lingers on certain old maps for the southern peninsula of Baffin Land. Their objective lay even beyond the British sea which Clement of Rome, and later Cotton Mather, called *Okeanos Aperantos*, "the Ocean which men cannot pass." The fable of Atlantis was in circulation; and the Argonauts were chosen as symbols, rather than Arthurian or European heroes, because they were more familiar material. It was the great age of English grammar schools, and every boy who had progressed beyond the three Rs knew what Michael Drayton meant when he called the Virginia explorers "Argonauts." Their leaders, many of them university graduates, used this terminology in their correspondence. The earliest voyagers likened the Indian idols to the oracles of Apollo; and nearly two hundred years later, the "Wilderness Zion" of the Puritans became an "Agrarian Utopia."

The Atlantis myth fitted perfectly into seventeenth-century projects for colonization, particularly those of the Virginians. Bacon's essay *Of Prophecies* set the seal on the discovery of the New World, with the aid of a famous passage from the *Medea* of the tragedian Seneca:

> Venient annis saecula seris,
> quibus Oceanus vincula rerum
> laxet et ingens pateat tellus,
> Tethysque novos detegat orbes,
> nec sit terris ultima Thule.[4]

William Strachey, first secretary of the Jamestown colony, who cited also the story about the Lost Atlantis in Plato's *Timaeus*, hinted that Columbus and others had "made good the prophecy of Reverend Seneca," and he himself translated the tragedian's lines:

> That age shall come, albeit, in latter tymes,
> When as the sea shall ope her lockt-up bounds,
> And mighty lands appear: new heavens, new clymes
> Shall Typhis bring to knowledge, and new grounds,
> New worlds display. Then shall not Thule be
> The farthest nor-west isle our eyes shall see.

The myth was now a fact. The historian Lopez de Gomara had identified Atlantis as America, and Sir John Denham celebrated its fulfillment:

> What the Tragedian wrote, the late success
> Declares was inspiration and not guess.
> As dark a truth that Author did unfold
> As Oracles or Prophets e'er foretold.
> At last the Ocean shall unlock the Bound
> Of things, and a New World by Typhis found,
> Then Ages far remote shall understand
> The Isle of Thule is not the farthest land.

Fifty years after the Virginians had rhapsodized over the promise of America, a New England Puritan recalled the same symbol, expressing the hope that the Christian message might triumph over native ignorance. Benjamin Tompson alluded to "Unheard of places, like some New-Atlantis,/ Before in fancy only, now Newlandis."

As to the location of the Lost Atlantis, fable is still fable. The Canaries, the Azores, "the Happy Western Isles," a large continent sunk beneath the sea, all have stirred the imagination of geographers. As late as 1771, the poet Philip Freneau, besides other references to the future greatness of America, essayed a translation of the Senecan prophecy which

Bacon had put into circulation. There was, of course, occasional protest when the fable was overworked. Nathaniel Morton, in his epistle dedicatory to *New England's Memorial*,[5] addressed to Governor Thomas Prince of New Plymouth, speaking of earthquakes and hurricanes, added whimsically as a footnote: "Thus was the Atlantic Ocean caused to be a sea, as Plato affirmed, who lived 366 years before Christ!" William Stith, the mid-eighteenth-century historian of Virginia and a reliable critic, enlarged upon the uselessness of such guesswork. James I, he declared, may have been a good classical scholar under the guidance of George Buchanan; but during his reign "the judges and Oracles of Law were, like the lying Oracle of old, much addicted to *philippizing*" (with concessions to the King of Spain in mind). For historical purposes, Stith regarded Hanno's voyage, Madoc's expedition, Plato's fable, and even Seneca's true prophecy as "learned trumpery." The realistic Thomas Jefferson discouraged any reliance on Geoffrey of Monmouth and his ilk, ridiculing "Moreton's deduction of the origin of our Indians from the fugitive Trojans."

Atlantis, however, had fulfilled its inspiring purpose. The prophecy of Charles Aleyn, historian of Henry VII, had been justified by the results of adventurers who became founders and of fable which became fact:

> About this time *our world* began to thinke
> Of a *New World:* 'twas an *Italian* Head
> Where this imagination first did sinck,
> That other Lands might be discovered,
> As *Blith Democritus* of old had done
> In his assertion of more worlds than one.

Search for the Golden Fleece by the Argonauts became the most appealing slogan after transatlantic colonization had begun.[6] Hakluyt's picturesque English advertised the "fertility of soyle, insinuation[7] of seas, multiplicitie of rivers, opportunities of habitations." Emigrating leaders of expeditions publicized their plans by reference to Roman colonization.

Even the matter-of-fact Swedes on the Delaware gave ancient names to their ships — *Fama, Mercurius, Neptunus, Achilles.* Oceanus Hopkins and Peregrine White were symbolically christened. The Fleece was allegory in dignified disguise for the scramble after precious metals and the English aim to drive treasure-laden Spanish galleons off the sea. Several *Argonautica* appeared in different nations, competing for transatlantic settlers. Prominent among these idealistic sales-men was William Vaughan, whose main concern was to combine Christianity with honest gain in the commercial field. In 1626 London saw his "Golden Fleece, transported from Cambrioll (Welsh) Colchos out of the Southernmost part of the Island commonly called the Newfoundland, by Orpheus Junior." In this region, the modern Colchos, "the Golden Fleece flourishes on the backs of Neptune's sheep, continually to be shorn." The reader of Vergil's Fourth Georgic will assume that the writer had in mind the seal fisheries or the Sacred Cod (although the latter is less likely).

These explorers refused to "stay at home like drones"; in search of "Apollo's Lawrell" they would become famous, like the old Romans, whose "Statuas or Images were set up in wax" to perpetuate their renown. The unidentified R. G., in his *Good Speed to Virginia* (1609), brackets the Biblical, "He shall not fail nor be discouraged," with the Horatian, "Time the devourer of his own brood consumes both man and his memorie. It is not brasse nor marble that can per-petuate immortalitie of name upon earth." Many adventurers along the Atlantic seaboard were of course disappointed: Captain Gorges left the new country, "scarce having con-tinued longer in the province than Tully's [Cicero's] vigilant consul, that had not leisure, during his whole consulship, so much as once to take sleep." [8] William Morrell, a temporary sojourner in the Gorges colony, published in 1625 at London a poem in praise of New England's resources, in both Latin and English versions. Mason, an Oxford man, was also frus-trated, after his Argonautic enthusiasm had tempted him into verse:

If hope of peace, of quiet life, or gaine,
May kindle flames within our mind againe,
Then let us joyne to seek this Golden Fleece,
Whose like ne'er came from Colchos into Greece.

A hastily improvised series of couplets is dedicated, in
Thomas Morton's *New English Canaan*, to the wonderful
Lake Erocoise (Champlain), with nymphs and naiads adorn-
ing its shores, including the inevitable Argonautic theme:
"Colcos' golden Fleece reject:/ This deserveth best respect."
The habit persisted: for Judge Sewall reports that Acting
President Hubbard, at the Harvard commencement of 1688,
"made an oration in which he compared Sir William Phips
(the finder of the sunken treasure ship) to Jason bringing
home the Golden Fleece." Cotton Mather hailed him as a
Knight of the Mythical Order: "The Stile [title] might pre-
tend unto some circumstances that would justify it." The
gold salvaged by Phips was real; but nearly all the precious
metal sought by the Virginia adventurers turned out, as
William Byrd later admitted, to be mica or crystals.

The first piece of real literary merit produced on the
Atlantic seaboard was a translation of Ovid's *Metamorphoses*
by George Sandys, the completed work published in London in 1626. Sandys was an Oxford man who spent ten years
in Virginia as a plantation owner, the treasurer of the Virginia Company, and a councillor under Governor Wyat.
Michael Drayton had given him a send-off in England, describing him as a pioneer in making America an outpost of
British culture:

Go on with Ovid, as you have begun
With the first five books; let your numbers run
Glib as the former, so shall it live long,
And do much honour to the English tongue.
Intice the Muses thither to repair,
Intreat them gently, train them to that air.

The spirit of the myth continued in the type of literature
that Sandys selected for his occupation on foreign shores.

Dedicating his Ovid to Charles I, he wrote: "It needeth more than a simple denization, being a double stranger sprung from the stock of the ancient Romans but bred in the New World, of the rudeness whereof it cannot but participate, especially having Warres and Tumults to bring it to light instead of the Muses."

The translation is an excellent one, by any standard. Thomas Fuller, in his *Worthies of England*, confirms the general opinion that "Ovid's genius may seem to have passed into Master Sandys." The English occupies little more space than the Latin, and there is force and drive to the verses. This is especially so in the ninth book, where, for instance, Deianeira bewails her fate on being deserted by Hercules for Iole:

> Shall I complain? Be mute? Shift houses? Stay?
> Return to Calydon, and give her way? [9]

Medea's debate with her conscience, whether to fly with Jason or to remain at home, is another impressive piece of translation:

> Fierce is my Father, barbarous my land;
> My brother a child; my sister's wishes stand
> With my desires; the greatest God of all
> My breast inshrines. What I forsake is small;
> Great hopes I follow: to receive the grace
> For Argo's safety; know a better place,
> And Cities which in these far-distant parts
> Are famous with civility and arts:
> And Aeson's son, whom I most dearly prize
> Than wealthy Earth, and all her monarchies.

Whether it is proper to rate Sandys as an American might be questioned. But a search through all of American colonial poetry reveals no one who is a more skillful master of the poetic art or who, if regarded as a Virginia resident, better deserves the title on the memorial tablet erected at Jamestown: PRIMO POETAE AMERICANO.[10]

The prompt transference and interchange of culture which

we have noted in Sandys is evident also in the large number of university men among the early settlers. One case out of many will suffice. The Reverend John Goodborne, who died in 1635 on the voyage over, brought a library which contained Homer, Aristotle, Ovid, Juvenal, Thucydides, Isocrates, Pindar, Seneca, Plautus, Terence, Persius, Horace, Cicero, Quintilian, Plutarch, Vergil, Suetonius, Justin, Caesar, Aelian, and the *Mythologiae* of Natalis Comes. The Plutarch was in Latin and English, Terence in English, Vergil in Latin and English.[11]

Another Virginian who played a prominent part in the affairs of the first settlement and in the field of classics was William Strachey, author of the *Historie of Travell into Virginia Britania* and translator of the above-mentioned passage from Seneca. Secretary of the Company, he sailed with Gates and Somers, amid farewell tributes from Thamesside as rousing "as a Roman triumph." By way of the "stillvexed Bermoothes" he reached Jamestown in 1610, making himself indispensable to the colony, codifying the laws and advertising the advantages of the province. He endeavored to extract from the "myth" all available items for the benefit of future planters. His style is picturesque, though rambling and at times awkward. The Christian message is uppermost, but for illustrative purposes his medium of description is largely classical. The title-page motto is taken from the *Epistles* of Horace,[12] wherein he proposes to discuss *res gestas, terrarum situs, flumina, arces montibus impositas,* and *barbara regna.* The aim is *Ecclesiae et Rei publicae,* and the well-worn epigram "As we are Angli, make us Angells too" indicates the dedicated spirit of the group. Describing the Bermuda storm, he invokes Horace's characteristic awe of the sea and its dangers: "May the wives and children of *our foes alone* be the victims of the rising South Wind and the roaring of the dark waters, and the beaches shaken by the blast! I know the murky waves of the Adriatic and the ominous signs of the clear West Wind." [13] These perils were no less awesome, according to Strachey, than "the fabulous drowning by Deucalion's floud, or burning by Phaeton, or synce the sincking of the Atlantic Islands."

The ambition of the voyagers was sharpened by recollection of past heroes. "Themistocles," says Strachey, "could not rest when he heard of Melciades' [Miltiades'] victory; and Caesar wept at the sight of Alexander's image." [14] What were dangers to true adventurers? Their friend, the poet Drayton, had said to them upon their departure: "When Aeolus scowls, you need not feare." Numa, Strachey believes, had the right answer when warned of an approaching enemy: "And we doe sacrifice!" The clamor of a centurion or two cannot disturb Numa Pompilius kneeling at the altar. The colonizers owed it to the ancients to show their mettle: "What overgrown satyrs would the British be if we had not been civilized by Roman settlements!"

The injection of classical scholarship into everyday activities is characteristic of Strachey's era. He himself was a graduate of Emmanuel College and a member of Gray's Inn. No reference is too farfetched for him, and one marvels at the range of his reading, which almost equals that of Cotton Mather. Indian women stain themselves with a kind of dye, "as is said of Greek women, how they colored their faces with certain roots called *Brenthyna.*" This item comes from Hesychius, the Byzantine lexicographer. The Indian boats remind him of the *monoxylum navigium,* the dugouts mentioned by Pliny the Elder, Xenophon, Polybius, and others. Their games bring to Strachey's mind the Trojans who taught the Latins "scipping and frisking at the ball." Their barley, sodden in water, is "not unlike that homely *ius nigrum* which Lacedaemonians used to eate — which Dionysius could not abyde to taste of." These Indians, children of nature, worshiped a devil, Okeus, "as the Romaynes did their hurtfull god Vejovis." Their chiefs, or "weroances," believed in metempsychosis, "not unlike the heathen Pythagoras his opinion." And in this connection Strachey condemns the Epicurean doctrine of the soul's annihilation after death: "The soule is not a meere quality of the body."

Strachey's handbook, *The Laws Divine and Morall*, confines itself more closely to rules and regulations. But it is inscribed with two mottos: *Alget qui non ardet* (He goes cold who does not glow with energy) and, a philosophical hint that the settlers must make the best of their difficulties, *Res nostrae subinde non sunt quales quis optaret, sed quales esse possunt* (Our affairs at present are not such as one might wish, but such as are possible). The dedication states that the author is presenting a "Toparchia or State of those duties, by which their Colonie stands regulated and commended," and hails the deputy governor, Sir Thomas Dale, as "Ethnarches."

Whereas the Massachusetts Bay settlers argued out their theological problems in an atmosphere of independence from the mother country, the Virginians followed a blueprint, as it were, from London. Sermons were preached to them on their departure: Daniel Price gave them farewell advice at Paul's Cross in May of 1609, blending economics with theology and hoping that the "Virginia Country may in time prove to us the farm of Britain, as Sicily was to Rome, or the garden of the world, as was Thessaly." The same motif persisted under Governor Harvey: "Virginia is become like another Sicily to Rome, the granary of all his Majesty's Northern Colonies." The home supporters of the Virginia Company hoped that the adventurers would make "Plutarch's *Poneropolis* an *Ouranopolis*, a savage country to become a sanctified company." The Church blessed the relief expedition of Lord Delawarr in 1610, with a glance backward at Roman history: "Look at the beginning of Rome, how poore, how meane, how despised it was; and yet on that base beginning grew to be the mistress of the world." Sandys himself appealed for support in the difficult days: "Those who upbraid us . . . let them take heed least they manifest themselves to be of the race of those Gyants who made warre with Heaven."

The way was hard and the discipline rigorous. Edward Wingfield, the first president of the Jamestown council, reported the jealousies and difficulties of a disappointed (and disappointing) official: "I was never dismayed, though I bethought me of ye hard beginnings which in former ages betided those worthy spirits that planted the greatest monarchies in Asia and Europe . . . with other of like history, then that venom in the mutinous brood of Cadmus, or that harmony in the sweet consent of Amphion. Even the brethren at their plantation of the Romaine Empire were not free from mortal hatred and intestine garboile." These pedantic allusions refer to the episode of the Dragon's Teeth, the story of Amphion, and the quarrel of Romulus and Remus. This historical parallel was repeated in 1663 by Sir William Berkeley, who visited England to secure a repeal of some harsh passages in the Navigation Act. He disagreed with certain critics who spoke of the colonists as "of a mean quality": "This to our malingerers we would easily grant, if they would consent to the *omen* of it; for was not Rome thus begun and composed? And the greatest honour that was given to Romulus and his City was this, that his severity and discipline in his time made them formidable to their neighbors, and his posterity masters of the world." [15]

Amid all the official statements and the strict prescriptions from London, which resembled the Roman praetor's edict for provincial administration, it is heartwarming to meet with Alexander Whitaker, the "Apostle to Virginia." His *Good Newes from Virginia* was published in London in 1613, through Crashaw and other of his friends. Had he so desired, they stated, he could have "written it in Latine or in Greek." We know little of his career in the province, but he toiled in spontaneous self-forgetfulness and transmitted his faith to the authorities at home. After six years at Jamestown and Henrico, perhaps having baptized Pocahontas, he is mentioned in the register book of Samuel Argall for June 9, 1617: "Mr. Whitaker being drown'd," an inadequate epitaph for such a devoted benefactor.

A fellow collegian of Winthrop and Cotton at Trinity in Cambridge, Whitaker is more sparing than they in his invocation of the classics. His book had two mottos: the Scriptural "Cast thy bread upon the waters" and the Vergilian *Aude, hospes, contemnere opes, et te quoque dignum Finge Deo*, which he translates, "Be bould, my Hearers, to contemne riches and frame yourselves to walk worthy of God." [16] A parallel from Roman history accompanies his account of the happy meeting with the relief fleet of Lord Delawarr, when Sir Thomas Gates in despair had already reached the river's mouth on the way home: "He had forsaken with *Hannibal's sighes* the first builded Jamestowne." His description of the settlers as living in a Senecan "contented poverty" is a manful attempt at optimism, particularly when we remember the sufferings of the adventurers. There are passages from the Latin Vulgate and both Greek and Latin versions of the proverb *Bis dat qui cito dat* (Charity, if prompt, is all the sweeter). Amid the flamboyant and mostly dictatorial leaders of the Jamestown experiment, Whitaker stands out brightly, brief though his candle was.

Captain John Smith has been a semimythical personality, resembling what the Greeks used to define as an *eponymous* and moderns as a self-made hero. Tradition portrays him as a bewhiskered fabricator of marvelous exploits and a fighting man with a slender background of education. But history takes him seriously as a constructive explorer and a tireless advocate of overseas settlement. America may claim him with some justification because three of his works were conceived and perhaps written on this side of the Atlantic. He is also significant, for our purposes, in that his medium of expression tends toward the classical themes which were familiar to Englishmen in the Elizabethan and Jacobean decades.

The parish register of Willoughby in Lincolnshire records his baptism, *ixth die Januarii*, 1579–80, in the usual semi-Latin terms. His father was a farmer in respectable circumstances, who allowed his son a grammar-school education at Alford and Louth. He evidently acquired enough learning to put up a good front, in both speech and writing, in the company of university graduates. In addition to the typical classroom Latin, he had access to many translations and to the florilegia, or "elegant extracts," which even highly trained students condescended to use. While resting between early campaigns at his Lincolnshire retreat, he read extensively, the books including the picturesque combination of Marcus Aurelius and Macchiavelli's *Arte della guerra*. That some perusal of Polybius was of practical use to him is evident from his application of the torch signaling at the siege of Olympach (Ober-Limbach) in Hungary against the Turks. With some changes, he followed the historian. Signalers on the mountain, visible to the town, flash with three torches to the governor of the town, seven miles away. The besieged flash back with three torches. In the code, the alphabet is divided into two parts, A-L and M-Z. The participants show and hide one torch "so oft as there is letters from A to that letter you meane." Two torches similarly take care of the interval M-Z. Three lights indicate the end of a word, and the answer is one light shone at the end of the message.[17]

Besides specific citations, there are hidden allusions which indicate familiarity with the classics, or at least a good memory. In his description of Virginia, Smith remarks on the climate: "The colde is extreme sharpe; but here the proverb is true that no extreme long continueth," — reminding us of the Epicurean proverb on pain, *Si longus, levis; si gravis, brevis*. Addressing his fellow explorers on the Potomac in 1608, he talks like a Roman general addressing his troops, or in the style of the *Miles Gloriosus* of Plautus. The preface to Smith's last work, *Advertisements for the Unexperienced Planters of New England* (1631), reinterprets the story of the shoemaker and the renowned Greek artist: "Honest reader, Apelles by the proportion of a foot could make the whole proportion of a man! Were hee now living, he might go to schoole: for now are thousands who can by opinion proportion kingdoms, cities, and Lordships, that never durst adventure to see them. And some try to tell what all England is like by seeing Milford Haven, as what Apelles was by the picture of his great toe." [18]

Roman heroism as a model for young Englishmen (a recurring motif throughout American colonial history) is a repeated theme in Smith's writings. In one of his exaggerated statements to the Worshipful Adventurers, he excuses himself by a boastful comparison: "I am not the first that hath been betrayed by pirates . . . Four men of warre have been sufficient to have taken Sampson, Hercules, and Alexander the Great, no other way furnished than I was . . . What made Rome such a Monarchesse, but only the adventures of her youth, not in riots at home but in dangers abroad." This sentiment is prefaced by a brave call to his countrymen, "A note for men that have great spirits and small meanes." One suspects a borrowing from Caesar's speech before the battle with Ariovistus: "It was not by staying at home or shirking their campaigns or avoiding their wars or pursuing their ease that our ancestors made the city so great: misfortune was nothing else than resting inactive." [19]

There is a delicate hint of Smith's own exploits in the dedication to the Duchess of Richmond in his *Generall Historie*: "When shall we looke to find a *Julius Caesar* whose atchievements shine so clear in his owne commentaries as they did in the field." England must conquer everywhere, as Rome did. One of Smith's colleagues wrote in a collection edited by the "Admiral":

> For the great Romans got into their hand
> The whole world's compass, both by sea and land,
> Or any seas, or heaven, or earth extended;
> And yet that nation could not be contented.

Immediate problems, however, were more pressing, and the Romans could also serve as a warning: "The *Romanes* estate hath been worse than this: for the meere covetousness and extortion of a few of them so mooved the rest that, not having any imployment but contemplation, their great judgments grew to such great malice, as themselves were sufficient to

destroy themselves by faction." At Jamestown, the varying
emotions of Phaedra, from Seneca's *Hippolytus,* are used to
describe the hesitation and the mutterings of the mutineers.
The council president himself was doubtful of the right
policy.

> I know those things thou sayest are true, good nurse,
> And fury forceth me to follow worse.
> My mind is harried headlong up and downe,
> Desiring better counsel, yet found none.[20]

These allusions, whether or not supplied by "ghost writers," were current coin to the intelligent adventurer. But we
may wonder whence Smith derived certain of his more rec-
ondite illustrations. For example, reporting on the competition with certain Dutch traders, he indulges in some deep
celestial physics: "The benefit of fishing is that *primum
mobile* that turns all their *spheres* to this height of plentie,
strength, honour, and admiration." It is either a credit to the
learning of the age or a bit of pedantry on the part of the
writer, when Aristotelian cosmology is introduced into what
we would now regard as a report to the Bureau of Fisheries.

Again, what could have been the extent of John Smith's
acquaintance with the Roman master of atomic philosophy?
When censuring those of little courage, he concludes with
Lucretius:

> It's want of reason, or it's reason's want
> Which doubts the mind, and judgment so doth dant,
> That those beginnings make men not to grant.
> John Smith writ this with his owne hand.

Here is a brave but almost incoherent handling of the Roman
poet's *Temptat enim dubiam mentem rationis egestas.*[21] I may
close these sketches of the Admiral's ventures into the classics
with some verses which he (or "Maister John Pory") cites in
order to get all hands in line and in harmony for purposes
of colonization. "Peruse this saying of honest Claudius"
(meaning Claudian), he writes:

See'st not the world of Nature's works, the fairest well, I wot,
How it, itself together ties, as in a true-loves knot.

Nor see'st how th'elements are combined, maintaine one constant
   plea,
How midst of heaven contents the Sunne, and shore contains the
   sea;
And how the aire both compasseth and carrieth still earth's
   frame,
Yet neither pressing burdens it, nor parting leaves the same.

The verse structure is too good, too literary, to be the work
of our noble adventurer: it displays the typical muscular
Elizabethan style. And, to show the closeness of the verses
to their classical source, in modern prose Claudian's lines
read as follows:

See'st thou not how the fair frame of the very universe binds
itself together by love, and how the elements, not united by violence, are forever at harmony among themselves? Dost thou not
mark how that Phoebus is content not to outstep the limits of
his path, nor the sea those of his kingdom, and how the air,
which in its eternal embrace encircles and upholds the world,
presses not upon us with too heavy a weight nor yet yields to
the burden which itself sustains? [22]

If we had nothing but Smith's own story, we might be
compelled to admit that in his case Fable had failed "to make
herself credible." But there is so much testimony to his
achievements that his deeds "take on the semblance of history." There are many contemporary tributes, illustrating
the pervasive classical atmosphere of the times and echoing
the myth motif discussed here. The poet George Wither, a
Lincoln's Inn man, heralded Smith's *Description of New England* in 1616. Another hailed the exploits of one who could
"In spight of Pelias, when his hate lies colde,/ Return as
Iason with a Fleece of Gold." The revised edition of the
Generall Historie enlarges further:

> Smith is here to anvil out a piece
> To after ages and Eternall Fame,
> That we may have the golden Jason's fleece.
> He, Vulcan-like, did forge a new plantation,
> And chained their kings to his immortal glory.

Richard James, approving the patronage of the Duchess of

Richmond for the publication of this same work, celebrated Smith's Caesarlike qualities, as did several other friends. His admirer Cartner offered a dedicatory verse:

> The old Greek Bard counts him the only man
> Who knows strange Countries, like his Ithacan.
> All these are met in thee.

Edward Jordan indicated his affection for the "Admirall of New England" by complimentary verses signed "Tuissimus." Samuel Purchas had greeted the adventurer in some awkward verses which alluded to Achilles and Pallas and the hero's expertness in "sword-grammar," implying optimistically that Smith was as clever with his writing as he was with his weapons. One would like to recognize, as a final example of these tributes, the couplet by "Io. Done": "Nor who doth better win th' Olympian prize/ Than he whose Countrye's Honor stirs his bloud?" John Donne, Dean of St. Paul's, was a stockholder in the Virginia Company, and he preached a hortatory sermon to the group in 1622. One of his sons served as an army officer in the West Indies and as an agent to the governor of Virginia; and there was a rumor that Donne himself at one time wished to hold some office. But the evidence is not sufficient to identify the Dean with this poetical tribute.[23]

This flamboyant atmosphere followed John Smith to the grave. The introduction to his *Advertisements for the Unexperienced Planters* contains a woodcut of a coat of arms, with Neptune carrying a trident and riding a dolphin, and the motto *Gens incognita mihi serviet*. On his tomb were his arms and the words *Accordamus, vincere est vivere*. So closely in those days did the "myth" combine with what Bacon called "the disposition and management of business." We may preserve what the lawyers call a learned doubt regarding the veracity of many of Smith's stories; but as a model Argonaut he has no superior. He is typical of the lively way in which the classical tradition colored the words and thoughts of the first American colonizers.

III

NOVANGLIA: CHURCH, STATE, AND THE CLASSICS

In the Old Dominion, with its established church directly responsible to the Bishop of London, there was little controversy over matters of doctrine. Nor did any of the Virginian clergy feel that the classical tradition must be kept subordinate to theology. It was to them a cultural asset. New England, however, born in an atmosphere of independence and Puritan reform, was ever watchful during its first decades to prevent any worldly interference with the Wilderness Zion, although the academic background of the settlers was superior to that of any community along the Atlantic seaboard. The atmosphere of early Virginia was suffused with mythological symbolism, but that of the Bay Colony was focused on the Scriptures. Men like Dudley, Saltonstall, Vane, and John Winthrop, Jr., are today thought of as having been primarily interested in civic affairs. Yet the majority of the leaders conducted their discussions in such a way that it is hard to tell whether the eyes, so to speak, of the controversial hurricanes were secular or religious.

The attitude of the conscientious John Winthrop on two well-known occasions may be taken as an illustration. In 1641 he objected to the principles "grounded upon the old Roman and Grecian governments" in Nathaniel Ward's election sermon, as a breach in the fortifications of the Biblical Commonwealth. In 1643 he declared uncompromisingly: "If we should change from a mixt aristocratie to a meere democratie, we should have no warrant in Scripture for it: there was no such government in Israel." [1] At the Hingham trial, when Winthrop was accused of exceeding his powers, he drew the distinction (with the aid of proverbs from Terence and Horace) between natural liberty or license and civil liberty or the reign of law, and won his case. This episode was hailed by Cotton Mather with Plutarchian praise: "If the famous Cato were 44 times called into judgment but as often acquitted, let it not be wondered at if our famous Winthrop were at one time so." Hutchinson, the historian of the Bay Colony, was equally sympathetic: "He had a little taste of what, in many other governments, their benefactors have taken a large potion. He would never have been accused had not the ostracism of the ancient Greeks been revived in this new Commonwealth." It was not until much later that the doctrine of natural liberty changed from an equivalent of chaos to a Ciceronian interpretation of the Law of Nature as applied to citizen rights, and the Divine Law as something having more than theological relevance.

From the start, however, voices were raised by educators and some of the clergy in favor of classical learning as essential material for the church as well as for the state. The Reverend Thomas Shepard wrote frankly to the governor, advising him to consult President Dunster of Harvard on the value of Greek and Latin for future ministers and civic officials. In 1655 Charles Chauncy settled matters with a statement that few leaders disapproved: "All truth, whosoever it be that speaks it, comes from the God of Truth. Who can deny but that there are found many excellent and divine morall truths in Plato, Aristotle, Plutarch, Seneca, etc.; and to condemn all pel-mel will be an hard censure . . . If one abolishes all the learning that the heathen men have uttered *out of the light of nature*, it will be a great oversight." This reconciliation of classics and theology was satisfactory to both scholars and clerics, for the essence of the Gospel message remained unimpaired as pulpit authority. As late as 1755, Harvard's President Holyoke, in the first Dudleian lecture, broad-mindedly set forth "three opinions as to the existence of the World: one, that of Plato, from eternity, flowing from God as Raies do from the Sun; second, Epicurus, a jumble of atoms without cause; third, that the World was formed by some great and excellent Being whom they called God."

It is worth while, before discussing the most significant controversy of the period — that between John Cotton and Roger Williams — to touch upon a few cases of support and opposition to the policy of the Massachusetts Bay Colony. An out-and-out champion of Winthrop's *perfecta res publica* was the colorful Captain Edward Johnson, whose *Wonder-Working Providence of Sion's Saviour in New England* was published in London in 1654.[2] It is a chronicle in prose and verse, defending the governor's "mixed company, part aristocracy and part democracy of magistrates." Johnson states that Christian soldiers, illustrated typologically by ancient heroes with generous borrowings from Plutarch, are busy at their noble task. If Greeks and Romans could find new worlds to occupy, so could English settlers — "such soldiers of Christ whose aymes are elevated by Him many millions above that brave warrior Ulysses." "If Caesar could suddenly fetch over fresh forces from Europe, Pompey to foile, how much more shall Christ call over this 900 league Ocean at his pleasure such instruments as he thinks meete!" The Puritan migration, Johnson declares, was caused by "Proud Prelates whose Pithagorian [oligarchical] philosophy caused the King to lose his life." This is an allusion to the small elite group ruled by Pythagoras with his *ipse dixit*, combining politics, religion, culture, and flavored with mysticism.[3] Johnson protested against the numerous heresies in New England which were springing up "like those famed heads of Hydra." President Dunster should be encouraged to enlarge the accommodations of his new university, which at present was equipped little better than the tun of Diogenes. Away with Sirens and the flighty worshipers of Venus and Bacchus.

There were many other tributes to Winthrop, among them that of Hugh Peter, who described the governor as "obedient to the law, a righteous soul, and a deeply reverent mind."

This is an obvious reminiscence of Persius' line, "A heart rightly attuned towards God and Man, a mind pure in its inner depths, and a soul steeped in nobleness and honour." [4] Still another supporter of the Bay's political theory was William Wood, an early visitor to the colony. He published his *New England's Prospect*,[5] with praise for the province's future and commendation of the settlers who, like beavers, *Multorum manibus grande levatur onus* (Lighten their heavy burdens by the shared work of many hands). He calls on Tacitus to show that revolutions in the home country made colonial independence easier, and he refers, with the poet Claudian,[6] to the coming happiness of those who will have "birth, life, and burying in the same place." Wood, who was probably a college graduate, dots his essay with phrases concocted from standard quotations made over into his own improvised versions — as in his description of the climate, *Nullum violentum est perpetuum*, a variation of the often mentioned proverb, *Si gravis brevis, si longus levis*. Plutarch appears in the book's dedication to Sir William Armine: the author hopes that he can catch inspiration from his patron as the common soldier Alexander drew strength from imitating his illustrious commander.

The reasons for Thomas Hooker's migration to Hartford and his dissatisfaction with the Bay policies are not entirely clear. But one may argue that Hooker was a mild rebel against New England theocracy and its limitation of the franchise to church members. No less strict in his theological views than his friends Winthrop and Cotton, he disagreed on the qualifications for full citizenship and voting privileges. Despite all of Hooker's emphasis on the Puritan tradition and his prominence as a religious leader, we detect a trend toward the democracy that characterized the secular side of the Hartford experiment, and there are some echoes of the classics in his writings. Thomas Hutchinson the historian was evidently critical of the venture: "They thought themselves at full liberty, without any charter from the Crown, to establish such sort of government as they thought proper, and to form a new state as fully to all intents and purposes as if they had been in a state of nature and were making their first entrance into civil society."

In a sermon preached before the General Court on May 31, 1638, Hooker was clear enough: "The choice of public magistrates belongs unto the people, by God's own allowance." And, "a general counsel, *chosen by all*, I conceive, under favour, most suitable to rule and most safe for the relief of the whole." But even here caution should see to it that there is a distinction between *ius naturale* and *ius positivum*. Hooker's *Survey of the Summe of Church Discipline*, published in 1648 by a group of his friends, contains much technical theology, much patristic Greek, and little Latin. We may glean, however, a few illustrations from ancient sources. On the indestructibility of true religion: "When you take away any part of the *Organicum Totum*, you lame the integrity of it, but you do not destroy the essence and nature of it. Socrates may loose a limb, an eye, and hand, so he is not an entire man, consisting of such members; yet he hath *totam naturam et definitionem hominis*, in regard of his essential causes." Matching this on the civil side, he declares: "*Salus Populi* is the highest law in all policy, civil or spiritual, to preserve the good of the whole." From current lawbooks he drew the proverb: *Quod ad omnes spectat, ab omnibus debet approbari.*

From Hooker we get one of the earliest colonial definitions of the Divine Law, in a letter of 1638 to Winthrop: "You will know what the heathen man said by the candle light of common-sense: 'The law is not subject to passion, nor to be taken aside with self-seeking ends, and therefore ought to be the chief rule over rulers themselves.'" This was a modified rendering of Cicero's standard interpretation of the Divine Law. We have seen that Hooker deprecated sermons overloaded with learning. He modestly declared that it could not be said of himself as it was said of Jerome by Erasmus, *Ciceronianus non Christianus*, "My rudeness frees me wholly from this exception." Whether or not his associates agreed with his views, he commanded universal respect. Cotton Mather recognized his outstanding qualities a half century later: "As Solon was pointed out to Anacharsis the Scythian visitor as the Wonder of Greece, so would Thomas Hooker be pointed out as the Wonder of New England."

There are many more such controversial episodes (of the kind which William Bradford of Plymouth tried to avoid) in early New England annals, but one more will suffice. It is an affair taken humorously by most readers, but its underlying threat was as serious as any. Thomas Morton of Clifford's Inn irritated both Puritans and Pilgrims with his contraband Indian trading and his Anglican propaganda. In 1627 he set up the Maypole at Wollaston and gathered about him a company of "Epicureans" dedicated to frivolity, quaffing "nectar" and dancing with squaws "in a corus, every man bearing his part." The Puritans censured him for celebrating "a Sabath like the Heathen to Venus, Bacchus, and Ceres." Endicott and Winthrop denounced him for "reviving anew and celebrating the feasts of the Roman goddess Flora, or the beastly practices of the mad Bacchanalians." But an objective view indicates that there was a deeper meaning in Morton's activity than the mere wish to preside at Horatian revels. A letter from the adventurer to Judge Jeffries in England, intercepted by Winthrop, shows his political hand: "If Jove vouchsafe to thunder, the charter and kingdom of the Separatists will fall asunder . . . I have uncased Medusa's head and struck the brethren with astonishment . . . the laws that are established in these parts are contrary to the dictates of wisdom (*invita Minerva*)." Morton's *New English Canaan*,[7] decked out with ancient mythology, the Trojan Horse, the Capitoline Geese, and a Ciceronian call to patriotic duty,[8] is a plea for free trade and for the enforcement of royal and parliamentary government. His schemes were failures, and he died at Agamenticus (York) in Maine, a disappointed pauper.

It is only proper, before discussing at length the most significant religious controversy of the period, to look about for an impartial viewer of the situation in Massachusetts.

Apart from the stylistic eccentricities that have already been mentioned, we find in Nathaniel Ward, author of *The Simple Cobler*, a frank commentator on the theological and political affairs of the Bay. His part in framing *The Body of Liberties* (1641) to the satisfaction of Winthrop marked him out as a constructive critic. Ward was no democrat, except for his insistence that the rights of the common man should be respected. He was a compound of lawyer, clergyman, and businessman, with experience in European diplomacy, a friend of Bacon, Sir Nathaniel Rich, and Elizabeth, the mother of Prince Rupert. As a Puritan he had suffered under Laud; but he aimed at a sensible compromise.

Nor was Ward particularly tolerant: he advocated a sort of liberal conservatism, *Nullum malum peius libertate errandi* (There is no greater evil than the freedom to make mistakes). Final decisions should be made by the upper magistrates, *Inter optimates penes quos est sancire leges* (By the leaders whose duty it is to approve the laws). Instead of a "colluvies of opinionists," he desired the age-old combination of ruler, council, and commons. He is, however, no less frank with the king than with the Seekers and extremists. He rebuked Charles for upsetting the balance: "*Majestas Imperii* has interfered with *Salus Populi*." Two years before the king's tragic end, Ward saw a faint chance for reform and parodied an epistle of Horace: "As you put up with your fortunes, so, Charles, shall we put up with *you*." [9]

Ward runs the gamut of classical and contemporary ideas. "Truth and Peace are the Castor and Pollux of the Gospel." Puns occur frequently. *Pax quo carior eo charior*, a manufactured epigram, is translated by the author: "A peace well made is likeliest then to hold/ When 'tis both dearly bought and dearly sold." Petronius, Ovid, Martial, Plautus, Vergil, Homer, and many other ancients find their way into his pages. His imagination runs riot in one table, with parallel columns of heretics classified according to their denominations: Erastians–Dryades, Anabaptists–Potamides, Enthusiasts–Pegasides, Seekers–Heliconiades, Antitrinitarians–Hamadryades. The remedy for the whole lot is: *Haeresis dedocenda est, non permittenda* (Unlearn your heresies; forbid them). God's instruments should be corrected "in his own mould, *ad amussim*" (to exact measurement by the spirit level). His use of alliteration, paradox, and caricature is abundant, but the classics also affected his political thinking.

A civil war, in the Cobler's opinion, is futile: "In civil Wars 'twixt subjects and their king, There is no conquest got by conquering." Ward's versatile training, flavored with his thorough knowledge of classical philosophy, had given him a human approach to legislation. He was an impartial observer. The triple balance of ideal government was well described by this Aristotelian critic: *Pura Politeia neque unum admittit soloecismum, neque valet praescriptio in politicis aut moribus* (The ideal state must be flawless, and special orders have no place in politics or ethics).

The well-known pamphlet debate between John Cotton and Roger Williams affords an excellent view of all these controversial details. Was "separation" or "nonseparation" the better way? Was the Old Testament an adequate guide for the régime of "Moses his Judicialls"? How far could the heritage of Greece and Rome serve as useful testimony and basis for action? Was the doctrine of "types" an adequate or helpful procedure? [10] (Winthrop was called a "Lycurgus"; Samson and Gideon were types and Christ the prototype.) Have civil governments a right to enforce religious policies? May the Church give orders to civil magistrates? Or was the real issue a conflict between oligarchy and an incipient democracy? Since the complicated theology of New England has been skillfully analyzed by recent historians, we may concentrate our attention here on another facet — the classical tradition and its effect on these two devoted spiritual leaders. The two men are particularly significant in that they set the stage for a drama which finally played itself out by 1700, when church and state, without further entanglements, became independent of each other.

This was no ivory-tower affair. Both Cotton and Williams were Cambridge-trained, at Emmanuel and Pembroke respectively. They were finished classicists. Cotton had held his congregation spellbound at Boston in Lincolnshire and subsequently as a partner in the Puritan colony. Williams, at home in cities or in the wilderness, started as a law apprentice to Sir Edward Coke. He was master of seven languages and a successful negotiator of two provincial charters, from two such different characters as Cromwell and Charles the Second. Cotton was serenely entrenched in his pulpit, with only occasional problems to bother him, such as the Anne Hutchinson episode. Williams, the restless radical, could both win the confidence of Indian tribes and hold his own with John Milton.

Besides Cotton's sermons, and letters or short pieces by both men, there are three tracts with which we are particularly concerned. Williams, after some bitter exchanges on the subject of his exile from the Bay Colony, opened the debate in 1644 with his *Bloudy Tenent* [doctrine] *of Persecution*, answered in 1647 by Cotton's *Bloudy Tenent Washed and Made White in the Bloud of the Lamb*, and culminating in 1652 with the Rhode Islander's *Bloudy Tenent Yet More Bloudy*. Cotton, politically in sympathy with the governing authorities, was primarily theological in attitude and interests. Williams, founder of a new experiment, employed a wider variety of knowledge, more classical, more historical, more diffuse, and less denominational.

In England Cotton had abandoned the fashion of sermons laden with Greek and Latin references. In the New World John Norton commended him for leaving off "rhetorical ornaments" and for preaching plain repentance, criticizing those who "prefer the Muses before Moses, and taste Plato more than Paul, and relish the Orator of Athens [Demosthenes] far above the Preacher of the Cross." Cotton expressed this idea in his pamphlet, *The Pouring out of the Seven Vials*: the early Christians "were glad to renounce their Jupiters and Junos." After such a conversion, "all the

Gods of the Gentiles shall not be able to provide any more offerings to be brought unto their alters, neither Apollo nor Jupiter nor Hercules."

If we compare the political beliefs of Cotton and Williams, we find them dealing not with the "mixed" form of government which they had studied in college, but with the extremes — the one oligarchical and the other democratic. According to the former, the magistrate has power over the souls as well as the bodies of the citizens. "Democracy," Cotton declared, "I do not conceive that ever God did ordain as a fit government." It may "be *status popularis* where a people choose their own governors; yet the government is not a democracy if it be administered not by the people but by the governors." "A democratical government might do well in Athens, a city fruitful of pregnant wits, but will soon degenerate to an *Anarchia* amongst rude common people." Whether Williams or Nathaniel Ward was the person he had in mind, we are not certain, but Cotton wrote: "It is unworthy the spirit of so godly learned a man as maketh this objection, to preferre Athens before Jerusalem, pregnant wits before sanctified hearts." The Aristotelian model of monarchy, aristocracy, and democracy would have to wait until the Constitution makers and the *vox populi* could combine forces in a truly republican document. The Reverend Mr. Stone had summed it up, with perhaps unconscious humor: the church is a "speaking Aristocracy in the face of a silent Democracy."

In justice to Cotton, however, we should note that he disapproved of a "mere aristocracy" or a *perpetua dictatura* which might fall into unfit hands. When Lord Saye and Sele, with Lord Brooke, projected a colony in the Bay region with a hereditary nobility and gentlemen of confirmed sincerity and worth, both he and Winthrop objected: it ran counter to the theocratic concept and was soon abandoned. Cotton illustrated his opinion with a line from Ovid: *Turpius ejicitur quam non admittitur* (It is more disgraceful to throw it out than to refuse its admission).[11] The historian

Hutchinson quoted the same passage, agreeing with such a policy. There must be a standard of character and a religious test, even for the nobility. But the example that Cotton and the Assistants particularly disapproved of was the Athenian Ecclesia, with its ballot privileges for every citizen. He agreed with Polybius that this procedure meant mob rule.[12]

Cotton's illustrations are mainly Biblical and patristic, dealing with Greek New Testament terminology. What is the meaning of the "bitterness" that came between Paul and Barnabas? How do we define heresy, sin, service, teaching, proof, refutation, love, faith, belief? What is the significance of the Greek word for "subverted"? Both men agree that these fine distinctions must be taken seriously. *Eutrapelia*, or courtesy, was all very well; but there should be no mixing of jest with earnestness — *Non est major confusio quam serii et joci.* Cotton is an opponent of all frivolity: when he condemns *ludicra*, he means not only stage plays (as the Romans defined the term) but all unprofitable distractions. His *Reply to Mr. Williams* is full of brief coinages, tossed off from his store of theology and classics. His Providence rival is *authades*, "self-pleasing, selfe-full, self-willed," like some of the bishops Paul describes in the first chapter of Titus. Superstition is a *cultus supra statutum.* Pastor and flock should work together *ex mutua alterius affectione.* A key phrase is penetratingly clear: *Non poena sed causa facit martyrem. Maius lumen extinguit minus.* These epigrammatic supports to his arguments, frequent in all his writings, are a kind of compensation for his sacrifice of the Greek and Roman authors whom he loved and quoted in his days as a Fellow of Emmanuel.

The Boston preacher could not entirely blot out his affection for the studies which had occupied his earlier years. His *Exposition of the Book of Canticles*, dealing with sacred love, welcomes a pagan comparison: "Thou hast Dove's eyes, that is, Chast and loathing uncleanness, as Pliny [the Elder] reports the doves to be." A line of verse from Ovid strikes a similar note: *Aspicis ut veniant ad candida tecta columbae*

(See how the doves come only to a clean dovecote).[13] Also, with reference to the first Christians: "What a sweet testimony doth Pliny [the Younger] himselve, though a persecutor, give of them, when he said he could find no fault with them, but that they rose early and went into the woods to sing hymns to one Jesus."

Cotton's offhand use of Latin is rare. Proverbs like *nodus in scirpo* (knot on a bulrush) escape him occasionally. In a letter to Williams he remarks that, because of suspected sympathy with Anne Hutchinson in the 1637 controversy, he had thought of leaving Massachusetts because this doctrine of union was "the Trojan Horse, out of which all the erroneous opinions and differences of the Country did issue forth."[14] When Williams printed a private letter of his concerning a Newgate heretic, Cotton had recourse to Pliny's epigram on the subject of personal communications: "It is one thing to write to an individual; it is another thing to address the public."[15] In his pamphlet *Keyes to the Kingdom*, he borrows the Roman rule for the appointment of a dictator — "to preserve the state from harm." Mere report and rumor are, as in Vergil's phrase, "as greedy for what is false and base as they are conscious of what is right."[16] Duties are duties; and citizens are duly assigned to their proper tasks, "each in his own place, as in Tully's *Offices*" (Cicero's *De officiis*). Most of these sayings are memory passages from old English schooldays, rather than specially presented aids to his arguments.

Cotton differed from Williams on certain historical issues. To the former, the Divine Law concerned church affairs only and did not apply in the Platonic or Ciceronian sense. The two men were poles apart in their interpretation of the attitude of Roman imperial officials toward the Christians. Cotton commended the law that "the accuser should show himself face to face," and believed that the Edict of Antoninus Pius was a reward for loyal service in the army; but the founder of Providence thought otherwise. The Edict ordered that "no Christian should be punished merely for that he was a Christian," unless some other crime against the civil state could be proved against him; and Cotton ascribed Rome's later troubles to image worship and Byzantine politics. Williams, however, as we shall see in the case of Constantine's Edict, held that official decrees did not cover the field of religion and that the ecclesiastical and the governmental were two separate functions. His opponent frankly stated that the magistrate had a double duty, a *judicium publicum,* wherein the judge must determine both what is right before men and what is right before God. For the same reason the Church must investigate crimes and errors. *Dedecus* (disgrace) is not *scelerum varietas aut atrocitas:* it is *scelerum impunitas.*

Roger Williams goes farther afield for his supporting material and much deeper into classical sources. He ransacks patristic works for definitions of "heathen" and "gentile," with perhaps less accuracy than Cotton. He is more general, making a distinction between plain piety and the holy earnestness which embodies full understanding of God's word. The term *kakon* is explained as that which is opposed to civil goodness in a commonwealth and should not be contrasted with "Spiritual Good or Religion in the Church." He separates *bonum temporale* from *bonum spirituale* (this is the kernel of his creed). Still more vividly he declares: there is no divine right of kings, for the state begins "in a community-consciousness." The family is a social growth, as Aristotle taught him, the base of society, "self-supporting in all that conduces to a good state of life in political association." Polybius fortifies this idea: there must be community protection for the family, safe from crude nature but under nature's higher law, where man is not subservient to "the might of the stronger." [17] Here Williams seems to be a predecessor of James Wilson, who a century and a half later urged that this arbitrary overlordship be provided against by the Constitution. The dictum of Protagoras, "Man is the measure of all things," is approved. The Stoic principles of equality and natural right, discussed by Cicero, are also touched upon in the works of Williams, who was as much at home in a political gathering as he was in a council of churches. The climax came when he declared in the *Bloudy Tenent* that "the Soveraigne, original, and foundation of civill power lies in the people." In so saying, he sealed his own theological death warrant as far as Massachusetts Bay was concerned.

The founder of Providence delighted in sharp, incisive phrases:

> To say that the civil and the spiritual are like *Hippocrates' Twinnes,* born together, grow up together, laugh together, weep together, sicken and die together, is a most dangerous Fiction of the Father of Lies.
>
> When Mr. Cotton confounds spiritual resistance with guns, swords, etc., he speaks too like the oracles of Apollo, which will be true however the event fall out.

Williams is a pioneer in the use of the famous *Lex Insita Naturae* of Cicero, "A Law of Nature, written in the hearts of all mankind, yea, even pagans."

In opposition to Cotton, Williams holds that the Edict of Antoninus Pius was misleading,[18] that real progress in Christianity took place when the martyrs suffered under Nero and Domitian, and that "dictation within the Church [under Constantine] was worse than oppression from without." Constantine's zeal "did more harm than the raging fury of the most bloody Nero." (Governor William Bradford of Plymouth, incidentally a far more learned scholar than he has been given credit for, agreed with this opinion. He held that the persecutions of Christians by the heathen and their emperors "were not greater than those of the Christians one against the other." [19] Bradford supports his statement by reference to Socrates of Constantinople, a fifth-century church historian.) Furthermore, in order to prove that secular and spiritual control are essentially different, Williams calls ancient history to witness. Successful political systems existed in pre-Christian times; there were heathen governments which had "civil peace and quiet, notwithstanding their religion was corrupt." "Master Cotton confesseth the flourishing of states ignorant of Christ, from age to age, yea even two thousand years in Athens, six generations before it heard of Christ, and fourteen generations since. . . . The Commonwealth of Rome flourished five hundred years together before even the name of Christ was heard in it: which so great a glory of so great a continuance mightily evinceth the distinction of the civill peace of a state from that which is *Christian Religion*." This statement, which might at a later date have been confused with deism, was merely Williams' way of saying that the *true* Gospel is far above the secular law.

Paul's request for a trial as a Roman citizen was a purely technical matter, in Williams' view. So was the question of the unoccupied territory which the Puritans appropriated from the Indians, arguing that these "voyd places" were wide open on the ground of *vacuum domicilium cedit occupanti*. The objection of the Rhode Islander to this policy was one of the reasons for his banishment. Legal matters could be thrashed out in court, but the rage of persecutors can be resisted. Even though *furor* and *ira* are short-lived, Jerome was right in holding that heresies must be "cut off, not by human law but by the sword of the spirit." [20]

The famous simile of Williams — a ship that carries men of many faiths but needs guidance by an expert captain, whatever his creed may be — is fortified by mention of Plato's "Gubernator," who must be a trained pilot and in this capacity issue such orders as he sees fit for the physical welfare of passengers and crew. This principle of segregation, emphasized in *The Bloudy Tenent*, made a profound impression in England, where Williams spent several years in association with Cromwell and Milton. It was a "clear-cut distinction between the Order of Grace and the Order of Nature." The symbolism, or typology, was well understood by those who attended the conferences held at Putney or Whitehall.[21] It was proper for him to praise "the gentile Prince Cyrus" as a restorer of God's people and "an instrument of mercy to the faithful." He also gave Gallio some credit for his decision that Paul's case should be dismissed,[22] and that spiritual mat-

ters were "out of his province." Ancient history furnishes
the radical Roger with several other parallels: "The civil
state of Ephesus was essentially distinct from the worship of
Diana in the city." In a passage remarkable for its daring universality, he declares: "Caesar, as a civill supreme magistrate,
ought to defend Paul from civill violence and slanderous ac-
cusations about sedition, mutiny, disobedience, etc. And in
that sense who doubts but God's people may appeale to the
Roman Caesar, an Egyptian Pharaoh, a Philistine Abimelecke,
an Assyrian Nebuchadnezzar, the Great Mogol, Prester John,
the greate Turke, or an Indian sachem!" Ovid's punishment
by the Emperor Augustus was a purely civil matter, inflicted
because he taught "The Wanton Art of Love."

Among the many activities of the founder of Providence
was his friendly relations with the Indians. It was owing to
his unselfish diplomacy that Canonicus, the *morosus ac bar-
barus senex,* became reconciled to the English. He advised
leniency to the conquered Pequots in 1638, adapting a line
from Juvenal to read mercy rather than vengeance — "a light
penalty is more blessed than life itself." [23] "The Lord," he
wrote in 1637, "drew the bow of the Pequot War against the
country," a figure of Apollo in the *Iliad* used by many
colonial historians. Much later (1656) a letter to the General
Court urges patience with the Indians, for *dies et quies sanant
hominem* (time and tranquillity are the best cure for mankind). Dashed off with his usual speed on a voyage to England in 1643, his *Key to the Indian Language of America* is a
unique document. He compares Indian dialects with the
Greek, using grave and acute accents and indicating parallels
to the classical forms (some of them farfetched). Native
words are sometimes given their Greek equivalents; he notes
that the Bear constellation is based on the same metaphor as
in the Greek. Their communal life impresses him and evokes
the overworked Senecan commonplace: *Concordia parvae res
crescunt, discordia magnae dilabuntur* (Harmony makes small
establishments grow; discord makes great ones crumble).[24]
The Indians see a mystic power in nature; it seems like pan-

theism — *Praesentem narrat quaelibet herba deum,* which Williams translates, "Every little grass doth tell/ The sons of Man, there God doth dwell."

It would be monotonous to record all the parenthetical classical allusions, mostly quoted from memory, and the almost macaronic coinages found not only in the two pamphlets we have discussed, but also in Williams' private correspondence. They often occur as afterthoughts, to drive home his arguments. Writing to his friend John Winthrop, Jr., he emphasizes obedience to civil law, with a tag from Terence: "We mortals deteriorate if we are under no restraints." At a critical time in 1649 he reminds the same correspondent of *Hoc momentum unde pendet aeternitas,* fortifying these words by "Proverbs 6." "Again, while we are here, noble sir, let us *viriliter hoc agere, rem agere humanam, divinam, Christianam.*" To Governor Endicott in 1651, after the almost Neronian treatment of some strangers of other faiths, he waxes more than indignant: "He was a tyrant that had put an innocent man into a bear's skin and so caused him as a wild beast to be baited to death."

Compared with Cotton, Williams' style is diffuse, eccentric, sometimes illogical. He was fond of alliteration, such as *Ratio est rex legis et lex est rex regis.* He invokes the "maxim of Queen Experience: *Secundae cogitationes meliores.*" He plays with words: *Sicut fluctus fluctum, sic luctus luctum* (As wave follows wave, so woe follows woe). We meet with innumerable echoes from his reading and study, transmuted into his own informal English. Seneca, an author whose style bears some resemblance to his own, furnishes material for some unacknowledged remarks on friendship, on the readiness to face death, and on the transient nature of human existence.[25]

These reactions of Cotton and Williams to the Greco-Roman tradition lead us to several conclusions. Cotton, highly trained in the ancient languages, abjured them in favor of a conservative theology, a settled position of leadership, and a strict theologically oriented government. Williams, just as earnest in religious matters, combined his use of mystical symbolism with a wide sweep of classical illustration, going far afield into linguistics, law, and diplomacy. Their differing beliefs, equally sincere, are an early landmark in the "segregation" controversy, the question of the separation of the civil and the religious function. Neither can be neglected as a man of weight in public affairs. Their debate, full of the dogmas and doctrines of a bygone age, reveals the difference between the oligarchic, or aristocratic, policy of the leading guardian of New England puritanism and the belief in democracy and popular will which found an outlet in the Providence experiment. The eighteenth century, with its blend of reason and enlightenment, provided an answer to the dilemma.

IV

COLONIAL REACTIONS
TO A CLASSICAL EDUCATION

THE type of education offered to the youth who attended colonial grammar schools and colleges was uniform and standardized. Compared with present-day elective systems, there was little differentiation or attempt to suit the work to the individual. Although a few "extras" crept into the curriculum by degrees, providing an occasional choice of subjects, the Greek and Latin languages were the passwords for admission into colleges and for progress to the bachelor's degree. Beyond the elementary stage they were the main academic diet.

In the compass of this chapter, a haunting question must be answered: How did this trivium of grammar, rhetoric, and dialectic, with three quarters of the quadrivium (arithmetic, geometry, and astronomy), the direct descendants of medieval scholasticism, fit into the American scene? Was it a springboard or a hurdle? Our main theme recurs, like Plato's "sound of the flute in the ears of the mystic," and we shall attempt to find out how this academic monopoly, linguistic and metaphysical, amplified itself in the later lives of its students into such a variety of ideas and differences of opinion.

After we examine the requirements for admission to the nine pre-Revolutionary colleges, and the schedules of the colleges themselves, we may apply this recurrent refrain to the mature workings of the colonial mind. We meet, in a span of nearly two hundred years, an astonishing preponderance of college men as political leaders. We note that the classical tradition becomes a partner rather than a servant of theology. We find a conscientious democratic desire to give the Indians the benefit of this formidable training. Throughout the provincial period the abstract speculation found in the classroom and in senior theses deals increasingly with practical politics. There is an intellectual activity which goes far beyond mere imitation or influence: it proliferates into the lives and interests of several generations. Colonial educators were not concerned, as we are in the twentieth century, with the debatable issue of "mental transfer"; nor did they weigh the respective values of accumulated knowledge in contrast with aptitude and intelligence testing. We note a sharp dividing line between the conceptual world of the Enlightenment, with its theory of progressive excellence or its Chain of Being, and the empirical and statistical methods of today. We cannot adequately explain the difference, but we can let colonial America speak for itself.

Solidly classical, the college entrance requirements remained the same for about one hundred and seventy-five years. The only addition was a dash of arithmetic. When John Winthrop's nephew, George Downing (who gave his name to the London street), applied to Harvard, he was asked to "understand Tully, Virgil, or any such classical authors, and readily to speak or write true Latin in prose and have skill in making Latin verse, and be completely grounded in the Greek language." Most of the textbooks were written in Latin, and that language was used on all academic occasions. Downing was so well trained that later he was able to converse at length with Cardinal Mazarin in Latin. John Jay, who entered King's College (Columbia) in 1760, had to give a "rational account of the Greek and Latin grammars," read three orations of Cicero and three books of the *Aeneid*, and translate the first ten chapters of the Gospel of John into Latin. In mathematics he was supposed to be "expert as far as the Rule of Reduction." As late as 1816 Horace Mann, entering Brown University, had to jump a similar hurdle:

"Upon examination of the President and Tutors, the candidate must read accurately, construe, and parse Tully and the Greek Testament and Virgil, and shall be able to write true Latin in prose, and hath learned the rules of Prosody and Vulgar Arithmetic, and shall bring suitable testimony of a blameless life and conversation." When planning the program for the University of Virginia, Jefferson approved Dr. Cooper's statement: "It should be scrupulously insisted on that no youth can be admitted to the university unless he can read with facility Vergil, Horace, Xenophon, and Homer: unless he is able to convert a page of English at sight into Latin: unless he can demonstrate any proposition at sight in the first six books of Euclid, and show an acquaintance with cubic and quadratic equations." They agreed that a lower standard than this would make the proposed institution "a mere grammar school."

There was no change in the classical requirement of the colleges. The Boston Latin School (as well as resident tutors or neighboring clergymen in the south) answered the challenge. In 1710 a boy who had reached the seventh year on this ladder of learning was reading Cicero's orations, Justinian, the Latin and Greek New Testaments, Isocrates, Homer, Hesiod, Vergil, Horace, Juvenal, and dialogues in Godwin's *Roman Antiquities*, as well as turning the Psalms into Latin verse. The last-named accomplishment was sometimes omitted by special permission. The prevalence of this classical atmosphere is evident in the funeral tribute paid to Headmaster Cheever of Boston Latin by an alumnus, Cotton Mather, who loved him as Crito loved Socrates:

Having learnt an oration made by Tully in praise of his own master [the poet Archias], they should not be outdone by a pagan in gratitude . . . Verrius the master to the nephews of Augustus had a statue erected for him; and Antoninus obtained from the Senate a statue for his master Fronto. I am sorry that mine has none. And Cato counted it more glorious than any statue to have it asked *Why has he none?* But in the grateful memories of his scholars there have been, and will be, hundreds erected for him.

In these examples Mather ranges characteristically over Plato, Cicero, Suetonius (*On the Grammarians*), Fronto's *Letters,* and Plutarch's *Cato Major.*

Good schoolmasters lived before and after Ezekiel Cheever, but none with greater influence or distinction. He was not only thorough: he was original. In his elegy Cotton Mather paid tribute to his high standards of teaching: "Do but name Cheever, and the Echo, straight/ Upon that name, *Good Latin* will repeat." This "Corderius Americanus," as Mather called him, was born in London in 1614 and schooled at Christ's Hospital and Emmanuel College, Cambridge. Settling in New Haven in 1638, he became a force in the religious and civic life of the town. Unfortunately for Connecticut, but luckily for Massachusetts, his independent views on church matters led to an ecclesiastical trial and to his departure for the Bay Colony. Here he taught for the rest of his long life, at Ipswich, Charlestown, and the Boston Latin School, active at the last-named from 1670 to 1708. Judge Sewall's tribute to him is characteristic of both men: "A rare Instance of Piety, Health, Strength, Serviceableness." Many anecdotes imply that Cheever was, for his time, a "progressive," who taught "Latin without tears." His *Accidence, a Short Introduction to the Latin Tongue,* circulated in new editions and reprints until 1838. One of its objects was to simplify the famous Lily's Grammar, which Shakespeare parodies through the absurdities of Holofernes and Sir Hugh Evans. Nor did he become a slave to classroom routine, as is proved by his manuscript log of four hundred pages containing copies of ancient masterpieces, experiments in Greek and Latin verse, and critical comments.

This Boston program seems to have been still more intensively classical a century later. Jonathan Homer "entered Lovell's in 1776 at seven years, and studied Latin from eight o'clock to eleven and from one till dark. I entered college at the age of fourteen and was equal in Latin and Greek to the best in the Senior class." Ezra Stiles, the President of Yale, held back the precocious John Trumbull, who was ready for college at the age of seven and a half. He had finished off his requirements with "Cordery, Tully's XII Select Orations, Vergil (*Eclogues* and all the *Aeneid*), and the four Gospels in Greek." [1]

By 1750 grammar schools in the larger cities were approximating the Boston standard, such as the Hopkins Grammar School of New Haven and the Penn Charter School of Philadelphia. Private instruction in the south modeled itself upon the same program. The many boys who were sent across the Atlantic to English schools, to Westminster, Eton, Wakefield in Yorkshire, or St. Bee's in Cumberland, were fed on the same pabulum. A letter from John Laurens, that most attractive young colonial, to his father, later the president of Congress, tells of the homework required at Westminster: "Little Harry sits by my side, making his verses for Monday morning . . . a little while at making one or two quicker than he is accustomed . . . he exalted and exclaimed 'Apollo favors me tonight.' " [2] John Laurens himself, though his father was skeptical of such a concentrated schedule,[3] had studied at Geneva "Latin, Greek, French, Italian, Belles-Lettres, Physics, History, Geography, mathematics, experimental philosophy, fencing, riding, drawing, and reading the Civil Law."

There were plenty of polite rebels, such as Jacky Custis, the stepson of Washington, and Ben and Bob Carter of Virginia who fought a genial rear-guard action against the system. The list of books which the Reverend Jonathan Boucher, the tutor of Jacky, suggested to Washington for entrance into King's College indicates a heavy burden for a boy of fourteen: Terence, Horace, Cicero, Livy, Martial, Grotius, the Greek Testament, *Clavis Homerica* (Key to Homer), grammars, Blackwell's *Sacred Classics*, Hooke's *Roman History*, and Kennet's *Roman Antiquities*. Ezra Stiles, always on the lookout for genius, having examined Lucinda Foote (aged twelve) in Greek and Latin, presented her with a certificate stating that if she had been a boy she could have entered the freshman class at Yale.[4]

From early days, however, there were two popular forces at work on this formidable curriculum. The first was the gradual growth of the belief that interest was no less important than industry. Many attempts were made to enliven curricula: there were "Colloquies," "Nomenclators," and "Sententiae Pueriles." The *Moral Distichs* of Cato, a composite collection dating from the fourth century A.D., was popular for centuries: it was translated by James Logan and published by Franklin. Cotton Mather recommended Sebastian Chateillon's *Dialogorum Sacrorum Libri Quattuor*, which set forth stories in Latin taken from the Scriptures for "molding the language and the characters of youth." A *Phrasium Poeticarum Thesaurus* appeared in London in 1642. Parents asked for the *Ianua Linguarum Reserata*, the "Door to Languages Unlocked," by the progressive Comenius. William Fitzhugh of Virginia described to a friend in 1698 an experiment he had tried with his son, wherein a French minister taught the boy Latin in the French language, confining English to vernacular home-talk.[5]

One can always trust Roger Williams to do something original. He tells us, in a letter of July 1654 to John Winthrop, Jr., that:

> It pleased the Lord to call me for some time and with some persons to practise the Hebrew, the Greeke, Latine, French, and Dutch. The Secretarie of the Counceill (Mr. Milton) for my Dutch I read him, read me many more languages. Grammar rules begin to be esteemed a Tyrannie. I taught 2 young gentlemen, a Parliament man's sons (as we teach our children English) by words, phrazes, and constant talk, etc. I have begun with mine own three boys (who labour besides). Others are coming to me. Ever yours, R.W.

Here is a clear case of what is pedagogically defined as "the direct method." Anthony Benezet, the Philadelphia Quaker, objected to the amoral tone of Horace and Ovid: Numa was a better model than Romulus; Plutarch and Xenophon were satisfactory for youthful pupils. The Reverend Hugh Jones, in his *Present State of Virginia* (1724), held that there should be more science, along with commercial and agricultural courses. Old Dominion lads should have "polite and mathematical learning conveyed to them in English, without going directly to Greece and Rome." "They may be good scholars without becoming Cynics, as they may be good Christians without appearing Stoics." William Penn, a Christ Church classicist, who quoted Greek philosophers in support of his doctrine of the Indwelling Spirit, recommended the study of "things" rather than "words" for young pupils, advising the postponement of Latin until age twelve.

A second force or trend began to manifest itself in colonial educational circles, in step with increasing prosperity and the growth of industry. This was what we now call "vocational training." There were of course many who could not write, and many who, after elementary schooling, chose the farm, the sea, or the counting house. New ventures, privately supported, sprang up on the secondary level. Most of them attempted to cover the Latin requirement for higher education. But at sea-going Portsmouth in New Hampshire we find navigation, "gauging," and "tonnage" added to the grammar-school curriculum. In mercantile Philadelphia there were extra subjects such as "indentures, accounting, and bonds," as well as trigonometry and "plain, parallel, and current sailing." A Maryland school offered, besides Greek and Latin, "merchants' accounts, surveying, and navigation." Charles Peale, father of the portrait painter, added to this fare lessons in fencing and dancing, under special masters. Theophilus Chamberlain, a college graduate, in 1768 advertised a private school in Boston, "to fit boys for entering any college upon the Continent." A compromise, not leading to higher education, was arranged for in the will of the Virginian George Mason.[6] His nephews were to be taught at home until age twelve, studying elementary subjects and modern languages, "then to be kept at learning the Latin language, book-keeping, mathematics, and other useful branches of literature till the age of 18," with a business career to follow. Men training for army service could find classes in fortification and gunnery. In the libraries of Standish, Greene, and Washington there were included the military treatises of the ancients, especially Caesar, who was conspicuous by his absence from most secondary curricula until the beginning of the nineteenth century. Some schools made no pretense at being anything but vocational and paid no attention to college preparation. It was a far cry from the offerings of present-day public schools, which present a hundred permutations and combinations of courses, or from our private academies where, in one case, out of a graduating class of sixty-one pupils only ten had exactly similar schedules.

As to literacy, in certain well-settled regions the proportion of those who could read and write was as high as 90 percent: on the frontier the ratio was much lower. At all events, the ambitious individual could rise on the educational scale. The Moravians provided schoolmasters who would prepare youth for the Latin courses at the seminary in Bethlehem, Pennsylvania.[7] Zinzendorf's *Unitas Fratrum* combined the *collegium musicum* with a liberal education which acknowledged the guidance of Halle and Jena. George Fox, the Quaker champion of a "guarded education," laid the seal of his approval on the publication of his *Institutiones Pietatis*, in 1676: "The chief Principles of the Latin tongue being added." Peleg Folger, ambitious to be Nantucket's schoolmaster, took his classics with him on his whaling voyages, despite the banter of a shipmate who scribbled in one of Peleg's books: "Peleg Folger is a rum soull for writing Latin." This young relative of Benjamin Franklin attained his objective: he gave up whaling and taught Latin to the young Nantucketers.[8] A rapid glance at the careers of Edmund Pendleton, George Wythe, and Patrick Henry makes it clear that mastery of the classics was not confined to college graduates. Henry, studying at home with his father and his clergyman uncle, read Livy and Vergil in the original and continued his "homework" with Grotius, Bacon, Horace, Juvenal, Homer, Ovid, and translations of Demosthenes as a model for oratory. The case of Roger Sherman, Connecticut cord-

wainer, surveyor, and calendar editor, who held his own in
all three of the legislative bodies although he was not a college man, speaks for itself. The apocryphal story concerning
James Gibbons, the Pennsylvania farmer who conducted a
school in Chester County, has probably gathered momentum
after nearly two centuries. A group of British officers, after
the battle of Brandywine, challenged him on his linguistic
knowledge. Gibbons answered them in French and Spanish,
capping with a Horace quotation and "routing them all with
a knowledge of Greek." [9]

The first completely recorded college curriculum, with
detailed courses and textbooks, was that of Harvard in 1723.
Freshmen reviewed "the classic authors learned at school."
New Testament Greek, logic, and rhetoric occupied the
attention of those who were "cohabiting for scholastic com-
munion whereby to actuate the minds of one another." Greek
and Hebrew were food for sophomores. The third-year men
(or boys) were exercised in disputations on ethics, metaphysics, geography, and Heerebord's *Meletemata Philo-
sophica.* Charles Morton's *Compendium Physicae,* taught
from a manuscript, continued the Aristotelian tradition
(though by degrees Aristotle's metaphysics were modified by
the more natural doctrines of Ramus). Keckermann's *Systema
Logicae* was a compromise between these two authorities.
Chaldee or Syriac was available, but not popular. For seniors,
Alsted's *Comprehensive Encyclopaedia* provided the geometry, and their natural philosophy (physics) was made scrip-
turally safe by the *Medulla Theologiae* of William Ames.
Every two weeks or thereabouts, debates in Latin took place.
A final thesis wound up the work for the baccalaureate; and
after the three-year interval many presented *quaestiones* for
the final accolade of a master's degree. In the period between
1642 and 1723, we find some astronomy, "the nature of
plants" (a summer field course), politics (a partner of ethics),
and "Divinity Catechetical." There were florilegia, or anthologies, to be read extracurricularly: Nathan Bailey's
Polyanthea was a short cut to those seeking quotations. An

amusing volume had appeared in London in 1603: *Carminum Proverbialium totius humanae vitae status breviter delinian-tium loci communes in gratiam iuventutis selecti* (Commonplace sayings from Poetical Proverbs which described briefly every situation in the life of man, selected for the edification of youth). For a patriotic diatribe there was Nikolaus Reusner's *Symbola Heroica Imperatorum et Caesarum Romanorum.* A divinity student could quite properly get some help from Musculus' *Commonplaces of Christian Religion,* published first in 1563. There was also free time to browse in modern literature or to copy into a commonplace book favorite passages from one's reading.

The Princeton program was even more classical. As described by President Witherspoon on a money-raising tour of Jamaica in 1770, it announced "First year: Latin, Greek, classical antiquities, and rhetoric; second year: one ancient language, geography, philosophy, mathematics; third year: language, mathematics, natural and moral philosophy." The final year was more flexible: "the higher classics, mathematics, natural and moral philosophy, history, literary criticism, and French if desired."

By this time the outside world had entered the classroom. Though earlier authorities had rejected "an ergasterium for mechanic fancies," the Copernican theory, first taught in 1659, was accepted. Bacon, Newton, and Descartes edged their way into the curriculum. The political rather than the metaphysical Aristotle began his impressive influence as an analyst of "mixed government." By 1738 John Winthrop established himself as a leader in the trend toward the march of science and academic laboratory courses. Telescopes, globes, hydrostatics, the orrery, and electrical apparatus became popular. David Bushnell, a Yale sophomore, invented a *Machina quae ad naves Bostoniae portu pulveris pyrii explo-sione distruendas nunc est fabricata* (a device which has been built for the purpose of blowing up the [British] ships in the port of Boston by means of a charge of gunpowder).[10] But economics, government, and shop-work courses were creations of a later day. Home chores, the forum, the state house, and independent invention furnished the "life-experience" material. Presidents gave extracurricular lectures on every conceivable subject; and undergraduates, all taking the same academic program, explored outside the college schedule in their informal conferences and abstract debates. The College of Philadelphia led the way with a medical school, though still insisting on the classical base, and as a concession to modernism set up a special mathematics division. But the new prospectus for King's College endeavored to break the mold in the process of higher education. In 1754 Samuel Johnson outlined the program:

It is the design of this college to instruct and perfect Youth in the learned languages and the Arts of reasoning correctly and speaking eloquently; and in the arts of numbering and measuring, of surveying and navigation, of Geography and History, of Husbandry, Commerce and Government, and in the knowledge of all Nature in the Heavens above us and in the Air, Water, and Earth around us, and the various kinds of Meteors, Stones, Mines, and Minerals, Plants and Animals, and of everything useful for the comfort, the convenience and Elegance of life . . . and finally to lead them from the study of Nature to the Knowledge of themselves and one another.

There could be no more Socratic or comprehensive climax to education than this. Even the magnificence of the unfulfilled claims demands our admiration. Had Johnson himself offered a specific course for each of these fields, he would have been presiding, *mutatis mutandis*, over the equivalent of a twentieth-century university.

To repeat the initial query — how was it that such a rigid curriculum produced so many outstanding and original personalities in colonial affairs? Anyone who has read deeply in American biography cannot help being impressed by the proportion of college graduates whom historians agree upon as representative of the provincial period. One writer describes eleven early New Englanders, nine of whom were college-bred. Another sketches the careers of thirty-three men (from all the colonies), thirty of whom were products

of higher education.[11] The Massachusetts Bay region contained one hundred and thirty British alumni by the year
1646. A collection of portraits of emigrants to America before 1701 shows one third possessed of university degrees.
Virginia clergymen were in many cases trained in the home
country. Ninety-eight Americans during the colonial period
attended Oxford or Cambridge. One hundred and eighty-one
were registered at the Inns of Court in London, with Virginians and South Carolinians well in the lead.[12] The Middle
Colonies were especially interested in the medical school of
Edinburgh, where theses were required to be written in Latin,
although a canny Scot connected with the university Latin-
ized them on a black-market basis "for a consideration." Dr.
John Morgan in his inaugural discourse at the University of
Pennsylvania in 1765 recommended "Greek, in which were
the original treasures of medical science, Latin as the common
language of physicians and scholars, and French, as needed
for current professional literature." Leyden was also prominent in its appeal to medical students.

The record of the signers of the Declaration of Independence and the Constitution, with their frequent invocation of
classical testimony, reveals the close connection between
their studies and their political activity. Twenty-seven men
with college backgrounds out of fifty-six at the congress
supported the Declaration (Harvard furnished eight), and
twenty-three out of thirty-nine (with nine from Princeton)
committed themselves to the Constitution. Nine champions
of federal union had studied law in London. If we add to
these groups a numerous body of Tories, in the main American-born, the facts are striking. Furthermore, we must include many of the "self-starters" already mentioned as attain-
ing familiarity with the ancient tradition, such as the first
Governor Wolcott of Connecticut who, according to President Stiles, "did not go to school, but knew Latin." [13]

This proportion is still more striking if we go back to
those who organized and led the first settlers. The individuals
mainly responsible for British migration were with few

exceptions the product of Oxford or Cambridge. Coddington of Newport and Oglethorpe of Georgia seem to be the only front-rank founders with no academic experience: and even the latter had matriculated at Oxford before entering the army. Baron De La Warr, who might be called the first real governor of Virginia, and John Mason, the disappointed patentee of "Laconia" (now New Hampshire), hailed respectively from Queen's and Magdalen of Oxford. Among the pioneer Germans, we may include Pastorius, Muhlenberg, Peter Miller, and Count Zinzendorf. The 1801 cabinet of Jefferson was composed entirely of college graduates — the President from William and Mary, Madison and Robert Smith from Princeton, Lincoln from Harvard, Granger from Yale, and Gallatin from the higher schools of Geneva.

A second question raises itself at this point, as in one of the old Roman *controversiae*. How does this prominence of college graduates in colonial affairs harmonize with the great American democratic dogma? The degree-less conquerors of the frontier, the happy New World farmers whom Crève-coeur sketches so charmingly as emancipated from Roman ruins and classical decay, the immigrant in general — all these are historically important. They made their way in a land of opportunity. But this very opportunity was also available in the educational field. Bacon's proverbial saying, that "the generall Counsels and the Plots and Marshalling of affairs come best from those that are learned," left the leadership wide open to all. Free tuition for many local schools (except in certain backward regions), the Bay Colony law of 1647, the Pennsylvania statute of 1683, the compulsory education of apprentices, indicate that the colonists were on the watch for youth of promise. The farm lad whose term bills were paid in grain or pigs or cider, the "log colleges" in the Middle Colonies and Virginia, with special funds for "poor and pious youth," prove that any able individual was welcome. John Wise, the son of an indentured servant, worked his way through Harvard and spoke of his alma mater as "the place, if not of the goddess Minerva or Apollo, yet the Bethel and temple of God Himself." [14] When Hugh Brackenridge, applying to Princeton, apologized to the president for his poverty and quoted the famous lines from Juvenal — *Haud facile emergunt quorum virtutibus obstat Res angusta domi*[15] — the kindly Witherspoon replied: "There you are wrong, young man; it is only your *res angusta domi* men that do emerge!"

There were social levels based on property; but there was no class cleavage in the old-world sense. The classical program was an intellectual instrument for both conservatives and radicals (as in the case of Governor Hutchinson and Samuel Adams), for Tories and Whigs, for the ambitious immigrant and the comfortable proprietor. Roger Williams, the extreme "leftist" of New England, drew upon the ancients much more copiously than did his opponent John Cotton, the bulwark of theocratic aristocracy. Jefferson, the arch-exponent of agrarian democracy, urged a complete system of public education for his native state, culminating, as we have noted, in a university program which took for granted a knowledge of Greek and Latin. He wrote to his nephew some formidable recommendations for pre-college reading, which included nearly all the Greek and Roman historians, the poets and dramatists of major importance, and some philosophy. As if this were not enough, he bade the boy not to omit Shakespeare, Milton, Pope, and Swift.

The prevalence as well as the democracy of this classical prescription is proved by the fact that it was regarded as the duty of the settlers to offer its advantages to the Indians. Here was what we might call "an error in the fourth dimension." In the early Bay Colony youthful Indians were catechised by Wilson, Shepard, and Eliot in the form of queries which derived from the problems posed by the Stoics two thousand years before — for example, in Seneca's fifty-seventh *Epistle*, "If a man should be inclosed in iron a foot thick and thrown into the fire, could the soul come forth or not?" or the famous paradox of Socrates, "Suppose two men sin, of whom one knows that he sins and the other does not know it, will God punish both alike?" One Indian received the B.A. degree at Harvard; one fell by the wayside; and one died in college. The successful candidate became an expert in Greek and Latin verse. Similar pains were also taken by Governor Spotswood for the training of friendly Indians, with indifferent results. William Byrd, on a journey inland, sent back word to William and Mary College, recommending "two Nansemonds, two Nottaways, and two Meherrins to go to the Colledge."

Dartmouth College seems to have been more successful. A visitor to the Indian camp after Wayne's victory at Fallen Timbers told of a conference with Chief White-Eyes, who had attended Dartmouth and read Greek books in the wilderness.[16] Ezra Stiles in 1762 recorded a conversation with Captain Tucker of Newport, who had been on the Mississippi. Tucker met there an Indian who spoke French and English and wrote Latin. He was said to have commanded the Indians against Braddock in 1755 and "had been a student at Harvard College in New England."[17] This was indeed drawing a long bow! One distinguished classicist, however, adopted quite a different policy. James Logan of Pennsylvania, translator of Cato's *Distichs* and Cicero's *De senectute* for Franklin's press, welcomed the Indians to his country place at Stenton, but made no attempt to reform their culture.

If we agree that this classical curriculum was both democratic and conducive to leadership, our next query or, to use Plato's phrase, our "third wave" may concern itself with those elements in the curriculum which trained for service to the community. Yale's early degrees qualified a man as *instructus ecclesiae* or *ornatus patriae*. The climax of this higher education was the bachelor's graduation thesis and the master's *quaestio*. Here is a chronological mirror of the colonial mind, from abstract metaphysics and academic dialogue to the burning issues of independence. It became gradually a training ground for the application of Aristotle, Cicero, Polybius, and other political scientists of old to the debates over the Declaration and Constitution. The thesis originated in Scotland, the *quaestio* from Oxford. The former was an acid test of technical reasoning, in Latin, on a given subject dealing with logic, rhetoric, philosophy, physics, or mathematics. As time went on, *theses politicae* became more frequent. A broadside sheet was distributed or posted. A query was to be attacked or defended. These were medieval inheritances, descendants of the ancient *suasoriae* and *controversiae*. The theory of mental training was implicit, and it was assumed that the required skill would carry over into the meditations of the creative writer. The speakers knew the five points of an oration from Cicero and Quintilian — *exordium, narratio, refutatio, confirmatio, peroratio*. Some of the future ministers had read the *Ecclesiastes*, or *Ars concionandi*, of Erasmus, a book on homiletics. Those who could "draw the heads" of a sermon had modernized the ancient formulas into text, application, doctrine, division, and use.

Theses and *quaestiones* in the first three American colleges were seldom political, for obvious reasons, until church and state grew independent of each other. Early topics were metaphysical and speculative: *Universalia non sunt extra intellectum*, or the standard *Quicquid est in intellectu prius fuit in sensu*. One student contended that matter and form could not exist separately. William and Mary College, few of whose theses are extant because of a fire, rebelled at the Aristotelian syllogism; but records of its early debates show extensive use of ancient history. "Was Brutus justified in having his son executed?" "Is an agrarian law consistent with the principles of a wise republic?" Yale ran to science and theology, Princeton to rhetoric. For some students this was heavy going: in 1663 we find some mock theses. A Harvard scholar declared *Geometres est Nebulo Angularis* (A geometrician is a cross-grained blockhead). Another defined ethics as *vitiorum emplastrum corrosivum* (a mustard plaster to cure vice). Later, at the University of Pennsylvania, a wag maintained that "A too rapid succession of ideas is often the cause of insanity." But the issues of the day began to creep into the cloister. Dudley Woodbridge asked the old Roman question in 1699, *An Salus Populi Sit Suprema Lex?* and answered in the affirmative. The *quaestio* of Andrew Eliot in 1740 claimed that "absolute and arbitrary monarchy is contrary to reason." Matthew Cushing's topic (1742) was: "Civil laws which are against nature are not binding on the conscience." In 1698 monarchical government was defined as "the best"; but in 1723 a speaker said no to the question, "Is the Royal power absolutely by divine right?"

Between 1743 and 1762 five orators held that civil government originates from compact, as did John Adams in 1758. The bachelor's thesis of Ezra Stiles at Yale (1746) was *Jus regum non est iure divino haereditarium.* A "syllogistic debate" in Latin, was held at Princeton approving the dictum of the legalist Ulpian: "All men are free by the Law of Nature." Theology had eased its fetters, for we note an address holding that "No religion is rational without liberty of conscience." A Brown graduate of 1769 opposed taxation without representation, and another from the same institution declared that a defensive war was justified. This was in 1774, the same year in which a Princeton student applied the popular slogan *Bellum servituti anteponendum.* Discussions on matter and form had given way to declarations such as the Brown thesis of 1773: "Have not the American colonists the same rights as the inhabitants of Great Britain?" The word *democracy* was sparingly used, but its equivalent was often in evidence.

A thorough reading of all possible material between 1607 and 1789 leads us to the conclusion that this educational program, with its manifold by-products, was relevant to the cultural and civic needs of a new national experiment.

A realistic confirmation of this point may be found in the career of John Witherspoon, president of Princeton from 1768 to 1794. He was not as thorough a scholar as Dunster of Harvard or Stiles of Yale. But he was an "original" because of his combined accomplishments in three fields — academic, clerical, and political — fortified by the common-sense philosophy which added power to his public efforts. More than any other American educator, he made Greek and Latin a functional part of the nation's literary style, as well as a vital element of training for both pulpit and public service. A Scotsman and a graduate of Edinburgh, he had followed the regular round of Greek, Latin, Euclid, logic, rhetoric, the *Poetics* of Aristotle, Longinus *On the Sublime*, plus moral and natural philosophy. Witherspoon took his degree in 1739 with a Latin thesis *De Mentis Immortalitate*, dedicated to the Marquis of Tweeddale. After a series of parish promotions and some hot arguments with the "moderates" of the Scottish Church, he accepted the Princeton presidency, to the great joy of Benjamin Rush, who wrote home in Horatian ecstasy announcing his success. He was of course aided by the advantage of entrance upon the American scene at its most dramatic period. But this man who served twelve years as an energetic member of the Continental Congress and in the provincial legislature of New Jersey proved conclusively that in his case Clergy, Congress, and College formed an impressive *aes triplex* of accomplishment.

Witherspoon's first commencement address left no doubt about his policy: "The remains of the ancients are the standard of taste." The same point of view characterized his extra-academic activities. He corresponded with his son David in Latin; he wrote essays for the *Pennsylvania Magazine* under the pseudonym of "Epaminondas"; and in the short-lived *Druid*, which he published and edited himself, he stated roundly: "A man is not, even at this time, called or considered a scholar unless he is acquainted in some degree with the ancient languages, particularly the Greek and Latin." They are, he holds, useful not only for purposes of literature and oratory, but also "to fit young men for serving their country in public stations." He is the only clergyman whose name appears on the Declaration of Independence.

Witherspoon's lectures to his seniors bear reading today, with allowances for the heavy Johnsonian style and the personal prejudices which he frankly announces. He follows Quintilian in recommending "for the complete orator a combination of natural talent and acquired skill." Pericles,

Demosthenes, and Cicero are ideal models, to be studied, not merely noted and pigeon-holed. The figures of Personification, Euphemism, and Propriety are all vividly illustrated. Even the proper use of *clausulae*, or rhythmic sentence endings, the straightforwardness of Livy, and the plainness of Xenophon are discussed almost in laboratory fashion. Cicero's *Archias* is cited as the last word: "All the arts that concern humanity have a certain common bond." Was poetry more ancient than prose? What is the most appropriate research for the statesman, the journalist, the man of letters? Can the procedures of a large province or nation be conducted like those of an Hellenic city-state? (This anticipated the later debates of 1787 on the definitions of *democracy* and *republic*.) John Adams, who was always chary of praise, benevolently and waggishly noted that "Witherspoon had *wutt*[18] and sense and taste." His pupil, Philip Freneau, the ranking poet of his time, may have shocked the old man with his radical views; Hugh Henry Brackenridge would have upset him when he was accused of complicity with the whiskey rebels of Western Pennsylvania; but his effect on all his students was profound. His lectures set young minds speculating on current issues, and the form of their dialectic, under Witherspoon's tutelage, was centered on reality, not too far inclined in a metaphysical direction.

This Scotch clergyman had some strong prejudices. One was a rooted dislike of Tom Paine, whom he regarded as an infidel and an enemy of the classics. His disapproval of the theater prompted "A Serious Inquiry into the Nature and Effects of the Stage." He called to witness "the best and wisest men, both Heathens and Christians," including Tertullian, Augustine, Plutarch, and Seneca. A third object of attack was deism. Moral philosophy, he maintained, should welcome certain pagans for their intellectual and civic contributions, but "what an inconsistency, for a Christian minister to speak of the Lord Redeemer in such style as to put Him upon a level with Socrates or Plato!" Although we do not find him quarreling on this point with Franklin or

Jefferson, his attack on the moderates of the Scottish Church, who welcomed stoicism and other ancient systems as partners of revealed religion, was daring satire for a clergyman: "I believe in the Divinity of L—S— [Lord Shaftesbury or Lucius Seneca], in the saint-ship of Marcus Antoninus, the perspicuity and sublimity of (A—e [Aristotle], and the perpetual duration of Mr. H—n's [Francis Hutcheson's] works." Scholarship, letters, and statecraft profit by the teachings of the ancient sages, but only as corroboration of the Christian message.

Witherspoon agreed with such New England puritans as Cotton Mather when he declared that "since the gospel's enemies make their attack by means of human learning, it is necessary that some should be ready to meet them and unravel the subtilty with which they lie in wait." In the last analysis, he grants the high value of Cicero, Plato, and others as helpful corollaries of the Scriptures. The prayer of Socrates for Alcibiades, that he should have an understanding heart, is parallel with Solomon's entreaty for the same understanding. If only, he declares, Cicero's *De natura deorum* were possessed of revelation, it would rank with any extant piece of sacred literature. Some grace is granted Xenophon, Marcus Aurelius, and Seneca, who "contain many moral sentiments," though lacking in the doctrines of Christianity.

The Princeton president's disputations and personal counsel bore rich fruit. What he desired was the *spoudaiotes* (earnestness) of the classical thinkers, studied and then applied to contemporary life. He so directed the minds of his undergraduates: "Some states are formed to subsist by sobriety and parsimony, as the Lacedaemonians . . . Public spirit in others, as in Greece, ancient Rome, and Britain." His discussions touch on all the issues of the day — divine rights, natural rights, compact, and other cardinal principles. He aims at a national standard which would prevent the fate of the Amphictyons and the Greek city-states. For all of Witherspoon's theological emphasis, it is interesting to note that, from 1769 to 1794, political theses prevailed and that the majority of Princeton alumni took part in public service. The results of this training did not stay in the classroom. It has been estimated that, besides Madison (Witherspoon's favorite pupil) and Aaron Burr (whose disgrace the old man was fortunate enough to predecease), his graduates, with considerable duplication of office holding, numbered ten cabinet officers, thirty-nine congressmen, twenty-one senators, twelve governors, thirty judges (three on the Supreme Court), and fifty members of state legislatures. In this case, the classical tradition was outstandingly effective. Other college presidents did their duty nobly, but in lasting influence Witherspoon was exceptional. His inspiration as a teacher and his wise counsel as a statesman can be illustrated by the proverbial remarks of a favorite ancient philosopher and a nineteenth-century journalist. Epictetus declared: "Whence, then, shall we make a beginning? If you will consider this with me, I shall say, first, that you must attend to the sense of *words*." [19] And William Hazlitt, in his "Essay on Familiar Style," carries the thought further: "The proper force of words lies not in the words themselves but in their application."

V

WILLIAM BYRD AND SAMUEL SEWALL: TWO DIARISTS IN THE ANCIENT TRADITION

It is an almost irresistible temptation to pair off two colonial Americans, as Plutarch in his *Lives* compared a Greek with a Roman. William Byrd II of Westover in Virginia and Samuel Sewall of Boston offer an interesting study in contrasts. The former was painted by Kneller and Bridges in a sparkling Restoration costume. The latter was extolled by Whittier as

> The judge of the old Theocracy
> Whom even his errors glorified —
> His black cap hiding his whitened hair,
> Samuel Sewall the good and wise.

Byrd the Cavalier was more of a Greek, and Sewall the Puritan was more of a Roman. The comparison is all the more justifiable because the mores of Massachusetts and Virginia were almost as different as those of Greece and Rome. The two provinces, though both American, were in closer touch with England than they were with one another. If, however, we are considering the likenesses of the two men, we shall find that both were prominent as public figures and that both were shining examples of devotion to the classics.

If we compare them on the basis of what the Romans called the *cursus honorum*, Byrd (1674–1744) and Sewall (1652–1730) were the chief all-round men of their day and their communities — although in this respect Increase Mather of Boston and James Blair of Williamsburg gave them some healthy competition. Byrd's 179,440 acres and Sewall's wife's dowry from her father, John Hull, of her weight in pine-tree shillings (according to the Hawthorne myth) allowed them a

good start in the race for distinction. Byrd was a vestryman
of the Established Church, Sewall a Congregational elder.
The former was schooled in England and Holland; his Middle
Temple training prepared him for the local and international
rough-and-tumble of politics. The New Englander's legal
career, after Harvard degrees and a brief teaching experience,
progressed by the informal and accumulative method peculiar
to lawyers in those early days, to freeman, general court,
council, and finally chief justice. The Virginian proceeded
from burgess to council, with such special offices as London
agent and receiver-general. Each was acting governor for a
short period. One was a governor of William and Mary College, the other a Harvard overseer. Byrd headed his county
militia; Sewall served as captain of the Ancient and Honorable Artillery. The one backed Sir Edmund Andros, the
other disapproved of him. Here resemblances cease, except
for each man's absorbing interest in classical history and
literature (the concern of this chapter). It is clear that, to use
a popular phrase, both of these distinguished amateurs could
have turned professional and occupied chairs in the colleges
which they served as trustees.

It was natural that the problem of slavery should occupy
their attention and that the Indian's status should be considered. Both men had their doubts about the traffic from
Africa and the critical problem of the Indians. Byrd, who was
strict but not cruel in his relations with his slaves, wrote on
July 18, 1736, to his friend Oglethorpe, congratulating him
on his exclusion of rum and slaves from the province of
Georgia; he himself hesitated to "keep a tort rein" on slaves.
There was ever in his mind, as there was in the minds of
several southern delegates to the later Constitutional Convention, the fear of another Spartacus and another Servile
War. He cooperated with the special arrangements at William and Mary for Indian education. With all his greed for
land, he, and his father, maintained good trading relations
with several tribes. With a good precedent in the case of
John Rolfe and Pocahontas, he recommended the French

policy of intermarriage. In his epigrammatic way he declared that a "sprightly lover" would promote interracial harmony. Sewall, whose conscience troubled him on the color question, went further. His well-known pamphlet, *The Selling of Joseph*, speaks for itself. Whimsically, or perhaps with unconscious humor, he suggests that the Negroes' color can be explained "through Ovid's fabulous cause," when Phaethon drove the Sun God's chariot too near the earth — "Thence arose the belief that the Ethiopians turned a black color because the blood was brought to the surface of their bodies." [1]

Sewall, on the authority of the great William Ames, held that the liberty of slaves would be *auro pretiosior omni*. In company with Cotton Mather, when a bill came before the Deputies against the intermarriage of whites with either Indians or Negroes, the judge "got the Indians out of the bill" and inserted a clause approving wedlock between Indians. Mather had on another occasion interceded "for Caesar that he might have his Diana." For the poor Indian student, Benjamin Larnell, who had been suspended from college, he manufactured an apologetic couplet to be presented on his reinstatement: *"Erroresque meos mihi condonate perosos,/ Absentique mihi precibus succurrite semper* (Pardon the mistakes which I now repent, and in my absence help me with your prayers).[2]

The moral element in Sewall is always uppermost. He entitled himself *censor morum* (as Franklin also did with didactic humor in his *Busy-Body Papers*) for the Muddy River section of Boston (now Brookline). On the deaths of aged men and women whom he respected, he noted their old Puritan standards in the words of Terence: *Antiqui mores, prisca fides*. In contrast with Byrd, who was a friend of Congreve and regarded life as a cynical drama, Sewall stood out uncompromisingly against "stage plays." In 1714 a request was made for the acting of a play in the Council Chamber. The judge declared: "I do forbid it. The Romans were very fond of their Plays; but I never heard that they were so far set upon them as to turn their Senate-House into a Play-House."

He reinforced this statement with the penitent lines of the exiled Ovid: *Ut tamen hoc fatear: Ludi quoque semina praebent/ Nequitiae: tolli tota theatra iube!* (Even though I admit this charge, the games also furnish the seeds of wrongdoing. Order the abolition of all the theaters!).[3] Sewall felt that everything must be considered on a moral basis. At the age of seventy-four, during a visit to his old college, he applied the Puritan criterion: "Notwithstanding the singular advantage Cambridge has enjoyed in their excellent Pastors and Presidents, yet it must be said: *Venimus ipsam Cantabrigiam ad stabiliendos et corrigendos mores*" (Even when I come to Cambridge it is my duty to strengthen and reform its standards of conduct).[4] This is simply a case of chastening while loving, for Sewall always looked upon Harvard as a spiritual and intellectual home. When an undergraduate, confined by illness at Newbury, he lamented to his friend Daniel Gookin, again in the words of Ovid, that he could not accompany him back to Cambridge: "Rome in all her pomp and glory could not be so much to so noble a Man and Poet as that town must be to me." [5]

Byrd's devotion to William and Mary was no less loyal, but it took a different form. He records board meetings, faculty gossip, occasional tilts with President Blair, dinners, recitals by students of Latin verses, as if his experience in the management of a college were simply another scene in life's comedy. All new developments in science or literature interested him and found their way into his library of nearly four thousand volumes. As a Fellow of the Royal Society, he thought in modern terms, whereas Sewall followed the old method of Charles Morton's *Compendium Physicae*. An example of the latter's fear of conflict between religion and natural philosophy occurs in one diary entry. When his friend Cotton Mather "went Copernican," he noted that "he thought it inconvenient [unsuitable] to assert such problems." [6]

The attitude of the two men toward death, reticent in the one case and emotionally expressed in the other, is illuminating. The colonel had a brief statement carved on his father's tomb at Westover, recording him as simply *Armiger et huius Provinciae Quaestor* (Receiver-General). Throughout his diaries and letters the subject of death is muted. Sewall, however, introspective as usual, and in a region where the mortality rate was higher, enters in his diary innumerable memoranda of losses of friends and relatives. Among his Latin verses is one laden with sorrow, on the family graves at Newbury:

> Anglica Jana[7] iacet germanis flenda duobus,
> Uni germanae; septimus iste dolor.
> Iam Nova Villa vale! Tecum pater est mihi nullus
> Nec mater, patriam qui statuere meam.
> Unum germanum, bis binas flere sorores
> Cogimur interdum; iam Nova Villa, vale!

These Latin elegiacs, correct enough in spite of the difficult identifications, may be translated:

> Here lieth, wept by brethren two and sister one,
> Our Jane, the British-born, our seventh loss.
> Farewell, dear Newbury! For in thee no more
> My parents live, who made this land my own.
> Meanwhile, one brother and four sisters bid
> Our tears to flow. Farewell, dear Newbury!

The sentimentality is obvious, but it is sincere and characteristic of the period. The only journal in colonial history which exceeds that of Sewall in the number of recorded deaths is that of Henry Muhlenberg, the Lutheran pastor of the Pennsylvania-German settlers. (These figures are of course surpassed by the appalling number of deaths in the earlier days of Plymouth and Jamestown.)

The Virginian, outwardly strict in his duties as a vestryman and frank in his dealing with the commissary in charge of the provincial clergy, shows little interest in matters of doctrine. His *Secret Diary* contains his prayers, included with the personal foibles he confesses or those which he chronicles in others, along with brief details of his reading in the classics.

A typical entry is that for September 18, 1709: "I rose at 3 o'clock and read a chapter in Hebrew and some Greek in Josephus. I said my prayers and danced my dance. I went to church; I read a little Greek in Homer. I had good health, good thoughts, and good humour, thanks be to God Almighty." The phrase "danced my dance" refers without doubt to setting-up exercises for keeping in condition. It is quite likely that Byrd got some hints from "the Priest's Dance" and "the Clothes-Cleaner's Jump" as described by the valetudinarian Seneca in his fifteenth *Epistle*. The Roman philosopher paralleled the Virginian's "good thoughts" in his eighty-seventh letter. One who would spend three hours a day on Pindar for a week, Dio Cassius for over a month, and Lucian intermittently for two years, with grammar and dictionary, might claim credit for firsthand knowledge of his subject.

The chief justice of Massachusetts was deeply devotional, at home in his Latin and (though not always accurate) in his interpretations of Greek Testament scholarship. He regarded the Quakers as heathens. He dreaded the inroads of Catholicism. When the former preferred a petition to the Governor's Council for the building of a meeting house (August 23, 1708), he recorded his outburst: "I opposed it; said I would not have a hand in setting up their Devil-worship." On the arrival of the tempestous George Keith, who appeared in Boston to draw converts to the Church of England, Sewall denounced him as a "Helena," a "destroyer." He looked askance at the latitudinarianism of Nathaniel Gookin — *Quaedam confidentia non est virtus, at audacia*. At the Harvard commencement of 1720 he objected to one of the theses which posed: *An Christus qua Mediator sit adorandus? Negat* (Should Christ be worshiped in His capacity as Intercessor? No).[8] Long before, in 1696, with his Apocalyptic studies already under way, he had suggested a topic dear to his soul: "Writ to Mr. Increase Mather, to desire that one of the Masters might hold the following Question at the next Commencement: *Res Antichristiana in America est Eu-*

phrates ille Apocalypticus, in quem Angelus Sextus effundit Phialam suam? Affirmat respondens S.S."

This difficult subject of the Beast and the Vials in Revelations, often discussed in New England studies and pulpits, backed by Sewall's readings in "Mead, Bullinger, Aretius, Illiricus, Pareus, Wilson, Cooper, and Cotton," resulted in his book, *Phaenomena Apocalyptica*. His diary records that on March 27, 1697, "I read to the Lieut-Governour my manuscript, and he licensed the printing of it." Confusing as all these speculations may seem today, the pamphlet was well received, and the judge wrote to John Wise in answer to his congratulatory letter: *Non deficiamus Evangelium praedicare, non deficiamus Dominum annunciare; usque in Idumeam extendam calceamentum meum.*[9] Ovid is welcomed as a witness to the immortality of the soul: *Morte carent animae, semperque priore relicta/ Sede, novis domibus vivunt habitantque receptae* (Our souls are deathless, and ever, when they have left their former seat, do they live in new abodes and dwell in the bodies that have received them).[10] This is the Pythagorean metempsychosis, or transmigration.

Sewall enters into his diary a specific prayer for almost every occasion. On his fifty-ninth birthday: *Aedes intravi et ibidem preces effudi* (I went home and then and there poured forth supplications). He altered the Stoic proverb to a Christian form: *Ubi Pater, ibi Patria* (Where the Father is, there is my Fatherland). While he writes and argues, admonishes and confesses, with doctrinal principles always in mind, he reduces everything to a standard of moral conduct: *Quid valet innumeras scire atque evolvere causas,/ Si facienda fugis, si fugienda facis?* (What does it matter to know or investigate a myriad of problems, if you leave undone that which you should have done, and do that which you should not have done?).[11] Sewall is never obscure in conveying his meaning; but he loves "sesquipedalian" words. *Aestuation* is a heated argument; *gravaminous*, burdensome; *Thrasonical*, braggart; *promoved*, promoted. He records with amusement, perhaps unconscious, the name of a certain skipper, "Arche-

laus Adams," as Byrd also was entertained by the nomencla-
ture of a woodsman, "Epaphroditus Bainton." Names from
ancient history were popular in those days. It must have been
a happy omen when two freed Negroes shipped from Portsmouth under John Paul Jones on the *Ranger* in 1777 — their
names were Cato Carlile and Scipio Africanus.

Turning from Sewall to Byrd is in some respects like going from a representation of Everyman to a Restoration
comedy. The Virginian takes his honors easily and describes
his duties with bored brevity. He is a stranger to theological
dogma, and his sophisticated cynicism seldom leaves him.
In his journal he speaks of himself as the scene of a struggle
between Venus and Diana, as acute as "the rivalry between
the Senate and the Plebeians." [12] This trait stands out in his
activity as commanding officer of a militia group. On April
27, 1710: "[At Williamsburg] I was appointed commander-
in-chief of the two counties." [13] At the age of sixty-six he
notes his reappointment as colonel, with Lawrence Washington as a captain. Byrd regarded this service as a game; but
Sewall took his as a religious duty, almost as an offshoot of
his studies. The latter enlarges upon his experiences. On a
certain training day he credits Ensign Noyes with the prize
for marksmanship: he himself had failed "to hit the butt."
The winner received a silver cup on which "I had provided
engraven *May 4, 1702, Euphraten siccare potes*" (Thou canst
dry up [or drain] the Euphrates River). We should give the
judge credit for a humorous sally, as we clearly do when at
a college declamatory exercise he adjourned the meeting by
quoting Vergil's orders to the farm boys: *Claudite iam rivos,
pueri, sat prata biberunt* (Close the sluices, lads; the meadows
are well watered).[14]

The donor of the cup, however, was serious in his ultimate
purpose. On a similar occasion Sewall presented to the Artillery Company a half-pike which, as he confided to his diary,
"will stand me in fourty shillings, being headed and shod
with silver: has this motto fairly engraven: *Agmen Massa-
chusettense est in tutelam Sponsae Agni Uxoris, 1701*" (For

the Massachusetts Artillery Company, for the defense of the Bride, Spouse of the Lamb). On reading this inscription, we find ourselves in the same atmosphere as that of Captain Edward Johnson's seventeenth-century call to militant Christianity — his *Wonder-Working Providence*, replete with Plutarch and historic heroes.

Byrd's *Secret Diary* entries are brief, staccato, matter-of-fact. The squire of Westover was not given to philosophical speculation. An early memorandum runs: "Feb. 7. 1709, read a chapter in Hebrew and 200 verses in Homer's *Odyssey*." Almost daily we find such entries. Thirty years later he rises, stays himself with a glass of milk, and devotes two pre-breakfast hours to Hebrew, Greek, French, and Latin. There is a continuity in his studies: during several weeks of reading Petronius he occupied himself with translating the Ephesian Matron's story. We note in his London diary a stint of translating certain of Lucian's dialogues while reading Hudibras as a diversion. On his return home in 1720, he devoted himself to Plutarch; and it should be noted that he used the original texts and the dictionaries which he possessed in abundance.[15] Herodian, Homer, Thucydides, and Sallust were read over extended periods, and the great Greek historian prompted him to indulge in one of his few publications. Byrd's *Discourse Concerning the Plague* appeared in 1721 at the press of J. Roberts in Warwick Lane, by "a Friend of Mankind," with the Vergilian motto *Dii, talem avertite pestem!* In this tract the writer gives a history of plagues, beginning with the scourge in the *Iliad*, when "Apollo, wroth with the king, sent down a pestilence." He proceeds at length with the Athenian tragedy described by Thucydides and the Roman epidemic referred to by Livy.[16] Lucretius is in part translated, with comment on the symptoms of the disease. These ancient accounts are balanced by modern authorities. Cleanliness, sobriety, proper sanitation, avoidance of panic, and occasional bloodletting or purges are recommended. But, like a good Virginian, he upholds the use of "fresh, strong, and quick-scented tobacco." There is little attempt at humor, and the essay is a contribution by a scientific amateur who got most of his material secondhand. The last two pages are something of a prose Ode to Tobacco; and the comparative freedom from epidemics in his time and region is naively ascribed to the blessings of the plant which Raleigh introduced into England and which made the fortunes of many dwellers in the Old Dominion.

For a whole half-year Byrd was engaged upon Dio Cassius, and it is singular that quotations from this classic are hardly ever recorded in the *Secret Diary*. The reflection of his reading is found in a few essays and letters, in the frivolous collection of *Tunbridgalia*, to which he contributed while at that English watering place, and in his *History of the Dividing Line*. His *Characters*, sketches of friends, rivals, relatives, and acquaintances, reveals distinct traces of Theophrastus; and his library contained a copy of that author. He kept a notebook of his reading, and he speaks of papers that he communicated to his family.[17] His skill in Latin is indicated in a diary entry of November 10, 1709: on a visit to the Accomac region he describes Parson Dunn as "a man of no polite conversation, notwithstanding he be a good Latin scholar." On the next day he whimsically pictures his wife's irritation at the Latin interchanges between her husband and the clergyman. The latter became angry at Mrs. Byrd and left the room in a huff. The Virginian resorted to innuendo rather than to direct quotation, as in a letter to Major Otway: "How does it fare with our honoured Mother [elsewhere nicknamed *Medusa*], who either has a constitution of English Oak, or else employs Apollo him-self for her physician?" [18]

His letter of proposal to his second wife, Maria Taylor, was written in Greek, and good Greek at that. It is worth reproducing in translation:

When I thought you knew only your mother-tongue, I was passionately in love with you; but when I learned that you also spoke Greek, the tongue of the Muses, I went completely crazy about you. In beauty you surpassed Helen, in culture of mind and steady wit, Sappho. It is not meet, therefore, to be astonished.

I was smitten with such grandeur of body and soul when I admitted the poison of Love through my eyes and ears. Farewell.[19]

And he added: "If you deem it to send any reply, you will write it in English to Mr. Ornis at Will's Coffee House in Bow Street, Covent Garden."

Certain fugitive pieces of Byrd's, mostly anonymous, do no particular credit to the writer, in spite of their abundance of classical allusions. Some are disguised addresses to reigning beauties, written during his visits to England. There is "Sabina" — Mary Smith, daughter of a London magnate parodied as "Vigilante" — who refused him, in spite of his claim to be guided by his "demon" (the daemon who inspired Socrates). "Parthenissa" might be Patty Blount, the friend of Pope. "Facetia" is Lady Elizabeth Cromwell. The Duchess of Montague resembles Prometheus in her gift of divine fire: Paris would have given her the prize over Aphrodite. Another woman would inspire Apelles to finish the portrait of Venus, "which he left but half done." To "Minionet" he wrote in 1722: "The Graces and Furys were both represented in the shape of women," as in the cases of Lucrece and Messalina. In the allegorical, witty, and sometimes coarse style of the period, Byrd's quips run the gamut of ancient mythology. To "Lucretia," an English relative, he writes: "Mix 9 grams of folly with 1 of wisdom, — that is the just proportion which Ovid and all the doctors in the deep science of Love allow to a woman that would be irresistible."

In his *Characters*, few men escape sarcastic portrayal. The Duke of Argyll and Sir Robert Southwell are affectionately delineated as "Dulchetti" and "Cavaliero Sapiente," respectively. Many others are lampooned, notably one who broke the Jockey Club rules and furnished a modern companion piece to the "thrown" chariot race in the myth of Pelops and Tantalus. The *Tunbridgalia*, the anthology of light verse published in 1719 in London, had only one redeeming feature, a motto from the poet Martial: *Sunt bona, sunt quaedam mediocria, sunt mala plura/ Quae legis hic; aliter non fit, Avite, liber* (You'll read here stuff that's good, or middling fair, or outright bad — that's how a book is made).[20] In the midst of this frivolity, however, Byrd records himself as occupied with "a translation of the Difficult Passage of Plyny concerning the Nightingale in the 10th Book of his Natural History."[21]

In the case of both diarists there are many indications that their classical learning was deep-seated. Sewall, praying for his wife and children, intercedes for them not as *umbrae* (extra guests at a feast) but on their own account. Nor was it strange that Byrd, writing to Patty Blount, should refer to Apollonius of Tyana, who knew the language of "Byrds" and the notes of the turtledove.[22] Like most of the Virginia planters, Byrd was not interested in publishing under his own name. There are traces of a history of Virginia, supposed by some to have been incorporated into Robert Beverley's *History and Present State of Virginia*. He furnished the material for attracting a group of "Switzers" to his Roanoke property, disguising himself as "Wilhelm Vogel," thus adding an alias to his Ornis, Black Swan, and Rara Avis. The pungent epigrams of the Westover squire and the moral sayings of the New England judge are beyond counting. Byrd, put out with certain orders from Williamsburg, denounces the "Devilsburg Dictators." When Sewall's relative Dudley was accused of sharp practice in trading with the French, a legal proverb resulted: *Qui non vetat peccare, cum possit, iubet* (He who does not forbid a crime, when he has the power to do so, bids it be committed).[23]

Colonel Byrd's *History of the Dividing Line*, the disputed boundaries of Virginia and North Carolina, is a work of distinction. It has a light touch, which we see in Franklin, Hopkinson, and Nathaniel Ward but in few others. It was written in its first form as a report to headquarters in England, then humorously personalized for fireside reading to his friends, and finally in a third version which was published from his private papers after his death. The colonel, with his extensive landholdings and his experience in "perambulation of bounds," reduced celebrities to size and brought little

episodes into witty perspective. A prefatory chapter is devoted to "the Distemper of Colonization," as Byrd called
the whole westward movement.

The second version is full of caricature. On the Virginia
side Irvine, the mathematical astronomer from William and
Mary College, was "Orion"; Mayo the surveyor was "Astro-
labe," reminding us of Lincoln's nickname for his secretary
of the navy, "Neptune." The North Carolina surveyor was
"Bo-otes." There was considerable disagreement; and the
Carolinians gave up the task after some 242 miles and 70
"poles" had been surveyed, but the job was completed after
a second expedition. The characters are pictured in mock-
heroic style: at Norfolk the people "looked upon us as Men
devoted, like Codrus and the two Decii, to certain destruction
for the service of our country." At an inn where citizens
were too freely entertained, "Such liberal supplys of strong
drink often made Justice nod and drop the scales out of her
hand." There is charm in a description of the forest regions
which the writer knew well: "There was a waterfall in the
river just by our camp, the noise of which gave us poetical
dreams and made us say our prayers in metre when we
waked."

For our purposes the final draft is significant because of its
habitual classical allusions and its reflection of the Greek and
Latin that Byrd had been absorbing throughout his life. The
party assembled at Currituck Inlet, off Albemarle Sound, on
March 5, 1728. The fifteen miles of no-man's land between
the Nottaway River and an obscure creek, including much of
the Dismal Swamp, were the bone of contention. The Colonel
noted that the "Dismal" was so foul that "not even a turkey-
buzzard will venture to fly over it, no more than the Italian
vultures will fly over the filthy Avernus." When the North
Carolina delegation arrived, Byrd poked fun at his associates:
their country offered a parallel in "what Ancient Rome did
before them, which was made a City of Refuge for all
Debtors and Fugitives." A muddy job lay before them, but
the men were undaunted: "Hercules would as soon have sold

the Glory of cleansing the Augean Stables, which was pretty near the same sort of work." One of the natives whom they met was "as unkempt as one of Herodotus' East Indian Pigmies." When the company made a fire to counteract the swamp exhalations, they built it up "as large as a Roman Funeral-Pile." Under a cliff they were confused by "that prating nymph Echo, like a loquacious wife." "The happy man whose lot it was to carry the Jugg of Rum began already, like Aesop's bread-carriers, to find it grow a great deal lighter." [24] A first-class amateur naturalist, when discussing the terms for flora and fauna on one occasion, the colonel could not resist the recollection that the myrtle, the laurel, and the bay tree were "sacred to Venus and Apollo." Fountain's Creek was named after an unfortunate who was drowned therein and "like Icarus, left his name to that fatal stream." The gravel bottom of the River Dan resembled the gold "of the river Pactolus in Lesser Asia."

It is not surprising that such allusions are recorded in the journal of this expedition and of his two other travels — the *Progress to the Mines* and his visit to the *Land of Eden*. It simply means that such material was familiar ground to Byrd and that Teutonic or Celtic elements were not in fashion until a later date. His property near the Falls of the James (Richmond) was safely situated above the river — "too high for any flood less than that of Deucalion's." The drill man at the mines was a "Vulcan"; a lazy weaver was in need of Minerva's inspiration "to make the most of a fine piece of cloth." The baggage men complained that they were, like Tantalus, "half-starved in the midst of plenty." When the horses grew weary, the colonel expressed a desire for "one of those celebrated Musicians of antiquity who could play an air that would make a jaded horse caper," affecting the animals as did the strains which caused Alexander instinctively to grasp his javelin. In the *Land of Eden* he draws an estimate from ancient history: the land is as fertile "as the lands were said to be about Babylon, which yielded, if Herodotus tells us right, an increase of no less than 2 or 300

an acre." The Nottaway squaws resembled "the Lacedaemonian damsels of old"; and the writer speaks of an Indian
princess of former days who "poisoned herself, like an old
Roman, with the root of the trumpet-plant." The cranes, at
Crane's Creek, fought the frogs and fish "more cruelly than
they used to do with the Pigmies in the days of Homer."
Over the campfire with his Indian guide Bearskin, he discusses metempsychosis, Elysium, Tartarus, the "venerable old
man" who sat, as did Rhadamanthus, at the parting of the
ways, one supreme God, and the immortality of the soul.
Byrd understood the Indians, and he ventured to declare that
the cruelty of Indian torture was no worse than Alexander's
treatment of the conquered Tyrians.

Many of these references would be almost automatic for
any well-educated colonist. But there are others which prove
that Byrd, a self-trained scholar and no mere dilettante, possessed more than an ordinary knowledge of Greek and Roman
antiquity. For example, he says that the *Varia Historia* of
Claudius Aelianus, which is catalogued as part of his library,
narrates the story of the fabulous Egyptian frog, which
would "carry a whole joint of reed across its mouth, that it
might not be swallowed by the ibis." In the original story
the frog's enemy was a watersnake. He also mentions the
heroic beaver of Pliny the Elder, which would "bite off its
glands to compound for its life." [25] The red ochre that tinged
the waters of Paint Creek is compared with "the river Adonis
in Phoenicia, by which there hangs a celebrated tale." This
stream, flowing from Libanus at Byblos, turns by sympathetic
magic a red color, in sorrow for the wounding and death of
Adonis.[26] So Lucian had heard; but Byrd adds that an old
inhabitant told him that the color was caused by dust storms
at certain seasons. One wonders also where the colonel found
the story of the Indian scalp towels, when he compares them
with those of the ancient Scythians. Athenaeus is the authority for this,[27] but there was no copy of that author on his
shelves. Perhaps he borrowed the volume or found the Mun-
chausen-like episode in some anthology. All of this suggests

a deeper familiarity with the classics than one would expect from his lighthearted allusions.

At the end of the two "processionings" he wrote a finis to the story: "Thus ended our second expedition, in which we extended the Line within the shadow of the Chariky [Cherokee] Mountains, where we were obliged to set up our Pillars, like Hercules, and return home." The *History of the Dividing Line* contains two hundred pages of wit, natural philosophy, history, and literature, told in a style that ranks with any provincial prose. The language is plain, free from the heavy baroque which was ceasing to be fashionable. The casual comparisons hark back to the early morning hours when Byrd absorbed himself in his favorite Greeks and Romans. Long words are used seldom and only as a rule for humorous effect, as in his reference to a "Podagrous" (gout-stricken) friend. Striking phrases occur: "Instinct the half-brother of Reason." When reviewing the manifold interests of the Westover squire, we might reverse the epigram of Chaucer and say that "he was always busier than he seemed."

Judge Sewall's diary has long been known as a precious storehouse of political and social material, familiar to all who are interested in New England history. There is, however, a side to Sewall that has not received the attention it deserves. This is his avocation of Latin verse writing. One Puritan tribute defines him characteristically as "Our Israel's Judge and Singer Sweet." We may call his poetical productions *Lyra Novanglica*.

We have seen that the writing of Latin, and sometimes Greek, verse was a definite part of the program in the two earliest American colleges. The quaint custom that, on every Fifth of November (Guy Fawkes Day), the faculty of William and Mary College should pay to the governor of Virginia two copies of Latin verses occasionally evoked some distinctive poetry. Most of this was abstract and exhibitional; but the writers sometimes touched on current issues, as in the poems presented to the Earl of Dunmore, containing a plea for reconciliation and the reform of the *Poplicolae quos strinxerat impius error* (the demagogues who are smitten with wrongheaded disloyalty).[28] The famous mock epic describing the westward expedition of Governor Spotswood in 1716, "The Knights of the Golden Horse-Shoe," appeared in a Latin version by Professor Blackamore, the convivial occupant of a chair at William and Mary, with an English rendering by the Reverend George Seagood. Harvard published a *Pietas et Gratulatio,* a collection of tributes in Greek, Latin, and English, on the death of George II and the accession of George III. From William Morell's Latin and English *Nova Anglia* to the stately and monotonous productions of Robert Proud, the historian of Pennsylvania, these tributes of celebration or sympathy are enough to fill many large volumes.

It was reported of George Moxon that even in his undergraduate days "he was so good a Lyrick Poet that he could imitate Horace so exactly as not to be distinguished without difficulty." John Eliot, apostle to the Indians, slipped automatically into the metrical groove when paying a tribute to Richard Mather: *Vixerat in synodis, moritur moderator in illis* (His life was spent in church councils, and he died presiding over them).[29] The handbook for such purposes, the familiar *Gradus ad Parnassum,* was on the shelves of many an academic or amateur composer. The habit was so prevalent that Benjamin Franklin humorously referred to elegiac tributes, "written by some young Harvard and ending with a *moestus composuit.*"

Samuel Sewall is noted not so much for the quality as for the quantity of his original Latin verses, which were written frequently and in seldom more than a few couplets for each effort. With all the creaking of his search for the appropriate word, there is a vividness to his subject matter and his modernization of ancient ideas. Of all the classical writers Ovid is his favorite, tempting him to imitation. Lamenting the death of his little son Hull, he goes straight to the story of Ceyx and Halcyone: *Si non urna, tamen iunget nos littera; si non/ Ossibus ossa meis, at nomen nomine tangam* (Even though not the funeral urn, at least the lettered stone shall

unite us; if not your dust with mine, still I shall touch you,
name with name).[30] At every turn some Ovidian reminiscence
occurs. When he sends a certain tract to a friend, he adds
veniam pro laude peto — meaning that he prefers the indulgence of his fellow men to a gushing of thanks. The topic of
Indian relations is a sensitive one: *Pax tamen interdum est;
pacis fiducia nunquam* (There may be a temporary peace;
but there is no assurance of it).[31]

Steeped in this author, Sewall produced an extensive assort-
ment of his own experiments in verse. He hid nothing from
the reader; he ran the gamut from excellence to fatuity, between careful workmanship and helter-skelter speed. Condensed and to the point is an original couplet, written in
honor of Captain Tuthill and circulated at a dinner party on
Castle Island: *Auris, mens, oculus, manus et pes, munere
fungi/ Dum pergunt, praestat discere velle mori* (While ear,
mind, eye, hand, foot, perform their task, it is vital to be
reconciled to death).[32] This couplet, repeated on several
occasions, was originally written in a commentary on the
Book of Job and, according to the author, composed itself
in a dream.

Horace, in his famous travel satire, records his arrival at a
town which, for metrical reasons, cannot be rendered in
verse.[33] Sewall, lamenting the decease of the Reverend Francis Goodhue, wrestles manfully with a collection of word
plays and place names.[34] As a literary curiosity I reproduce
the poem, with a prose translation:

> Libertas nomen, bonitas conjuncta colori
> Cognomen praebent; Insula-Longa gregem.
> Nascitur Ipsvici; dissolvitur inter eundum;
> Seconchae lecto molliter ossa cubant.
> Doctrina, officium, pietas, adamata juventus,
> Nil contra jussam convaluere necem.
> Pars potior sedes procedit adire beatas,
> Gaudens placato semper adesse Deo.

(His name [Francis] signifies *freedom;* in his family tree *Goodness* blends with *Color* [hue]. Long Island was his parish, Ipswich his birthplace. He died on a journey from one to the

other. His bones lie peacefully in their grave at Seekonk. His learning, industry, devotion, and youthful charm availed naught against his destined fate. The nobler part of him is on its way to a happy home, rejoicing in permanent fellowship with the God who has blessed him.)

On the death of Sewall's brother a couplet is entered in his letterbook: *Nos simul occidimus, nostra recidente corona,/ Autumni frigus nos tetigisse vides* (Death's moment comes; our dear home-circle shrinks, and on us autumn's chill has laid his hand).[35] As a bulwark of New England Protestantism, Queen Anne is hailed in a couplet which Cotton Mather approved as an antiheretical thought: *Oceani fluctus ANNA moderante superbos, Euphrates cedit; Roma relicta cadit.* This is followed by his own translation, with a reverent alteration: "Christ governing the mighty waves of the tempestuous main, Euphrates turns and leaves old Rome to court recruits in vain." [36] On the same page we find an excellent combination of Amphion and Ovid with Calvin and David.

Always inclined toward symbolism, the judge presented a ring to Governor Shute, "with this poesy, *Post Matrem Diligo Natam*, meaning that His Excellency would favor New England only in subordination to the crown." [37] When, however, he attempts some hexameters describing the designs on varicolored bills of currency issued July 6, 1715, he loses himself in a maze of *Niger, Ruber*, and complicated signatures. But it is unfair to expect clarity in a Latin poetical version of financial technicalities; Sewall is on the whole correct in his metrical experiments. His good friend Richard Henchman is gently rebuked for ending a hexameter line with *dominantur undique fraudes*, wherein the last syllable of the first word ought to have been long in quantity rather than short.[38]

Sewall was generous in his assistance to young students. We find him "mending some verses for his cousin Joseph Moodey" who wrote home asking for more books: *Tempore, quaeso, pater, libros mihi mittere dignes: Musaeum* [library] *vacuum est, et solus degere cogor.*[39] The New England elder by no means despised a pun. Telling of an episode in church when he missed the tune set by precentor John White, he tossed off a pentameter line: *Albus praecinuit: vox mihi nulla fuit* (White set the tune, but my voice broke down).[40] Royal anniversaries were patriotically observed. There was a distich for Mr. Stanton, chaplain at the Castle, who "was gone a-gunning": *Imbres nocturni decorant Regalia Lucis;/ Rex populum, tanquam gramina tonsa, riget* (As last night's showers enrich today's ceremonies, so may our King refresh his people, as the rain the mown grass).[41] This description of a beautiful morning after a stormy night may refer to the accession of George I.

Sewall was no specter at a feast, but a genial contributor to the festivities. On the marriage of one of his daughters, he presented a piece of the wedding cake "to Captain Crow, of His Majesty's ship Arundel, now riding at anchor in the Harbour of Boston," with these punning verses.[42]

> Ecce per antiphrasin vocitaris, Ductor Arundel.
> Nomen te Corvum dicit, natura Columbam.
> Et quoties opus est, pugnas virtute leonis.
> Undique sic Christi nobilitate viges.

(There is a paradox in your name, Commander of the Arundel. Your name is that of a crow, your nature that of a dove. Whenever necessary, you can fight with the valor of a lion. Thus in all respects you are manfully following Christ's example.)

There are many other of these experiments in Latin verse; but we may close our reading of Sewall's efforts with a charming epithalamium in the style of Ovid (or Catullus), written in 1724 for an old friend, Judge Edmund Quincy of Braintree, on his daughter Elizabeth's marriage to John Wendell of Albany.[43]

> Parvula cognatum conscendis epistula Montem,
> Connubiique faces Splendentes visere gestis.
> Et Sponsum et Sponsam iubeo syncere salutes;
> Perpetua vigeant conjuncti prole beati
> In mare dum currunt Hudson Carolusque profundum!

(O my little letter, you are ascending the Hill where my relatives live. You are yearning to see the shining wedding torches.
I bid you greet with full heart the Bride and the Groom. May
they flourish in harmony, with offspring who will carry on the
happy tradition, as long as the rivers Hudson and Charles run
to the sea!)

The matching of these two colonial magnates, William
Byrd and Samuel Sewall, on the Plutarchian plan may not
be so appropriate as was hinted at the start of this essay. The
differences are so great that nothing but their spontaneous
interest in the classics justifies a comparison. The public
prominence of the two men is a secondary consideration.
Their part in the complicated political and commercial activities of the period may be left to the historian. At any rate,
they kept pace with the cultural life of the colonies and in
some respects led the way. The ancient tradition found a
modern welcome on the banks of the James and the shores of
the Bay.

VI

COLONIES, ANCIENT AND MODERN

Two ancient ideas were regarded by pre-Revolutionary Americans as fundamental: the Greek concept of a colony independent of the mother state, in everything except sentiment and loyalty, and the Law of Nature which took precedence over any man-made legislation. The former, illustrated by Thucydides in his account of the controversy between Corinth and Corcyra leading to the Peloponnesian War,[1] was a standard slogan, invoked by many leaders from John Winthrop to Samuel Adams. The second idea was the higher law, and it became the focus of all colonial appeals, culminating in the Declaration of Independence. The one was a convenient, if not altogether accurate, analogy with the principle of self-government, and it cropped up from time to time as a useful parallel. The Law of Nature, however, had to emerge from its partnership with theology, and it was not seen as fully relevant to provincial purposes until James Otis brought it into concrete relationship with the quest for colonial rights.

Cicero's version of this law, preserved by Lactantius from the *De republica*,[2] may be regarded as the *locus classicus* for ancient and modern application:

True Law is Right Reason in agreement with Nature; it is of universal value, unchanging and everlasting. It is a sin to alter this law . . . we cannot be freed from its obligations by senate or people, and we need not look outside ourselves for an expounder. There will not be different laws at Rome and at Athens; but one eternal and unchangeable law will be valid for all nations and all times. God is the author of this law. Whoever is disobedient is fleeing from himself and denying his human nature.

All law flows originally from God, as James Wilson believed, quoting Cicero's dictum: "There is no race of men so uncivilized and no human being so degraded that his mind is not touched by some idea about the Gods." [3] This declaration appears in various forms from the *Antigone* of Sophocles to Blackstone.

Jonathan Mitchell, in his famous sermon of 1671, "Nehemiah on the Wall in Troublous Times," had combined the Scriptural "love thy neighbor" with an invocation of Cicero's *salus populi suprema lex*, "that maxime of the Romans." Mitchell's version was: "The eternal Law of God, that Eternal, Immutable, Moral Rule, engraven on the forehead of the Law and Light of Nature . . . This Law, being supreme, limits all laws and considerations . . . There is sunlight for this maxime, never doubted by any that hold to Rational and Moral Principles." By the end of the century, the ancient testimony was welcomed in both religious and secular circles. Jeremiah Dummer's *Discourse on the Holiness of the Sabbath Day* (1704) treated natural law in up-to-date terms: "Men know by nature the essential difference between good and evil"; and in support of this opinion he refers to "the best of ancient philosophers." The Age of Reason, with its belief in progress and human perfectibility, welcomed for all purposes this text of *natura optima dux* and *virtus nihil aliud nisi perfecta et ad summum perducta natura*. From this time on, until the final embodiment of the law in the Declaration, minute research took place in the classical historians and the Roman legalists.

John Wise of Ipswich, whose active career extended into the eighteenth century, applied the test of the natural law (and the principles of democracy) to the preservation of Congregational Church independence. The overtones of his theological arguments touch upon another type of independence — the right of the citizen to hold his own opinion as a member of the body politic. The title of Wise's most important work tells the story: "A Vindication of the Government of the New England Churches, drawn from Antiquity, the Light of Nature, the Holy Scriptures." His main plea was based on natural law, fortified by Pufendorf's *De Jure Naturae et Gentium,* Cicero, Plutarch, and numerous other classical authorities. He saw no antagonism between natural and revealed religion: "Academic learning we profess to be a very essential accomplishment in a Gospel ministry." An active, versatile man, he had been a chaplain with the forces at Quebec, a critic of Dudley's province tax, and a champion of paper money. It is advisable to regard Wise as a political no less than a theological writer, as we can see when we read a statement of his that, if made in 1637, would have sent him flying into exile more speedily than Roger Williams: "It seems most agreeable with the light of Nature that if there be any of the regular government settled in the Church of God, it must be a democracy." Or, "Aristotle's heroical kingdom is in no ways inconsistent with a demo- cratical state." A mixed government is satisfactory if it in- cludes a "noble democracy." This is a further development of Thomas Hooker's concept of political freedom.

Wise fortifies his argument by invoking Tertullian's early Christians, who "are a constituted body, associating them- selves into a group"; with Eusebius and Cyprian, he believes in the popular will. The divine and natural laws welcome the Ciceronian "true and primal law" as the foundation of all religions and, he implies, of all communities. Central management of the churches would bring on the fate of a modern Troy, repeating Vergil's "destruction to the re- sources of an unhappy kingdom." In this case the first Christians were right, and the advice of Boethius (freely translated by Wise himself) holds good: "Basely to leave the plain and good old way/ Turns into mournful night a joyous day." Cicero in many places stated the case for the "Original Liberty enstamped upon man's Rational Nature." There are at least four extensive passages appropriated from Pufendorf, to the same effect. Aristotle's Rule of the Superior was ac- cepted by the Ipswich minister, with the proviso, approved also by Cicero: "Nothing is more suitable to nature than that those who excel in understanding should rule and control those who are less happy in these advantages."

The style is picturesque; the vocabulary is quaintly dotted with Latin-derived words, reminding us at times of Nathaniel Ward. "Incogitancy" means "thoughtlessness"; "insults" signifies "overleaping the bounds"; "reluct" means "struggle against." A good man should not be "buried in a *miosis*" — a rhetorical term for "understatement" or "belittling." Legal Latin phrases are borrowed from Dalton's *Countrey Justice*, of which Wise possessed a copy. "A civil state is a compound moral person," as Aristotle declared. The Greek Amphictyonic Council, a parallel used almost ad nauseam during the colonial period, is commended as a force for interstate good will. But Wise does not merely leave his reader strolling along classical bypaths. He is after results. An "un-mixed government," the perversion of the ideal Aristotelian blend, when applied to ecclesiastical affairs, would end in either (1) Episcopacy or Papacy, or (2) Presbyterianism, and both would defeat the Congregationalism he was defending. Unlike some previous controversies, the debate between the centralizing Consociationists and the Ipswich parson ended peacefully. It was said of Wise (after Plutarch) that "his kind, condescending and most generous and obliging carriage has often brought to remembrance what was said of Titus Vespasianus the Roman Emperor, viz., that no man ever went out of his presence sorrowful."

The famous speech of James Otis on the Writs of Assistance was not the first to apply the Law of Nature and the charter rights of a province to colonial problems; but it was the first forceful and direct statement of the case. The scene in Boston's Superior Court of Judicature was one of America's dramatic episodes, when the orator denounced the search warrants of 1761. John Adams later recorded his impressions: "A promptitude of classical allusions, a depth of research, a rapid summary of historical events and dates, a profusion of legal authorities, a prophetic glance into futurity,

and a torrent of impetuous eloquence . . . On that day Independence was born, a sturdy infant, *non sine dis animosus
infans*." [4]

Otis was steeped in Greek and Roman precedents, as were
most of his associates. For two years after graduation from
college he had been in seclusion at Barnstable, reading avidly
in Greek, Latin, and the law. He then opened an office and
prospered, in spite of a nervous affliction which toward the
end of his life became madness. So classically inclined was
he that he published a book on Latin prosody in 1760; and a
similar work in Greek remained in manuscript. These lu-
cubrations are reflected in his speeches. It sometimes seems
as if he *thought* in Latin, often quoting from memory, with
an oral text of his own making. With a few reminiscences of
Pope, Milton, and Swift, and numerous citations from British
statutes and "The New Regulations Considered," the Greek
and Roman references outnumber those from Blackstone,
Vattel, Grotius, Harrington, and even Locke.

The preface to his *Vindication of the Conduct of the
House of Representatives* (1762) closes with Increase
Mather's spiritual advice to scholars: "Make a friend of
Socrates, a friend of Plato, but, still more important, a friend
of Truth." With all his fiery attack, he hoped for concessions
from a Parliament that had the right to be the final authority;
and he held to the Aristotelian combination of ruler, council,
and people. Martin Howard's *Letter from a Gentleman at
Halifax* stirred his ire, with its "virtual representation" and
its claim to tax unrepresented provinces. Howard believed in
the strictest Roman interpretation of provincial administration and even fewer privileges than the Romans allowed. In
defiance of this assumption, Otis unleashed the language of
Cicero against Catiline: "Do you dare to show yourself in the
light of day?" He declared that if a lawyer abuses the machinery of justice, he is "nothing unless he be a sharp legalist,
an auctioneer of briefs, a reciter of formulas, and a hunter
after gossip." [5] At times he supports the governor. At times

he threatens him with the furious words of Juno: *Flectere si nequeo superos, Acheronta movebo* (If I cannot win over the gods above, I shall raise the powers of Hell).

But Otis still desired harmony with Britain, even at the price of a free assembly. The clearly defined charter, if respected, would result in a partnership like that between the Trojans and the Latins: "Let all this tract, with a pine-clad belt of mountain height, pass to the Trojans in friendship; let us name just terms of treaty, and invite them to share our realm." [6] Next to the Law of Nature, the contrast between the Greek and the Roman way of handling colonial affairs was an obvious subject for discussion. The Greeks were "kind, humane, and just toward their colonies; but the Romans were cruel, barbarous and brutal toward theirs." This, of course, is only a half-truth, on both sides. But the Americans made the most of it. The colonists forgot, or sometimes pretended to forget, that Roman citizenship was gradually bestowed on non-Italians both individually and by communities.[7] Conversely, the high-handed procedure of Athens and Sparta, beginning in the early fifth century B.C., was no model for modern colonization. Otis recoiled with surprise at the "Gentleman's" remark that "There was a *natural* relation between ancient states and their colonies, and *none* between the modern states and their colonies." The latter's relationship was based merely on compact. Otis brought out and dusted off the case of the Corinthians and Corcyreans (from Thucydides, supported by Grotius) as an example of loyalty to a mother state. The fiery Bostonian invoked a passage from Dionysius of Halicarnassus, who reported King Tullus as saying: "We look upon it to be neither truth nor justice that mother cities ought of necessity and by the Law of Nature to rule over their colonies." [8] The independent growth of the Greek city-state was regarded by Otis as a significant hint from antiquity.

Otis was no supporter of unchecked popular democracy: "A tolerably virtuous oligarchy might be satisfactory." But a lesson could be learned from these same Romans, who "never had a proper balance between the senate and the people." Both extremes were, in his eyes, perilous — the tyrant and the mob. He would allow no "tribunician veto." Equally undesirable was the uncontrolled Rule of the Superior: *Hoc volo, sic iubeo: sit pro ratione voluntas* (This is my will and my command: let my will be the voucher for the deed).[9]

Many ideas in the Declaration of Independence are anticipated by James Otis. Caesar illustrates the danger of standing armies: "The supreme power in a state is *ius dicere* [administering the law]; *ius dare* [making the law] belongs only to God." With Aristotle, Locke, and Jefferson, he holds that people may alter their government by due legal process. Again, *salus populi suprema lex* is as old as the Twelve Tables and as young as the contemporary statesmen who proclaimed it. Cicero's *omnium consensus naturae vox* is a basic part of Otis' pamphlet *The Rights of the British Colonies* (1764). Elsewhere he stated that the British authorities who considered a search warrant to be a solution of imperial problems should remember (as we shall find Dulany stating) that the American provinces were not *their* colonies, nor were they won by conquest: *Nec gladio nec arcu nec astu vicerunt* (They did not win their way by sword or bow or strategy).[10]

Neither London nor America could agree on the advisability of actual resident membership in Parliament. Franklin suggested it, but it was geographically impossible. After the nonimportation agreement of 1768, an American-born member of the House of Commons was told that, since no Carthaginian would have been permitted to sit in the Roman Senate, so no Bostonian ought to be allowed to sit in the British Parliament.[11] Samuel Adams and the Massachusetts patriots emphasized the essential issue: the revolution of 1688 was meant *for the Realm*, but what of the dominions outside the Realm? [12] Hence internal policies should be decided by the Americans themselves, as they later claimed in 1774. Thomas Hutchinson regarded the colonies as feudatory; the colonists disagreed. The Revolution became an actuality only after the colonists refused to obey the Crown, following their refusal to obey Parliament.

There are few classical authorities whom Otis does not invoke and few situations that he does not foresee. The divine and natural law, the equality of human beings in abstract Roman jurisprudence, the right to resist unjust legislation, hints at separation of powers, the danger of dictators, the "half-gods" who contribute to the false deification of princes, the injustice of an unbalanced political machine — all these appeals are based on the tradition in which he and his fellow citizens were in so many cases trained. It is small wonder that John Adams praised Otis' "Prophetic glance into futurity."

This brilliant, nervous, and sometimes inconsistent patriot burned himself out in the fires of controversy. At one stage he echoes the cry of the marooned Greek in Vergil, warning the travelers of the Cyclops: "Flee the scene, ye hapless ones, and cast off your cable from the shore!" [13] He is always ready with an unrehearsed appeal to ancient history. We may overlook his brawls and inconsistencies and credit him as a pioneer, who, dramatically enough, died Ajax-like in 1783 by a stroke of lightning.

There were many colonial voices speaking out in favor of the theory that colonies should have the same franchise rights as citizens of the mother country. The Dulanys of Maryland claimed the privilege of colonists to share English laws.[14] The senior Dulany, a member of Gray's Inn, cited Paul's Roman citizenship, with Maryland as Cilicia and Annapolis as Tarsus, deploring the bondage of men who, like the ass in the fable, "are sure to be as heavily laden as they can possibly bear." Maryland, unlike many ancient and modern settlements, was not a conquered country: it was acquired by free men. Daniel Dulany, Jr., an alumnus of Eton and Cambridge, carried forward and intensified his father's argument. His pamphlet *Considerations on the Propriety of Imposing Taxes in the British Colonies*, published in 1765 at Annapolis, made quite a stir in England and was influential in Pitt's repeal of the Stamp Act. He began with lines from Persius, that rarely read Latin poet: *Totumque hoc verba resignent/ Quod latet arcana non enarrabile fibra* (That my words may render up all the love that lies deep and unutterable in my inmost soul).[15] Dulany is conciliatory, hoping "that the Maryland Lower House may be regarded as the guardian of liberty, like the Roman Senate." He also upheld mixed government; he cited, as a predecessor did, the declaration of Ariovistus to Caesar on the privileges of Teutonic freedom, according to which "all men have natural and all freemen legal rights which they may justly maintain, and no legislative authority can deprive them of." A king should have the right in a crisis to exercise the power of the Roman dictator so that *ne quid detrimenti res publica capiat* (the state shall suffer no damage). But no constitution would leave all the responsibility to the pleasure of that officer. Dulany's watchword is the hackneyed Horatian phrase, *nullius addictus iurare in verba magistri* (resolved to swear no allegiance to any master).[16]

There are, in Dulany's opinion, errors on both sides in the case of the Stamp Act. Persius again is invoked to illustrate its dangers: *Diluit helleborum, certo compescere puncto/ Nescius examen.* He himself translates this: "He infuses a dangerous drug, without skill to know the proper point between its good and ill effects." Nor should this same Stamp Act, if repealed, allow any modification in the interests of special favorites, who should, like Seneca's courtier,[17] be kept at arm's length:

> Ille superbos aditus regum
> Durasque fores, expers somni
> Colat.

(Let him cultivate the proud vestibules of kings and their in-hospitable corridors, sleepless in his ambition.)

This tax might drive manufacturers to America and force a new burden on the provinces. They would then say with the fabulist:[18]

O me infelicem, qui nunc demum intellego
Ut illa mihi profuerint quae dispexeram,
Et illa quae laudarem quantum luctus habuerint.

(O unhappy I, who now at length am sensible how the things
I had despised were of advantage to me, and how much mourn-
ing they caused after I had approved them!)

The tract closes with the hope for representation, or at least
adjustment, in the words of the long-suffering Aeneas:
Dabit deus his quoque finem.[19]

Richard Bland, a graduate of William and Mary and a
Virginia burgess from 1742 to 1775, spoke much the same
language as the younger Dulany in his *Inquiry into the Rights
of the British Colonies.*[20] He opens with a passage from
Lactantius on the wisdom of free inquiry: *Dedit omnibus
Deus pro virili portione sapientiam, ut et inaudita investigare
possent et audita perpendere* (God has given wisdom pro-
portionally to all men, that they might be able both to investigate things which they have not heard, and to weigh
things which they *have* heard). He agrees with his neighbor
Dulany on the evils of taxes controlled from outside the
province and also repudiates the thin disguise of "virtual
representation." As many others had, he notes the difference
between the Roman and the American provinces; but the
latter were founded by free men, supported by British rights
and royal charters. The Corcyreans again are brought in as
evidence. Like Dulany, he records the conversation between
Caesar and Ariovistus, and cites a chapter from the *Germania*
of Tacitus to support the ideal of liberty.[21] The Law of
Nature permitted men to make a new compact in a new
political society. But neither Bland nor Dulany objected to
the supremacy of Parliament, provided that its demands were
reasonable and that American assemblies could have financial
"home rule."

A third contemporary of Bland and Dulany deserves more
consideration than he has received so far. Joseph Galloway
of Pennsylvania was naturally *persona non grata* because of
his unbending Toryism and his transfer into the British

camp.[22] His plan for a general governor, a grand council, and local assemblies (an arrangement approved in 1754 by Franklin, Hutchinson, and Pownall) failed by only one vote at the first session of the Congress, and the defeat led to his permanent exile. As a matter of fact, Samuel Johnson, president of King's College (Columbia) in New York, had suggested in 1760 "a union to be formed on the general plan of a captain-general . . . with a council composed of two representatives from each province . . . like the Amphictyonic Council of the ancient states of Greece."[23] Galloway admitted that Britain should have settled all the colonies with full rights, such as the free Roman *municipia*, incorporating Pennsylvania, for example, as a "body politic" instead of a chartered community, with the semblance of independence but without any real citizen privileges.

He also declared, however, that "Pennsylvania should not have been settled on democratic principles without the mixture of a single ray of monarchy or aristocracy."[24] It is characteristic of Galloway that he criticized his English hosts, blaming the slackness of the Howes and attacking Charles James Fox in a series called *Letters from Cicero to Catiline the Second*, with ample quotations from the Roman orator. He rebuked British officials whom he accused of being halfhearted, entertaining "a truly ridiculous idea of English representation, drawn from the petty democracies of Greece." This last complaint was the burden of his *Fabricius*, published in 1782. The allegorical characters in this book were accompanied by bitter parallels from ancient Rome. The restless Galloway was never happy on either side of the Atlantic.

There were many other analyses of the colonial situation, but none more lucid than that of the author of *Letters of a Farmer in Pennsylvania* — a series beginning in 1767. John Dickinson stated the case for provincial rights with legalistic thoroughness. In 1764 he had urged patience and cooperative study of the problem, quoting his favorite Sallust to the local assembly: *Nihil vi, nihil secessione opus est* (No need for force, no need for separation). In an address to the Committee of Correspondence in Barbados (1766), he stressed his loyalty to the king: *Cara Deo Suboles* (a scion dear to God). He was still urging reconciliation when he drafted the letter from Congress (1774) to "The Inhabitants of the British Colonies in America," citing cases of unjust taxation and emphasizing the well-worn golden rule of Cicero.[25]

Letters of a Farmer was hailed as a masterpiece throughout the colonies. Samuel Adams greeted them with joy, and the almanac editor Nathaniel Ames devoted some space to them. A Boston town meeting sent Dickinson a vote of thanks for his "Spartan, Roman, British Virtue, and Christian spirit joined." Richard Henry Lee wrote the preface to a Williamsburg edition, indulging in the usual patriotic exaggeration: "Xerxes with his armed millions could not reduce to slavery the much weaker but free states of Greece." Dickinson had already referred to the primary provincial failing, lack of unity, in mentioning Philip of Macedon's threat to the Hellenic confederacies. Tacitus furnished him with a case of a similar sort, from the conquest of Britain: "Against these very powerful tribes there was no circumstance more useful than their failure to plan in common." [26]

We are struck by the welcome and the understanding of these letters by all sorts of provincial leaders. Statistics of contemporary literacy are not available; but one concludes that the "intelligence quotient" of the people in general must have been of a high order. Dickinson, "the Penman of the Revolution," tossed off from memory Latin epigrams and proverbial sayings. Private tutors and four years of the Middle Temple had equipped him with a wide mastery of the classics. He was at home in the company of social and political scientists, from Bacon, Locke, and Montesquieu to contemporary orators like Pitt and Camden and all the current pamphleteers. He cited decisions from all the standard legal authorities. He drew from Hooker on the law of God, from the volumes of parliamentary history, the *Florilegia* of

Stobaeus, the *Encheiridion Ethicum* of Casper Bartolini, and the *Archaeologica Graeca* of Archbishop Potter.

The "Farmer" writes briskly and crisply. Each of the twelve letters ends with a summarizing epigram, a classical refrain for the reader to remember (like the "chorus-endings from Euripides" which Browning cherished). The end text for the first letter is the well-known Senecan motto, popular throughout the colonial period and used, as we have seen, by Roger Williams, *Concordia res parvae crescunt;* the assumption is that the reader will recollect the second half of the quotation, *Discordia maximae dilabuntur.* The fifth letter closes with a wistful appeal for relief from the mother country: *Mens ubi materna est?* The sixth grows more emphatic: *Quocirca vivite fortes/ Fortiaque adversis opponite pectora rebus!* Dickinson here adds his own translation: "Wherefore keep up your spirits and gallantly oppose this adverse course of affairs!" Persius is used to warn the colonists, *Venienti occurrite morbo* (Meet the disease at the start). A final exhortation in the twelfth installment rings out in the words of Memmius, taken from the *Jugurtha* of Sallust: *Certe ego libertatem, quae mihi a parente meo tradita est, experiar; verum id frustra an ob rem faciam, in vestra manu situm est, Quirites* (I shall certainly aim at the freedom handed down from my forebears; whether I am successful or not in so doing is in your control, my fellow countrymen).

Specific problems are correlated with similar crises or solutions of the ancients. The Law stands above human interference: *Qui sentit commodum, sentire debet et onus* (They who feel the benefit should feel the burden also). This applies to the British government. The Stamp Tax and the nonrecognition of the New York Assembly indicated the danger to American liberties, like those which Demosthenes defended in his Second Philippic: "If any person considers these things, and yet thinks that our liberties are in no danger, I wonder at that person's security" (that is, carelessness). Cleons and Clodiuses, and Caesar's destruction of Roman freedom under the title of "tribunicial and dictatorial authority," are to be guarded against. The peril of standing armies and the tendency toward *prorogatio*, or continuation in office, are noted, with allusion to Livy and Macchiavelli.

Dickinson's second letter finds a parallel in Carthage's exploitation of Sardinia, matching the strait-jacket procedures of the Board of Trade in London: "When the Carthaginians were possessed of the island of Sardinia, they made a decree that the Sardinians should not raise corn, nor get it any other way than from the Carthaginians. Then, by imposing any duties they would upon it, they drained any sums they pleased." Nero's trick of remitting the tax on the sale of slaves simply resulted in a higher price and more hardship for the buyer.[27] With all his objection to the taxing powers of Parliament, Dickinson never forgets his respect for the British law when it is fairly applied. Britain's constitution was sound in concept, and only at fault when corrupted. He feels that there should be some remedy. In his twelfth and last letter Dickinson admits that "the legal authority of G. B. may lay hard restrictions upon us; but like the spear of Telephus it will cure as well as wound." England's policy should be in harmony with the Eternal Law. He turns to Vergil and Sophocles for support: the State is a living thing, and "A spirit within sustains the universe; and Mind, pervading its members, sways the whole mass and mingles with its mighty frame." [28] The Divine Law transcends any law of nations. Antigone expressed it in its highest form:

> I never could think
> A mortal's law of power or strength sufficient
> To abrogate the unwritten law divine,
> Immutable, eternal, not like those
> Of yesterday, but made ere time began.

These pre-Revolutionary discussions, from Otis to Dickinson, were analytical commentaries on the relation of a colony to its mother nation. But the duel between Governor Thomas Hutchinson of the Bay Colony, the conservative defender of British policies, and Samuel Adams, the advocate of popular sovereignty, was a fight to a finish, with no holds barred. Both violated the Aristotelian canon, the one supporting monarchy and aristocracy, the other often appealing to extreme democracy, or mob rule. The question was: Who is at the controls, King and Parliament, or the General Court and the New England town meeting? Each man was vulnerable before the court of history — the governor with his pluralistic officeholding and blind obedience to London, the other with his questionable record as a tax collector and his habit of closing his eyes to the excesses of the Liberty Boys. Both were the holders of masters' degrees from Harvard. Adams exhausted the list of Latin noms de guerre in the newspapers; Hutchinson is recorded mainly in his excellent *History of Massachusetts Bay* and his state papers. They were comfortably at home in Latin, and in Greek through translations.

Hutchinson believed in the Rule of the Superior. A typical statement in his *History*, of which the first two volumes were published in 1765, was enough to set Adams and his cohorts ablaze with democratic zeal: "However this account may appear to some readers . . . it may perhaps excite a laudable ambition in some of the descendants of the first magistrates to merit the honor of their ancestors; for altho' places and titles in the Colonies are not hereditary, yet, *caeteris paribus*, the descendants of such as have done worthily have some claim to be distinguished." A passage from Cicero's *De officiis* backed up this complacent remark.[29] On the whole, however, the governor tries to be impartial. His attitude toward the Indians is reasonable, like that of William Byrd. Horace, Tacitus, and Sallust are called upon for parallels. Indian polytheism was cumulative: "I began to suspect, from this instance of plurality of gods, something like the mythology of the ancients, where Romulus was taken into heaven as a new deity." He repeats Bradford's "vanity of that conceit of Plato's, that the taking away of property and bringing in community into a commonwealth would make · them happy." There is little humor in Hutchinson (or Adams either); but we detect a modicum of it in his comparison of the early Puritans who were added to the governing group with the *Dii Minorum Gentium,* the second grade of "divinities" or demigods in the Roman religious calendar.

Hutchinson's *History* contains many realistic references to early Puritan problems. Commenting upon their frequent fast days in times of trouble, he calls upon Cato to recommend a practical remedy based on hard work rather than on petitions to heaven. The Stoic doctrine, "nothing is useful which is not also honorable," is a cautionary watchword. When the Assembly brought forward an act to make drinking King Charles' health illegal, he fell back on a line from Ovid: "This is no slight insult to our ancestors." Describing hard times and low wages, he employs one of Lucan's brilliant epigrams: "The refusal of just rights is an invitation to armed force." Andros and Dudley, monarchists both, are denounced for their attitude toward Council and Assembly. "Nero concealed his tyrannical disposition more years than Sir Edmund and his creatures did months." Governor Belcher was a reasonable official, but his attempt to liken the case of Cato closed up in Utica to the Bay Colony under the restraint of royal orders was an unwise move: for Belcher felt that Cato should have submitted to Caesar.

It is when Hutchinson tries to defend the status of a colony that he encounters real opposition. We have already seen that, throughout the American colonial period, the Greek and the Roman types were continually contrasted, usually in favor of the former. Samuel Adams stated the case clearly: "Why the conduct of Rome towards her colonies should be recommended as an example to our parent state, rather than that of Greece, is difficult to conjecture . . . Greece was more generous and a better mother to her colonies than the former . . . we are willing to render to Great Britain respect and certain expressions of honour and reverence as the Grecian colonies did to the city from whence they derived their origin, as Grotius says, so long as the colonies are well treated." [30]

A decade later, Alexander Hamilton in his *Farmer Refuted* retorted to Samuel Seabury, in agreement with Adams: "The treatment of her [Rome's] dependent provinces . . . is one of the greatest blemishes in her history." [31] Three bland and perhaps naive statements by Hutchinson must have irritated the Boston town meeting. "I doubt," he said, "whether it is possible to project a system of government in which a colony 3000 miles distant shall enjoy all the liberty of the parent state." Then, "In a remove from the State of Nature to the most perfect state or government there must be great restraint of natural liberty." Finally, "The government in every colony, like that of the colonies of Old Rome, may be considered as an *effigies parva* [a miniature copy] of the mother state." One sympathizes with his difficult position as a servant of the crown; but one can also understand the objection of the Caucus Club, the taxpayers, and John Adams himself to such a remark as the following: "In our mother country, when disputes arise between the branches of the legislature upon their respective rights, parties are formed and the body of the people are divided; for in a well-constituted government it is of importance to the people that the share even of the popular part of the Constitution should not be raised unduly to the suppression of the monarchical or aristocratical parts."

Hutchinson, honest and courageous but without skill in handling a hostile faction, does not seem to have made any fundamental compromises, as his predecessor Pownall did. He touches again and again on the rivalry for office between the "patricians" and the "plebeians" in the Puritan province, which might have been settled by gradual accommodation. Trumbull of Connecticut was not insulting his native state when he warned his son "that Connecticut was not Athens." But the Bostonian, with bitter memories of several mobs which on certain occasions he had escaped by a hair's breadth, declared to a friend, "Remember, you do not live in the Commonwealth of Plato," and called the local gangs "the dregs of Romulus." [32] Alluding to certain rebellious activities in Boston, he instanced uprisings in Spain, Greece, Sicily, and Tarentum, instigated by Hannibal: "In the 27th and 29th books of Livy we find an instance of refractoriness in the Roman Colonies not altogether unlike to that of the British Colonies, and of the spirited and successful doings of the Roman Senate upon that occasion."

In 1774 Hutchinson, his position now untenable, retreated to England from a province which, though he loved it no less than Samuel Adams did, he could not cope with. He was at last free from "The Grand Incendiary" and his "Psalm-singing Myrmidons." He eased his soul with the famous Tacitean proverb, "You hate one whom you have wronged," and with the adage *Gubernatorum vituperatio populo placet.* Lamenting the death of his brother-in-law, Lieutenant Governor Oliver, he compared his situation with the tribute of Cicero: "This was a stroke mournful to his friends, afflicting to his country, and heavy to all worthy patriots; but the calamities which soon after happened to the State were such that to me it appears, the gods cannot be so properly said to have deprived Lucius Crassus of life as to have rewarded him with death." [33] Unlike Scipio, who withdrew from Rome after a misunderstanding, he himself would never forbid his ashes to rest in his native soil. Martial and other favorites come to his mind as illustrations of his feelings. At the news of his death, in 1780, a chorus of unjust classical opprobrium appeared in the American newspapers. But one of the dramatic ironies on our human stage is the award to Thomas Hutchinson of an honorary doctorate of civil law by Oxford, on July 4, 1776.

Enthusiasts who called Samuel Adams "the Cato of New England" were less accurate in their historical perspective than was Jefferson, who hailed him as "the Palinurus of the American Revolution." He was more of a tribune than a senator, and Jefferson's diagnosis was the correct one. Palinu-

rus, as Vergil's readers will remember, fell overboard after
piloting the Trojan ships to Italy and steering successfully
through all the dangers of the voyage. Adams was the pro-
tagonist in long-range planning for independence, with
Patrick Henry as partner; but he was inadequate as an archi-
tect for the building of a nation. Perhaps his biographer Hosmer was right in describing him as "the Antaeus of Democracy" — for he returned after every setback to the
Mother Earth of the town meeting, watching all the while
"lest another Caesar should arise and usurp the authority of
his master."

Adams began his political career with some cautious praise
of the British constitution, founded, as he declared, "On the
Law of God and the Law of Nature," according to Cicero,
the Stoics, Grotius, and his colleague James Otis. Awaiting
opportunities for democratic action, he may have had his
tongue in his cheek when he wrote: "We are far from desiring that the connection between Britain and America should
be broken; *Esto Perpetua* is our ardent wish." He claimed,
with some justice, that a proper balance of the three governmental functions would have postponed rebellion for many
years, satisfying both colonists and Englishmen on the cardinal principles of equal standing for all three. But he soon went
further in the direction of provincial reform, agreeing with
Otis' *Rights of the British Colonies* that "in the order of
Nature, immediately under God, comes the power of a
simple democracy." He made an observation similar to those
of Roger Williams and the agnostic Dr. Young, "providing
by illustrations from Greece and Rome that pagans could be
as great statesmen as Christians." To Franklin he wrote that
"the capital complaint of all North America is a subjugation
to as arbitrary a tribute as ever the Romans laid upon the
Jews or their other colonies."

Dotting his communications with well-known catch-
words — *Obsta principiis* (Meet the trouble at its start),
Vis unita fortior (Power with unity is more effective) — he
presented to his Sons of Liberty a set of slogans, and to his

better-educated readers a generous sampling of classical passages bearing on current problems. The Stamp Act was like the sword desired by the Roman emperor who would have liked to "decollate the Roman People at a stroke." He looked eagerly for the establishment of a "Christian Sparta" in Boston. He brought up the case of the pathetic dispossessed shepherds in the *Eclogues* of Vergil: *Fraudum sedes aula* (Courts are the abodes of iniquity). The heroic Helvidius or the incorruptible censors were models for imitation. Even when the general atmosphere of well-being blunted the edge of his denunciations, Adams would stage at the town meetings "a number of warm disputes to entertain the lower sort, who are in an ecstasy to find the Old Roman Patriots still surviving."

Samuel Adams at the age of twenty-one had said nothing new when he offered his Latin *quaestio* on the overthrow of tyrants for the Harvard master's degree. From Manegold von Lautenbach to John Locke, in varying circumstances the deposition of a ruler could be justified. Althusius, author of a popular textbook in early American colleges, had approved it in times of crisis. To the historian with a good memory such action was possible, *de jure* if not *de facto*. But Adams did not stop at this stage. Several samples of "near treason" can be assembled. Hutchinson was told that Adams, at a college gathering, had declared: "Every man has a good right to put an end to the life of a tyrant." If this gossip was true, our sympathies must go out to a harassed governor rather than to a rabble-rousing quoter of Plutarch and such ancient heroes as Harmodius and Aristogeiton. Before Bernard's departure from the governorship, he and Hutchinson drafted an affidavit that Adams was treasonable when he wrote: "The times were never better in Rome than when they had no kings and were a free state . . . We shall have it in our power to give laws to England." Perhaps there was treason as well in his praise of "the independent spirit of Brutus who expelled the proud tyrants of Rome." As "Candidus" in the *Boston Gazette* of September 23, 1771, he maintained that "the tyrants of Rome were the *natives* of Rome" — a palpable hit, though unjust. Massachusetts leaders could, however, hardly refrain from protesting against his remark that the action of Caligula's murderers involved a principle "which may prove as destructive to men who take the lead in a Commonwealth as to absolute monarchs."

There was no rest for the Bay governors after the incumbency of the popular Thomas Pownall. For Bernard, Adams pulled out of his magazine a devastating nickname: "Verres the tyrant-governor of Sicily." Benjamin Church, later a turncoat, had written a poem in 1769, "An Address to a Provincial Bashaw":

> Hie thee, poor tyrant, to that happy goal
> Where Verres, Andros, from resentment stole;
> Go share eternal infamy with those!

Epithets traveled back and forth. The town-meeting men were characterized as "Faneuil Hall, that celebrated school for Catalines [*sic*] and sedition." The milder-mannered Joseph Warren fell back on the curse of Allecto the Fury, as several had already done. Bernard was so harried that he withdrew to England; and Adams went on with his denunciations of Hutchinson. The emperor Galba and his associates and the tyrant Pisistratus were invoked as types. How different from that Roman hero and patriot, Lucius Quinctius Cincinnatus, who, "tho' vested with the authority of a dictator, was so moderate in his desires of a continuance of power that he resigned the dangerous office, which he might have held till the expiration of six months"!

It is too easy to dwell on such abuse of the official who tried his best to carry out his orders from London. Hutchinson regarded the "state of nature" as chaos (so did John Winthrop); but Adams made it, along with the idea of compact, the vehicle for freedom. The significant report of 1772, known as *The Natural Rights of the Colonists*, held that the provinces had the privilege of working out their own local procedures, and it cited Cicero and John Locke for support. Even the Roman colonial plan, it was admitted, had some redeeming features: for if Parliament could tax without the taxpayers' consent, "in this respect the provinces are being treated with less decency and regard than the Romans showed to the provinces they had conquered. For they only determined upon the sum which each could furnish, and left every Province to raise it in the manner most easy and convenient to themselves." But for Americans, the Law of Nature ("Right Reason in agreement with Nature"), with the claim for "no taxation without representation" and freedom from the several restrictions complained about for a decade before the Revolution, were matters calling for immediate attention.

After all this turbulence, and the later more dignified discussions, the "perversions" of the standard Aristotelian frame of government found their way into the Declaration and the Constitution. By 1776, according to Adams, "Monarchy was exploded." "The aristocratic spirit gives way to democracy." "Our senate may equal that of Athens, which was said to be the most sacred and venerable assembly in all Greece."

This controversy between Hutchinson and Adams may be regarded as a preliminary bout, but it was one of immense importance. The persistence and frequently unscrupulous propaganda of the latter stand in opposition to the consistent and frequently obstinate policy of a governor who was doing his duty as he saw it. Both were vulnerable. The one had to find his advice to the home authorities set aside, as in the case of the Stamp Act; for this he commands our sympathy. The other was a master of journalistic cleverness, and often employed devious means for encouraging mob action. The one dwelled on the aristocratic theme; the other spoke out uncompromisingly for democracy. Hutchinson's continual mention of patrician versus plebeian is in vivid contrast with Adams' out-and-out tribuneship of the people. Their main resemblance is in their love and use of the classics, and the relevance with which they applied the ancient tradition to the problems of their day. One must be wary of extreme

statements; but there is much in the idea that the audience of
Samuel Adams and the circle of Thomas Hutchinson "knew
the literature of Rome far better than they did that of England." [34]

VII

LOGAN, FRANKLIN, BARTRAM: HUMANIST, PRAGMATIST, PLATONIST

WITH that delightful condescension toward foreigners which breaks out from time to time even today, the Abbé Raynal remarked that America had produced "no good poet or mathematician or man of genius in a single art or science." Jefferson partially answered him in *Notes on Virginia*, citing the names of Washington and Franklin — he refrained from mention of his own versatile self — and declaring that colonial America provided proofs of genius in physics, political science, oratory, and painting.[1] Today, from a twentieth-century vantagepoint, we would nominate for addition to this group James Logan and William Bartram.

There are others who also made distinctive cultural contributions. John Winthrop, Jr., in seventeenth-century Connecticut earned a contemporary reputation in metallurgy, chemistry, and medicine.[2] Cotton Mather was a pioneer in the field of smallpox inoculation and took a keen interest in natural phenomena. Both men were members of the Royal Society. They represent progress from the Ptolemaic theory and the tradition of Pliny or Seneca to the principles of Copernicus and Newton. Latin was still the linguistic machinery, but the conviction began to prevail that religion is not an enemy of science. There was a graduation from astrology to astronomy and from natural history to a concept of empirical science. The college classroom eventually welcomed "fluxions" (calculus), laboratory physics, optics, and elementary mechanics.

The atmosphere of Philadelphia seems to have been especially receptive to individual experimentation. David Rit-

tenhouse, who is said (perhaps incorrectly) to have acquired
enough Latin to read Newton's *Principia* in that language,
made important discoveries in astronomy, magnetism, navigation, and surveying. Benjamin Rush, himself a Princeton
classicist, characteristically remarked that "if Rittenhouse
had had the usual round of advanced classical studies, he
might have spent his hours of study in composing syllogisms
or in measuring the feet of Greek and Latin poetry" — a
statement which Hindle calls "an example of unrealistic
primitivism." [3] Thomas Godfrey began as a glazier and im-
proved on Hadley's quadrant, under the patronage of Franklin. The *Instructor* for 1755 reflected contemporary opinion
among these mechanical pioneers: "Rome was at its best when
it only concerned itself with useful sciences. Athens was
never more foolish than when it swarmed with philosophers."

The famous garden on the banks of the Schuylkill, presided
over by John Bartram, William's father, was a center of
interest to many travelers. Joseph Breintnall, secretary of the
Library Company of Philadelphia, hailed Bartram in a poem
imitating the Sapphic meter of Horace's *Integer vitae:*

> Tho' now to piercing Frosts, now scorching Sunbeams,
> Now to unwholesome Fogs, tho' thou'rt exposéd,
> Thy Guardian Angel, Innocence, shall keep thee
> Safe from all Danger.[4]

Bartram's library, his collection of plants, and his journeys
to Ontario and East Florida made up amply for his lack of
academic training. He was King's Botanist for the Colonies,
but how much Latin he knew is debatable. He speaks of a
"neighboring schoolmaster who in three months taught me
enough Latin to understand Linnaeus." Hector St. John
Crèvecoeur, a devoted admirer, in his *Letters from an American Farmer*, reports that John Bartram requested him to
"read the kind epistle which the good Queen of Sweden,
Ulrica, sent me a few years ago." But the record of the Edinburgh and Leyden graduates who raised the colonial standards of medicine and combined the classics with their techniques makes impressive reading. Politely disagreeing with the

Abbé Raynal, we may enlarge upon three Americans who could stand in the company of their transatlantic counterparts.

It is difficult to decide whether James Logan was a classical scientist or a scientific classicist. Born in Ireland in 1674, son of an Edinburgh graduate, he was so thoroughly tutored in Greek and Latin by his father that he became headmaster of the Bristol Friends' School at the age of nineteen. A brief apprenticeship to a linen draper did not interfere with his studies, and it gave him a preliminary view of business in preparation for his work (after 1699) as secretary to Penn's colony, and ultimately chief justice, councillor, and acting governor (1736–1738) of the province. He was an easy writer and speaker of Latin. He read Greek comfortably and was qualified by the age of thirteen for any university in Britain or Europe. Perhaps in later life, when he sent his son back to Bristol for schooling, he expected too much of him. William was urged to finish, by the age of sixteen, Vergil's *Aeneid, Eclogues,* and *Georgics,* Cicero's *De officiis,* Thomas à Kempis, the *Consolation* of Boethius, some Tacitus, Seneca, Juvenal, Persius, and the Greek New Testament. He was also supposed to be familiar with Nizolius' *Apparatus Latinae Locutionis.* His tutor was instructed to send overseas some examples of the boy's Latin writing; but in some of these samples the parent complained that he detected "his master's hand." The absorption by Logan of the classics at an early age, with its carryover into politics and world affairs, is paralleled by the experience of James Otis, whose interest in classical scholarship was no less keen than his ability in the lawcourts. Logan's legal preparation, as we noted in the case of Samuel Sewall, seems to have been self-accumulated, a procedure common in those days to many a provincial justice.

Logan was among the first colonists to own and study Newton's *Principia.* When teaching at Bristol, he had mastered the *Cursus Mathematicus* of William Leybourne. He sent to the Royal Society observations on Godfrey's experiments with the quadrant, on provincial flora and fauna at the request of Sir Hans Sloane, and on Ptolemy's *Almagest*, which J. A. Fabricius presented to him in exchange for the *pelliculae* acquired by Logan in his extensive fur trade. His most significant production, written in Latin, was the *Experimenta et Meletemata de Plantarum Generatione*, on "Indian Corn or the Maize of America." This treatise was translated into English by his friend Dr. John Fothergill from the Leyden publication of 1739. Another pamphlet, on optics, appeared in Leyden. Linnaeus named a certain order of shrubs *Loganaceae*. Although he did not join them, he cooperated with the experiments of Franklin and Bartram in the proceedings of the American Philosophical Society.

One might speak of Logan as having attained a triple distinction. He was, first, a capable defender of Penn's long-distance control of the province and a genius in his peaceful handling of the Indians. In the second place, his experiments in natural history mark him out as more than an amateur follower of a hobby. He could turn from botany to philosophy, where, however, he was less at home. He warns his friends that his *Treatise of the Duties of Man as Founded in Nature* "should be considered only philosophically." In this essay he insists that the Divine Word is a higher principle than Reason. In another, he followed Aristotle rather than Hobbes in maintaining that man was intended for mutually helpful society. Corresponding with European scholars, he discussed the text of Euclid and the variant readings in Iamblichus' work *On the Pythagorean Life*.

Logan's third interest was perhaps his favorite one — the pleasure and serenity offered by the classics, in contrast to his harassed political life. Robert Proud, the historian, tells us that "he was well versed in both ancient and modern learning, acquainted with the Oriental tongues, a master of the Latin, Greek, French, and Italian languages." His library, now intact in the Library Company of Philadelphia, ranks on a par with those of Mather, Byrd, Adams, and Jefferson. In the proportion of Greek and Latin works it exceeds any other. Logan says of it: "About one hundred authors in folio, all in Greek . . . all the Roman classics without exception . . . Archimedes, Euclid, and Ptolemy." "I confess," he declared, "as I advance in years the Ancients still gain upon me and the Greeks particularly . . . As they give the only old accounts of time (besides the Scriptures) I am pleased to observe what the notions of men were at the greatest distance from me. For this reason Homer and Hesiod please me more than ever. Herodotus also . . . besides that I have a particular fancy for that language."

In 1735 he brought out his translation of *Dicta Catonis*, read at first to the family in his study. It caught the fancy of Franklin, whose *Poor Richard* it resembles in many ways, and it was published anonymously. In 1744 there appeared his English version of Cicero's *De senectute*, "for the entertainment of a friend less skilled in the language or the history of Rome," the Quaker statesman, Isaac Norris. Franklin, his publisher, called it "the first translation of a classic in this Western World." On grounds of quality, this is perhaps a justifiable claim; but Charles Evans records the printing by Franklin's arch-enemy, Samuel Keimer, of translations from Diodorus Siculus in 1725 and "Epictetus his Morals" in 1729.[5] Logan's style is excellent, and the English reproduces the Latin with graceful accuracy. There were many editions. Among those who praised it was Ebenezer Parkman, the minister of Westborough, Massachusetts. On May 12, 1779 he wrote in his diary: "I read Logan's Cicero of Old Age"; and the next day, "I am still engaged in Logan's Cicero of Old Age, with very useful notes." In August 1780 he records perusing the same work, "chap. xix." [6]

One does not find in colonial America the quality of Greek or Latin verse writing that distinguished Milton or Cowley or Johnson. But Logan can stand inspection with as much credit as any colonist, except for the author of the Virginia epic, *The Golden Horse-shoe*, or the contributors to the *Pietas et Gratulatio* published in Cambridge in 1761.

Samuel Sewall's elegies are respectable, but not always smooth.

A good example of Logan's hand is his lament for an infant daughter, written on the flyleaf of a copy of Heinsius:

> Sis licet in teneris abrepta parentibus annis,
> Vita exempta prius quam videare frui;
> At patris et matris pleno praecordia tangit
> Ictu discessus, cara puella, tuus.

(Though snatched away in childhood from thy home, removed from life before its joys were thine, thy parents, dearest daughter, weep thy going as deeply as the human heart can feel.)

Logan appears throughout his writings and correspondence as a skilled master of Latin prose. But his verses were regarded as private avocations or entertainment. He was challenged to compose a Latin epitaph for a friend of Jeremiah Dummer, the agent for Massachusetts: he went him one better by writing it in Greek verse with a Latin version appended. A particular crony of his was Governor Robert Hunter of New York.[7] They corresponded, says one biographer, "on all manner of literary and scientific topics, ranging from Gay's pastorals to the astronomical tables of Kepler and Tycho, from musical strings to an Italian translation of Cato's *Dicta de moribus*, from the poems of Lucan to the medical researches of Dr. Colden." Hunter sent his Philadelphia friend a Latin poem; Logan returned it in a Greek version, confessing the help of Scapula's dictionary. They coached each other on meters, comparing Homer and Euripides. When Hunter returned to England in 1719, Logan sent him a "propemptic" ode, in the manner of Horace — what we should define as a "steamer letter." There were few colonial Americans so versatile as Logan, in learning, statecraft, science, business, and application of the classical tradition to contemporary life.

Benjamin Franklin, who was a past master in the art of adapting to practical use everything that he read, saw, or experienced, caught up with the prevalent classical tradition by educating himself. A mere dash of elementary Latin at the Boston public school, before he was placed for two years in Brownell's reading and ciphering classes, was not enough for him. But he met the problem with such industry that, when his son was ready for Latin, he was qualified to help him. One of his first self-imposed tasks was that of modeling his style on some writer of distinction, as Stevenson followed Hazlitt and as Montaigne "drew upon Seneca and Plutarch as from a well." The *Spectator* was handy; in the *Courant* office were translations of Pliny's *Natural History*, Josephus, Vergil, the Roman historians, "Athenian Oracles," all waiting for an omnivorous reader. The situation was such, says Faÿ, "that in the eighteenth century a cultivated man could do without his shirt but not without his Latin quotations." [8] Plutarch was his first love for the hours stolen from the printing office or the Sunday services at the Old South meeting house. Pythagoras with his golden rules appealed to him, as he did to the young Jefferson.

First came his *Dogood Papers*, crude but remarkable for a youth of sixteen. With the skill of an adult he discusses the problem of free speech as it was met by Horatius, Valerius, and Cincinnatus,[9] and how Rome lost her liberty under the informers Sejanus and Tigellinus, partially regaining it under Titus, Nerva, and Marcus Aurelius. Franklin mentions a complaint of Pliny to the Emperor Trajan: *Queri libet quod in secreta nostra non inquirant principes nisi quos odimus* (How sad it is that only the princes whom we hate spy into our private affairs!).[10] For contrast he cites Tacitus on the good Roman emperors: *Rara temporum felicitate ubi sentire quae velis et quae sentias dicere licet* (How happy were the times when you could feel as you wished and say what you felt!).[11] It is possible that the young Franklin read Tacitus in a translation and hunted out the Latin to substitute for the English. In any case the illustrations he used reflected the independent ideas of the *Courant* editors. Many of the "Dogood" numbers were equipped with a proper classical motto. The editorial preface to the *Courant*, when Franklin took his brother's place (February 11, 1723), indicated his policy: *Non ego mordaci distrinxi carmine quemquam,/ Nulla venenato litera onusta ioco est* (I have never injured anybody with a mordant poem, not a letter of mine is dipped in poisoned jest).[12] A good "Couranter" should be broad-minded; like Janus, he can "look two ways at once." Hyper-carpus the critic, Clericus, Rusticus, and other characters with Latin names appear throughout.

The chief model, however, for Franklin's style and basic method of presentation was Xenophon's *Memorabilia*. From this and from translations of Plato he adopted the Socratic method of discussion. He tells us that he found the abrupt contradictory manner unsatisfactory and preferred to lead his opponent by suggestion rather than by challenge. Under the influence of this work he wrote an essay "to prove that a vicious man could not be called a man of sense." Besides Xenophon, we note an indebtedness to Plato and Plutarch for practical encouragement to the good life.

Poor Richard is full of proverbs based on *The Wisdom of Syrus*, a collection which began at the end of the Roman Republic and grew by accretion. In the issue of 1734 we find the standard saying: "He does not possess wealth; it possesses *him*." This epigram goes back to the Greek philosopher Aristippus. Even at the end of Franklin's life we find the same Platonic irony and directness in a letter from "The Elysian Fields" to Madame Helvetius.

The *Busy-Body Papers*, with their *Spectator* style, carry on this tradition. We meet with burlesque characters like Ridentius, Eugenius, Titan Pleiades, and Cato, the exemplar of sturdy integrity. Franklin announces himself as a *censor morum*, as Samuel Sewall did more seriously in Boston; he states, through one of his interlocutors, that he will copy the Roman emperor who cried that he had wasted his day if he had not done a good deed. The motto for February 18, 1728–1729, is Horace's "Instans Tyrannus" ode; for March 4, it is from the satirist Persius: *Vos, o patricius sanguis, quos*

vivere fas est/ Occipiti caeco, posticae occurrite sannae (O ye
blue-blooded patricians, you who have to live without eyes
in the back of your head, turn round and face the gibing in
your rear).[13] For March 27, he culls out the Vergilian phrase
which appears everywhere in colonial writings: *Quid non
mortalia pectora cogis,/ Auri sacra fames!*[14] His skit "On
Shavers and Trimmers" (*Pennsylvania Gazette*, June 23,
1743) incorporates appropriately the lines from Horace on
the city man who tried his hand at farming, only to return
in disgust to his auctioneer's stand at Rome.[15] For his little
diary of the thirteen virtues, he uses as a motto Cicero's
apostrophe: *O Vitae Philosophia Dux! O Virtutum indagatrix
expultrixque vitiorum!*[16] His "Poor Richard" slogan is prophetic of his future mastery of science: *Sapiens dominabitur
astris.*

Franklin cared nothing for what was not applicable to the
matter in hand, whether literary or scientific or political. He
did not worship the classics; he simply found them an adequate channel of expression. "It is better," he said, "to bring
back from Italian travel a receipt for Parmesan cheese than
copies of ancient historical inscriptions," thereby agreeing
with Crèvecoeur, who deprecated the worship of Roman
ruins and the idolizing of past civilizations. He utilized an
ancient language as an effective medium for his message, just
as Madison and the men of 1787 regarded Greek and Roman
governments as ground material for debates on the framework of a new nation. If "elegant extracts" and florilegia
were handy, he availed himself of them.

Wishing to discriminate between what De Quincey called
the literature of knowledge and the literature of power, he
spoke out plainly when proposals were afoot for the new
College of Philadelphia: "Latin being the language of learned
men in all countries . . . All intended for Divinity should
be taught the Greek and Latin; for physic the Latin, Greek
and French; for law, the Latin and French; for merchants,
the French, German, and Spanish." As he grew older, he
made some exceptions for the mathematical and scientific

professions. And in the end he defined the classics as the *chapeau bras* of modern literature, the "full-dress" subject which should not be the only way to intellectual salvation. Many prominent men took a hand in the commemoration medals so fashionable in those days. On the settling of the entente with France, Franklin suggested a representation of the infant Hercules in the cradle, strangling two serpents (Burgoyne and Cornwallis!), with Minerva sitting by as his nurse, equipped with spear and helmet — a "record of extinguishing two armies in one war." The motto was Horace's *Non sine Dis animosus infans,* the phrase used by John Adams for the birth of independence when James Otis made his famous speech on the Writs of Assistance.[17]

His mind was stocked with ancient comment on scientific matters. In a letter to a friend he remarked: "I had when a youth read and smiled at Pliny's account of a practice by the seamen of his time, to still the waters by pouring oil into the sea"; and he instanced modern cases of success in this same experiment.[18] He associated an ancient sepulchre found in Russia with the story told by Herodotus (IV.71) of the Gerrhians and their manner of preserving the bodies of kings. With another friend he discusses the *tessera hospitalis,* the indented identification-disc, as an example of harmony between their sons. His idea of a gunboat fleet at the start of the Revolution was suggested by the Roman triremes. He signs himself "Columella," the Roman agriculturist, in an open letter on the price of corn. He burlesques, speaking through the voice of the king, the purchase of Hessian mercenaries: "Do you remember that of the 300 Lacedaemonians who defended the defile at Thermopylae, not one returned? How happy could I be if I could say the same of my brave Hessians!"

One gets the impression that Franklin was much more at home in Latin than has been supposed. He corresponded in that language with Paullus Frisi of Milan. He presented a Baskerville quarto Vergil to his friend T. Hubbard of Boston, and he warmly thanked Don Gabriel of Bourbon for a deluxe copy of Sallust. Franklin reveals the extent of his reading in a letter to Galloway in 1775 on the error of merging British and American trade, citing the tortures devised by the tyrant Mezentius, who "coupled the dead with the living." [19] Logan presented Franklin with an Italian translation of Lucretius and recommended to him a French version of Polybius. Reporting to Jared Eliot on the success of his new academy, Franklin quotes offhand from Xenophon, Vergil, and Horace. He agrees to Logan's request that the librarian of the Library Company should have "learned at least some of the books of Virgil, and could translate the *Colloquies* of Erasmus into English." In his *Plain Truth* (1747), an argument for preparedness against the French, Franklin devotes half of the title page to a passage from Sallust's *Catiline* (in the Latin), spoken by Cato as a warning to aggressors, and some space to the tragedy of Pompey's siege of Jerusalem as described by Josephus.

The American sage modestly deprecated the praise of M. Nogaret, who hailed Turgot's tribute to his electrical experiments, *Eripuit caelo fulmen, sceptrumque tyrannis,* which he evidently did not know was a partial loan from the Roman astronomer Manilius. D'Alembert had rendered it in diffuse French, which Franklin politely accepted:

> Tu vois le sage courageux
> Dont l'honneur et mâle génie
> Arracha le tonnerre aux Dieux
> Et le sceptre à la tyrannie.[20]

These classical sources are applied in an up-to-date fashion. As John Dickinson did also, Franklin pointed out the trade monopoly of Carthage at the expense of the conquered Sardinians. He congratulated Georgiana Shipley on her translation of a despondent Horatian epode and its bearing on England's critical situation.

Most significant of all is his correspondence with his British friend, David Hartley, who was closely associated with him in the peace conference of 1782.[21] Hartley assumed that his Latin references to ancient politics would be understood.

In a flash of enthusiasm Hartley prayed for the abolition of defenses and armaments: *Aspera compositis mitescent saecula bellis* (Savage ages will become civilized when wars are peacfully settled).[22] He wrote to the American a sort of *cento* of their aims: *Consulere patriae, parcere afflictis, fera caede abstinere, irae tempus dare, orbi quietem, seculo pacem suo: Haec summa virtus, hac caelum patet via* — a rich medley of many Latin expressions of hope for peace. The bees in Vergil's fourth *Georgic* furnish a parallel to the rage of militant Europe: *Spicula caeca relinquunt/Adfixae venis animasque in volnera ponunt* (In thy veins implant a hidden barb, leaving behind their own lives in the wounds they give).[23]

It would, said Hartley, be bad for America to be dragged into a general European war; America could then apply to France the apostrophe of Horace, speaking in the person of Helen to Paris — *non hoc pollicitus tuae* (in other words, "this is not what you promised").[24] Hartley, a courteous gentleman, would never have tried to patronize or impress Franklin with language he could not recognize or understand. Franklin's reply was characteristic: "America would be as happy as the Sabine girls if she could be the means of uniting in perpetual peace her father [England] and her husband [France]." One leaves the study of Franklin, and tosses aside the quip of the Abbé Raynal, with the feeling that he was three persons in one — the scientific benefactor of humanity, the public servant who used the classics as a whetstone for his journalism, and the statesman who absorbed the Greco-Roman heritage to the exact extent of his needs. To prove the philosopher's soundness as well as his knowledge and his essential modesty, I may quote from his letter to his friend, Alexander Small: "You do me too much honour in naming me with Timoleon. I am like him only in retiring from my public labours."

William Bartram, who was born in Philadelphia in 1739 and whose life overlapped the colonial and national periods of United States history, would doubtless have regarded with surprise the inclusion of his botanical and ornithological journal as one of the masterpieces of American literature. Still more so would he have been astonished at being studied not only as a scientist but as a reflector of the Greco-Roman tradition, both in style and content.[25]

The Argonauts of transatlantic discovery had done their work, and the adventures by sea had given way to the beckoning of the western frontier. There were men like the poet Freneau who altered their "myth" from the slogan of an overseas Atlantis to the celebration of a new Utopia of the west and its possibilities for the future. The Red Man, with a few irritating exceptions, had turned into the Noble Savage. The spirit of the Enlightenment had reached its climax. The state of nature as a political motif had been thoroughly scrutinized. In Bartram we have one who was still exploring, engaged in a sort of *Argonautica Botanica* among the rivers and swamps and savannas of the southeastern colonies, full of new ideas and author of a journal of the first order.

In 1791 there appeared the *Travels through North and South Carolina, Georgia, East and West Florida.*[26] The quality of this work establishes Bartram in the canon of notable American writers. The book won the enthusiastic approval of Coleridge and Wordsworth, who quarried from its contents,[27] and we should also remember the statement of Carlyle to Emerson, that he read it from cover to cover. This son of John Bartram, who was himself a botanist of distinction, set out in 1773 for the purpose of exploring and describing "the rare and useful productions of Nature." Thus a technical journal became a literary classic.

Whereas John Bartram, the pioneer collector,[28] had acquired his education by self-teaching, his son "Billy" was persuaded to leave his favorite flower drawings long enough to attend the "Old College" of Philadelphia, where he studied under the scholar Charles Thomson, later secretary of the Continental Congress. His father, who had organized a neighborhood library, including such classical authors as Vergil and Seneca, succeeded in keeping the boy at school long enough to "learn his Latin and French." William's own bookshelf comprised the works of Aristotle in translation, Ramsay's *Travels of Cyrus*, Jefferson's *Notes on Virginia*, Hume's *History of England*, and many botanical books. On his trips he read widely, even in the midst of hazards, and recorded his observations on the spot. Dr. Alexander Garden, the well-known Charleston scientist, describes his meetings with the Bartrams and Cadwallader Colden of New York in enthusiastic terms. These men were *Animae quales neque candidiores terra tulit* (Souls as noble as the world has ever produced).[29]

Young Bartram felt toward the Indians, as he did toward the nature he loved to study, a sympathy common also to his fellow Quaker, William Penn. He has no truck with men like the early Virginia settler Stockam, who would have recourse to Mars and Minerva instead of the "verbal Mercurialls" (kindly interpreters): their method was that the Indians be kept at arm's length until their "priests and ancients" had their throats cut.[30] Bartram, who sticks pretty closely to the botanical field, raises the question of whether bullying the Indians into the ways of Europeans is not far less desirable than reaching a cooperative understanding with them. He points out "the propriety of sending men of ability and virtue, under the auspices of the government, as friendly visitors . . . let these men be instructed to learn perfectly their languages, and become acquainted with their customs and usages, religious and civil, their system of legislation and police, their traditions and history. These men, thus enlightened, would be qualified to make true reports . . . and offer to them a judicious plan for their civilization and union with us." A wiser Virginian than Stockam, William Byrd approached the vexing problem from the same viewpoint.[31]

There is no direct mention of the Revolutionary War in Bartram's *Travels*, and little consideration of any troublesome problems between the colonies and the mother country. The only "Sons of Liberty" are "the generous and true sons of liberty who dwell securely on the banks of the Alata-

maha." The journalist is evidently reminded of the Grecian
city-leagues when he describes the sacred capital of the Creek
Indian confederacy, "where a general peace is proposed and
deputies assemble from all the towns in the confederacy." [32]
Also, he regards the desire for bloodshed or the craving for
plunder as less provocative of war than the urge to absorb
other nations into their own hegemony. This applies, he feels,
to the Indians no less than to "the renowned Greeks and
Romans" or the modern civilized nations.

His journal is a curious assemblage of exact scientific observation, couched in a style as classically ornate as that of
any colonial writer. His ultimate objective was the collection
and description of specimens for Dr. John Fothergill, the
English Quaker botanist and friend of Franklin. But he was
no mere collector, and no mere rhapsodist. With all his praise
of the simple life and his yearning for the primitive,[33] he
knew how well his philosophy harmonized with the Enlightenment of the eighteenth century. He has been called a deist
or a Neoplatonist, but he is probably nearer to the pantheism
of the Stoics; for to him nature contains God and is alive —
an emanation of a benevolent Deity. To the Stoics the universe was a manifestation of divine reason: the individual
person or thing was a part of the whole. Original Being is
not a physical process, and Bartram's plants are living things
rather than metaphysical abstractions. Plato and Cleanthes
also fit into his philosophy.

There are many applications of this idea, although the
reader (and the writer) must be careful to avoid tempting
analogies. The *Dionea Muscipula*,[34] the flower that closes up
to catch "incautious deluded insects," serves to bring the
vegetable world into a class with the animal world, "or-
ganical, living, self-moving bodies," in harmony as man is
with the forces of the universe. To the same agency is
ascribed the vital flow of the fountains which Coleridge
copied for his subterranean caverns in *Kubla Khan*. "At the
return of the morning, by the powerful influence of light,
the pulse of nature becomes more active, and the universal

vibration of life insensibly and irresistibly moves the wondrous machine." [35] Bartram balances reason with emotion; he believes in "the more essential principle . . . which animates the illimitable machine which gives them motion . . . This must be divine and immortal." As a student of Vergil, he applies and reflects "the Inner Spirit, Mind which moves all matter and blends into the mighty framework of the universe." [36] The doctrine of Inner Light and the Divine Guide of Socrates (the daemon) are essential: "Learn wisdom and understanding in the economy of Nature, and be seriously attentive to the divine monitor within."

Bartram rejects the Aristotelian doctrine of the strong leader, thereby agreeing with statesmen like James Wilson,[37] who would have no encroachment on the will of the people. The Mico of the Muscogulge tribe is elective; but, unlike the monarchs of the old world, he is put at the top because of his character and the respect he inspires. Their "police" (that is, system of government) "follows the simple dictates of reason." Here the traveler ennobles the Noble Savage beyond his deserts. Even the birds in Georgia and Florida live in an allegorical commonwealth, more practical, he implies, than the Cloud-Cuckoo Land of Aristophanes. The often quoted comment on the habits of doves by the elder Pliny catches his attention: "How chaste, never known to violate the conjugal compact!" [38]

One can find countless apostrophes couched in elaborate form and verging on that perilous borderline between genius and bathos. This is one reason why Bartram is so intriguing: it is hard to tell whether he is a classicist or a romanticist. We may simply remark that the eighteenth century, with Burke in the lead, developed the idea of the Sublime and that this botanist was among its most distinguished masters.[39] But with all this elevation of style, this ornate writing, he was fundamental and plain in his meaning. The sun of Plato's *Republic* and the perfection of beauty sketched in the *Phaedrus* or the *Symposium* are apostrophized in a passage worthy of Sir Thomas Browne, describing a triumph of sun over

storm on the Alatamaha River: "The higher powers and
affections of the soul are so blended with the inferior passions
. . . Thus in the moral system which we have planned for
our conduct, as a ladder whereby to mount to the summit
of terrestrial glory . . . and from whence we perhaps meditated our flight to heaven, some accident surprises us. But let
us wait and rely on our God, who in due time will shine forth
in brightness and reveal to us how finite and circumscribed is
human power!" [40]

Technical terminology must be carefully distinguished
from stylistic embellishment. The *spatula* of the *branchio-
stega* of the red-bellied sunfish; *umbelliferous* tufts; *ocelle*
(an eyelike spot on an insect or fish); *villous lingulate* leaves;
trifid ferns; even the jaw-breaking Latin-derived word *in-
fundibuliform* (funnel-shaped) — all these are botanical, Lin-
naean, part of the traveler's research equipment. On the other
hand, Bartram affects a colorful use of words, as rich as the
brilliant plumage of the birds he so admires: "the *fulgour*
and rapidity of the streams of lightning"; *fulgid* sunbeams;
arbustive hills (covered with shrubbery); "*circumambient*
aromatic groves"; *decumbent* branches. *Nectariferous* tubes
is clear enough, whether technical or imaginative. A certain
riverbed is a *prolific nidus* for the growth of amphibious insects. He calls the famous Manate Spring a *Nymphaeum*,
punning on the Nymphaea Nelumbo which lines the banks.[41]
When he pushes away the *exfoliated* smoking brands of his
campfire, he falls back on certain involved phrases which
remind us of Cotton Mather's heavily laden sentences, such
as: "The disorder in my eyes subverted the plan of my
peregrinations." It is hard to tell whether the explorer is
humorous or bombastic when he describes his feelings at the
threat of "a thundering absolute crocodile."

There is hardly a quotation from any author, ancient or
modern, in the *Travels*. Everything is indirect and allusive,
the property of the writer, stamped with his own seal. On
his voyage to Charleston a storm overtakes them, "powerful
winds rushing forth from their secret abodes," calling to

mind the Vergilian Aeolus. The flowers of the Nymphaea Nelumbo resemble the Cap of Liberty. Of the curious Snake Bird, Bartram remarks: "If this bird had been an inhabitant of the Tiber in Ovid's days, it would have furnished him with a subject for some beautiful and entertaining metamorphoses." Bird migrations remind Bartram of Roman auspice-taking: "The knowledge of the passage of birds was the study of their priests and philosophers."

A singing Indian is "a young Orpheus"; the bridal chamber of a Creek couple is "a sacred mysterious thalame." Bartram's patch is too purple when he describes a young Seminole, resting on a "verdant couch guarded by the Deity," where Liberty and the Muses inspire him with wisdom and valor. A young trader and his wife, an attractive couple, evoke the same exaggerated compliment: "What a Venus! — What an Adonis!" The public square where the chiefs meet is an *Areopagus*. "Elysiums" are of frequent occurrence. The beautiful Vale of Keowe is as celebrated as the fields of Pharsalia or the Vale of Tempe. When Bartram kills a rattle-snake, his Seminole friends go through a whimsical ritual in order to "appease the *Manes*" of the dead victim.[42] It may also have been this scholarly interest of Bartram's that inspired certain investigations of the ornithologist Alexander Wilson, who is said to have studied the statements of Aristotle and the Elder Pliny that swallows become torpid in trees or caves and sink into the river mud for their hibernation period.[43]

It is the style, the refraction rather than the reflection of the classics, that explains any impulse to define the writings of this self-made craftsman in the science of flowers and words. There is a continuous bouquet of what ancient grammarians called the "Asianic," the full style rather than the simple and condensed Attic form. Bartram has left us a distinctive product of sentiment fresh from the Enlightenment, with the vehicle of the Noble Savage used to express that sentiment. This vehicle might also be called classical, for critics have found in the literature about the Noble Savage many a throwback to the ancient tradition; and the studies in primitivism already mentioned indicate that the journalist's attitude was nothing novel. As a scholar per se, Bartram is not at ease in the way that some of the New England writers of "rarities" were; he is flowery but never artificial. Bartram's utopia is full of fact, though sometimes descriptive aspects are overemphasized. There is a Stoic reverence and a Platonic mysticism, blended with deep Christian feeling, evident throughout his journal — he feels the humanness of the world of nature and the need for man's unity with it. As is the case with many of his eighteenth-century contemporaries, the Old World and the New go hand in hand.

VIII

THE TRANSATLANTIC MUSE

It is evident to anyone who reads widely in American colonial literature that the fields of politics, theology, and education, as well as experimental science, were enriched by the classical tradition. It is also clear that a considerable body of first-class prose can be identified as such even by the most exacting of critics. Franklin's *Autobiography*, Bradford's *Of Plimouth Plantation*, Woolman's *Journal*, Jefferson's state papers and *Notes on Virginia*, Paine's pamphlets, Bartram's *Travels*, William Byrd's *History of the Dividing Line*, and the recently published Adams-Jefferson letters do not suffer in comparison with British or European masterpieces of the period.

But what of colonial poetry? Perhaps it was so passively imitative of ancient models that the statement of T. S. Eliot applies only in reverse: "Not only the best, but the most individual parts of the poet's works, may be those in which the dead poets, his ancestors, assert their immortality most vigorously." [1] Did provincial verse, which began so haltingly with Rich's *Newes from Virginia* and ended with the early productions of the Hartford Wits, merely echo ancient sources, in contrast to the splendid loans from Greece and Rome which the great English poets turned into original creations? We might as well confess that much of this criticism is correct. But in reply to the notion that American poetry begins with Bryant and Emerson, we may single out some distinguished predecessors.

It was not easy for an original poet to emerge. There was, during the colonial period, no American London, no metropolitan center or clearinghouse. Problems of government and trade were demanding. The Indian menace, the French wars, and the westward movement absorbed the settlers' energies. The classics as models for imitation were ready to hand, but there was no challenge to transmute them into creative form. Although some discovered the trail up Parnassus, the majority remain as museum pieces in American anthologies.

Benjamin Tompson, in the Boston of the late seventeenth century, posed this question: "Pray what brave artist here can understand/ What one intends that takes a pen in hand?" A Philadelphian, Nathaniel Evans, looking wistfully across the Atlantic, lamented the absence of an understanding public and hence free play for his original inspiration:

> Shall famed Arcadia own the tuneful choir,
> And fair Sicilia boast the matchless lyre?
> Shall Gallia's groves resound with heavenly lays,
> And Albion's poets claim immortal bays?
> And this new world ne'er feel the Muses' fire,
> No beauties charm us, or no deeds inspire?
> O Pennsylvania! Shall no son of thine
> Glow with the raptures of the Sacred Nine?

Local conditions were no help. There was the "day of doom" shadow in New England, the scientific and mercantile trend in the middle provinces, and the feeling in Virginia that the planter might enjoy a good library but should not publish under his own name. There was verse in plenty, but it was apt to be occasional — epithalamia, anagrams, threnodies, celebrations of public events, ballads, satires, tributes, and prayers in times of trouble.[2] Writers of verse were often encouraged and were sometimes prominent in the public eye; however, their sources of inspiration were limited.

A careful examination of the poetry written during the colonial period reveals isolated fragments of high quality. There is the tribute to the Virginia rebel, Nathaniel Bacon, "By his Man." The dirge by Urian Oakes in memory of Thomas Shepard stands out among the many Puritan songs of lamentation. The vitriolic but gifted stanzas of the Tory Jonathan Odell arrest our attention. Graceful pastorals and *vers de société* sometimes rise above the average, in circles where amateurs cultivated the muse as an avocation. I am not including the many instances of excellent Latin verses, which college graduates turned out in profusion; nor should we claim as native American the masterly performance of George Sandys, the translator of Ovid's *Metamorphoses*, whose rhythmic version still remains unchallenged. From the early Baroque to the smooth couplets in the style of Pope, there was a continuous flow of verse from colonial pens, with respectable technique but little original genius. The background was in most cases classical; but the best poetry was independent of ancient models.

Opinions may vary as to the provincial poets who deserve special consideration. But I believe that seven of them should be discussed as significant: Anne Bradstreet, Edward Taylor, Benjamin Tompson, William Livingston, Francis Hopkinson, John Trumbull, and Philip Freneau. They all react, in different ways, to the Greco-Roman heritage. Each of them, except for Anne Bradstreet, held a college degree, and she herself lived in an atmosphere of gracious learning. I am discussing them not in chronological order, but in what I might call "harmonic progression," in terms of lesser to greater mastery of verse technique.

Francis Hopkinson, a graduate of the College of Philadelphia in 1757, was a master of metrics and a finished Latinist. Author of numerous prose satires and essays on current events, he was a virtuoso on the harpsichord, a collaborator with Franklin in several inventions, an Admiralty judge, a member of Congress, and a signer of the Declaration of Independence. His volume of songs, dedicated to Washington, who acknowledged the honor in a note which sustained the metaphor of Orpheus throughout the first paragraph, is no whit inferior to many English Elizabethan madrigals: "My generous heart disdains/ The slave of love to be." He was "master of ceremonies" for the most cosmopolitan of all the colonies.

He produced the usual ode in 1761, praising the new monarch as "The Roman Boast, the Generous Titus, joy of human kind." A poem of 1762 on the benefits of science opens with a Horatian tribute, making mention of the Muses, Helicon, Maecenas (in the guise of Lieutenant-Governor Hamilton), and Aeneas, with descriptions of an ideal college curriculum. After the Easton conference with the Indians, he praised (in his verses on "The Treaty") their powers of debate: "See from the throng a painted warrior rise,/ A savage Cicero." He referred to the Olympic games, and to contortions of the Delphic priestess, which he compared to an Indian war dance. Pageants were Hopkinson's forte. He wrote the classics-laden libretto for the *Temple of Minerva* in 1781 and the "Ode in Celebration of the Constitution" in 1788.

"The little man with a head no bigger than an apple, but genteel and well bred, and very social," as John Adams described him — and whom Nathaniel Lewis called "that little musical poetical witling" — was at his best when dealing humorously with public affairs. His well-known "Battle of the Kegs" in the strained period of 1778, with his prefatory metaphor of the Trojan horse, supplied welcome laughter to worried Philadelphians. His satire, "Date Obolum Belisario," pictures Britannia seated by the roadside in rags begging for alms: her son George has thrown the empire away, and his mother must subsist on charity.

Like Trumbull, Hopkinson satirized the dry grammatical teaching of Greek and Latin. At the age of twenty-five he reviewed the grammar of Andrew Stuart, finding "157 Capital Blunders in 137 pages," wittily producing a burlesque set of rules for the gender of declensions:

> The third are males in -*er*, -*or*, -*os*, -*n*, -*o*;
> Long words are Feminine in -*do* or -*go*;
> Most nouns in -*io* likewise *haec* procure,
> With -*as*, -*ans*, -*es*, -*is*, -*x*, and -*s* impure.
> Nouns ending in -*cal*, -*er*, -*ar*, -*men*, -*ur*, -*us*
> May to the neuter kind be placed by us.

> But from such music, from such heavenly squall,
> Good Lord deliver me, him, them, you, us and all!

Almost a cross between Horace and Petronius, he is seldom serious, as in his "Camp Ballad" of 1778 and in the patriotic lines on "The New Roof" (the Constitution), where it is his hope that "Science shall flourish, genius stretch her wing,/ In native strains Columbian Muses sing." Hopkinson himself would have been the first to smile away any pretensions to poetic prominence; but we are thankful for his light touch and his characteristic blend of amusement and instruction.

William Livingston, a graduate of Yale in 1741, wrote a pastoral poem, "Philosophic Solitude, or The Choice of a Rural Life," as a relief from the busy career of a statesman. He was governor of New Jersey from 1776 to 1790 and was one of the Whig group which prepared for independence with editorials in newspapers, Latin letters to friends, and satirical articles. Mottos for this poem were Seneca's *Otium sine literis mors est* and Vergil's *Nobis placeant ante omnia silvae.*[3] This "escape" was popular and was reprinted as late as 1793. His college classmates appended testimonial prefaces, with a host of mythological figures — such as "All Arcadia opens to our view." They credited him with "Pope's nervous phrase and Homer's sacred fire." Livingston's concept of nature is that of a well-cultivated garden, in the tradition of Tibullus, whose style and content he follows closely: "No trumpets there with martial clangor sound,/ But white-robed Peace and universal Love."[4] This is in the prevalent eighteenth-century cult of the simple life and the return of the Golden Age, when Saturn was king.

The country dweller, Livingston believed, must have a well-stocked library, containing books for pleasure, such as Vergil and Dryden ("whose lips were moistened in Parnassus spring"), and for profit, such as Locke, Thucydides, Tully, and Seneca ("Corduba's Sage, who fell by Nero's unrelenting rage"). This retreat should be spoiled by no frivolity, no temple of Venus. Here he would welcome a maiden for his wife, "Unblemished as the white-robed virgin quire/ That fed, O Rome, thy consecrated fire." If all this should fall to his lot, the poet would die happy at a ripe old age: "No warbling Syrens should retard my flight/ To heavenly mansions of unclouded light."

This verse making was to Livingston a recreation, unlike the serious efforts of Trumbull or Freneau. The poet-governor was in deadly earnest when he wrote prose for journals over the name of "Hortensius," and when he insisted that the Revolution originated with the people, who, "as a certain historian describes them, all joined forces as if for the purpose of putting out a wide-spreading fire." [5] Like Hopkinson, who wrote for entertainment, he would expect no crown of laurel; but as a cultivated man of letters and a statesman of distinction, he played a helpful part during "the times that tried men's souls."

Benjamin Tompson was born in Braintree in 1642 and died in Roxbury in 1724. He was an interpreter of life as he saw it in the Bay Colony, from his positions as schoolmaster, amateur physician, and town clerk. Funeral elegies, epics of Indian wars, local foibles, and gossip, were all grist to his mill. Like the Roman Janus, he looked both ways, backward to the old customs and forward to the broadening of the New England horizon. A graduate of Harvard, he applied in realistic fashion the material of the classics, and he was, like many other academic or clerical men, trained in the tradition of Latin verse writing. Critics see in his poetry a reflection of Dryden and Quarles, without the direct clarity of the former. His contemporaries must have thought highly of him: for on his Roxbury tombstone he is entitled "The Renowned poet of New England, *mortuus sed immortalis*."

Tompson was regarded as a poetical spokesman for his community. He took part in the pageant in honor of Lord Bellomont, who visited Boston in 1699 as the governor of New England. Costumed as the well-known Nathaniel Ward, the "Simple Cobler," he delivered the address of welcome, offering his service for any repairs and improvements which the noble lord might suggest. He introduced an Indian chief as a "Super," who had on "Hearing your lordship was to come this way,/ Begged Pluto's leave." Everyone, including farmers, joined in the greeting:

"Corydon to gaze deserts the Plough" and the brisk "Sons of Mars" await His Excellency's order to attack Quebec. This performance indicates Tompson's standing in the province as a gifted maker of verses, whose product was in demand. He was, in short, an officially recognized poet.

When his favorite pupil Cotton Mather published his *Magnalia*, that priceless record of New England notables, Tompson gave it a prefatory sendoff in a Latin poem, excellently phrased and redolent of Vergil's *Eclogues*. I hazard a hexameter English version, with a respectful bow to the original:

Since thou hast called from their dwellings on high these spirits departed,
Mather, the forest-born Muses with gratitude hereby reward thee.
Here a new offspring, in guise of the ancients, descending from Heaven,
Brought back to earth by the skill of thy pen, stand here in thy honor.
With hearts that are grateful to God, we thank thee in bountiful measure.
The glory and name of a Mather shall bide with us now and forever.

Tompson's "Grammarian's Funeral," in memory of two devoted teachers, is so filled with classical detail that the reader almost fancies himself back at school. Mythology and grammar go hand in hand, in the writer's quaint semi-baroque style. Gods come from heaven to attend the ceremonies; Vergil and Cato march in the procession.

Ovid from Pontus hast's Apparrell'd thus,
In Exile-weeds bringing *De Tristibus*.
That such a train may in their motion chord,[6]
Prosodia gives the measure word for word.

The death of "that Occidental Star, John Winthrop, Esq., Governour of Connecticut," evokes a manifold tribute. He is hailed as another Theophrastus, a Hermes Trismegistus, in his roles as astronomer, healer, philosopher, and ruler. Winthrop was all that and more — "a master of Apollo's art," a "Chiron skilled in teaching," and "a Scaevola in Court, an ancient consul."

The critical situation of New England inspires Tompson's sympathy and indignation. Here he turns to Vergil's last six books of the *Aeneid*. The curse of King Philip's War had thrown the colony into a state of disorder, into an Aristotelian *ataxia*, the opposite of *eupraxia* (well-being). "New England's Crisis" and "New England's Tears" went to the heart of the struggle. Part of the trouble arose from the abandonment of the simple life lived by the founders. The episode of Nisus and Euryalus repeats itself in the sufferings of the frontier settlers:

> Euryalus his soul reaks through the wound
> Of Nisus gasping by upon the ground,
> While the Rutilian,[7] like Enraged bears,
> The garments, with Men's Skins, asunder tears.

Messengers bring "quotidian gazets" of burnings and tortures. Families are decimated:

> Six of our leaders, in the first assault,
> Crave readmission to their Mother's Vault;
> Who had they fell in ancient *Homer's* dayes,
> Had been enrol'd with *Hecatombs* of praise.

Savages, "Whose locks Medusa's snakes do ropes resemble," could not be adequately described even by the artist Zeuxis. He could not paint "The phrenzy glances of the sinking saint." Such grim messages should be converted into a *celeusma militare* — a slogan for rallying citizens in defense of the province.

Tompson's many instances of Puritan suffering bring out the close connection between the poet and his community. His rough and often awkward lines impress us with their sincerity. There is no escape motif in his verses, and though we cannot rate him high in the list of American bards, we can praise him for his deep interest in the welfare of New England.

John Trumbull of Connecticut, as we have seen, holds the colonial record for precocity in studies. As a poet, he was essentially an academic product, but his window always looked out on a world viewed in the light of the laughing philosopher Democritus, coupled with a quite Churchillian irritation at its follies. His reading habits were voracious, in classics, French, and English; and his writings were voluminous. He spent a year in the law office of John Adams and, after some pamphlets on current affairs, turned his attention to politics.

Trumbull's first serious poem, "The Progress of Dulness," published in 1772–73, is now forgotten. Its author had mastered the octosyllabic couplet in the manner of Swift and Butler. The aim of the work was to attack the deadening routine of the teaching of classics and mathematics. A schoolboy "diets long on husks of Lily," proceeding "From thence to murdering Virgil's verse/ And construing Tully into 'farce.'" Hopkinson touched lightly on this subject, but Trumbull hammered it home. The remedy, he declared, was: "From ancient languages well known/ Transfuse new beauties to our own." Such an understanding of ancient literature would keep Tom Brainless, the parson, from boring his congregation, when "Glib-tongued Mercury in his hand/ Stretched forth the sleep-compelling wand." The poet advertises for sale "the arrows and darts of Cupid." He would let Homer tell his stories, Plato give wise philosophical advice, and Horace please by his wit. He would

> Give ancient arts their real due,
> Explain their faults, and beauties, too;
> Teach when to imitate and mend,
> And point their uses and their end.

On this basis, studies would be a part of life itself.

The events of the year 1774 furnished material for Trumbull's classical pen. His "Elegy on the Times" laments the Boston port bill and the sufferings of that city. While enemies "Quaff streams nectareous in the domes of state,/ The hostile beaks affright the guarded shore." But patience and wisdom will win in the end.

> Now meet the Fathers of the Western clime,[8]
> Nor names more noble graced the rolls of fame,
> When Spartan firmness braved the wrecks of time,
> Or Latian virtue fanned the heroic flame.
> Not deeper thought the immortal sage inspired,
> On Solon's lips when Grecian senates hung;
> Nor manlier eloquence the bosom fired,
> When genius thundered from the Athenian tongue.

Like Paine's *Common Sense*, Trumbull's *McFingal* was welcomed by Washington as a campaign document and went into countless editions. The meter of *Hudibras* is skilfully handled; the energetic drive of the cantos, crude as to subject-matter, is in the tar-and-feather tradition. The poem cannot be called great in any sense. But it is typical eighteenth-century farcical satire, in a profusely classical setting. Honorius, perhaps modeled on John Adams, is the patriot, the Coryphaeus. McFingal is the Tory squire, gifted, like his Scotch ancestors, with second sight: "No block in old Dodona's grove/ Could ever more oracular prove." His strength of lungs surpasses Stentor's. His speech to the Tory mob rises above the hubbub like the eloquence of Demosthenes over the roaring of the sea, as if "warmed with Homer's nectared liquor." Capitoline geese, the epic of the frogs and mice, and other allusions fill the pages. Waverers are accused of Penelope's delaying tactics: "As that famed weaver, wife t' Ulysses,/ By night her day's-work picked to pieces." Finally there is a fight between the two factions round the liberty pole:

> As faméd Ovid paints the adventures
> Of wrangling Lapithae and Centaurs,
> Who at their feast, by Bacchus led,
> Threw bottles at each other's head.

McFingal's sword fails, just as the sword of Turnus was shattered by the armor of Aeneas. The Tory is felled to earth, *ad terram duplicato poplite*, "with his hamstring mus-

cle cut, he sags to the ground." The gods are against him.
And when he is hauled up struggling to the top of the pole,
the poet rather inappropriately thinks of Socrates aloft in his
basket. Claudian's *Gigantomachia* is drawn upon to illustrate
the tar-covered wretch, who looked like "Plato's two-legged
animal without feathers." This heavy artillery grows monotonous. The frequent Greek and Latin allusions become
purely exhibitional. In the previous century Tompson's classical tears were appropriate to the sufferings of the Bay colonists and, while not so impressive in metrical skill, were
more poignant than the belly laughter of Trumbull the
"bestseller."

It is at this point that the honest critic must take stock.
The four authors we have been discussing drew on classical
satire or pastoral or epic in generous amounts, reflecting or
imitating the ancient fashion to the satisfaction of their
readers. Their work cannot be regarded as of high quality,
but it suited the provincial public. In the case of the remain-
ing three, however, whose best work is superior, we meet
with a paradox. The better the quality, the less does their
poetry rely directly on the classics for inspiration. The
Greco-Roman heritage is apparent — more so in Freneau
than in any of the whole group — but it is not blended ef-
fectively as it is, say, in Milton's *Lycidas* or Shelley's *Hellas*.
This final trio, however, when we scan them closely, seems
to have followed the advice of Philip Sidney: "Look in thy
heart and write!"

Anne Dudley Bradstreet, the daughter and wife of Massachusetts governors, entered the poetical world with a warm
welcome, not only as a woman pioneer on Parnassus but
as a highly regarded personality in the Bay Colony. Her first
volume, with the title of *The Tenth Muse Lately Sprung
up in America*, published in London in 1650, elicited many
tributes. Among her sponsors was Nathaniel Ward, for-
merly a neighbor in Ipswich. Ward pictured an Olympian
competition, between *La Semaine* (the seven days of Crea-

tion) of her model, the Calvinist Du Bartas, and the poems of Anne Bradstreet herself. Mercury and Minerva present these two candidates, with Apollo as judge. The god, examining both volumes through his spectacles, gives up in despair and declares the contest a tie. Others praised her work, calling it as sweet as the Hybla bees, spoiled by no frivolous Venus or Daphne allusions, and enhanced with the dignity of Orpheus and Arion.

These first poems were the creation of a scholar-poetess. They were quarried from Joshua Sylvester's translation of the popular Du Bartas, the world history of Walter Raleigh, and such treatises as Pemble's *Period of the Persian Monarchy* or Crooke's *Mikrokosmographia*. In her *Quartets* she covers the Four Elements, the Four Humours, the Four Ages of Man, the Four Seasons of the Year, and the Four Monarchies. The Puritan Bible is fundamental, and the illustrations or figures are apt to be classical. The Greek background has a particular appeal for her: "Let me name Grecia: 'tis my heart." The prologue to the first edition opens with a tribute to Demosthenes: "Nor can I, like that fluent sweet-tongued Greek,/ Who lisped at first, in future time speak plaine."

Anne Bradstreet's method is based on cases from ancient history and mythology, but she personalizes the material upon which she draws. Among the four elements, Fire shows its powers in the world of nature, as in the Vesuvius eruption which caused the death of Pliny the Elder and made a Roman emperor cower with fright. Earth is arbitrarily credited with the glory of Greece: "For learning, arms, and arts I love it well,/ But chiefly 'cause the Muses there did dwell." But with this praise of the pagan world she qualifies her adoration: the classics are welcomed for illustration but must not compete on equal terms with the Christian message:

> So do I more the sacred tongue esteem,
> Though plain and rural it do rather seem
> Than schooled Athenian and divinity.[9]

Her "Four Monarchies" is a résumé, half of it from Raleigh. The opening lines are reminiscent of the classical praise of the Golden Age, when "Man did not proudly strive for sovereignty." There is the usual debate between the flesh and the spirit, and some mention of current affairs in the "Dialogue between Old England and New." Her hero is Sir Philip Sidney. Though Queen Elizabeth was "the English Minerva" (a greater woman than Dido), the noble knight stood first, with the inspiration of Mars, Minerva, and all the Muses.

If this were all, we should leave Anne Bradstreet among the blue stockings. But we must remember our injunction — that the poet's art must transmute his ancient models into vital and imaginative forms and that the weakness of American colonial poetry was its imitative reliance on these very sources. This New England poetess is at her best when she throws away Du Bartas or Raleigh or even the Greco-Roman writers on mythology and history, and speaks from the heart, as Sidney recommended. With her increasing years, mere philosophy is not enough. Its shortcomings are expressed in the "Vanity of All Earthly Things":

> What is it then, to do as Stoicks tell,
> Nor laugh nor weep, let things go ill or well?
> Such Stoicks are but Stocks, such teaching vain.
> Where shall I climb, sound, seek, or search or find
> That *Summmum Bonum* which may stay my mind?

The 1678 edition of her poems indicates this change.

The later poems deal with nature, her happy family life, and the triumphs of a woman over the hardships of a region that contrasted vividly with the English comforts with which she had been reared. Her husband Simon Bradstreet is a source of continued inspiration, in this case Homeric:

> He that can tell the starrs or Ocean sand,
> Or all the grass that in the meads doth stand,
> The leaves in th' woods, the hail or drops of rain,
> Or in a cornfield number every grain . . .
> May count my sighs.

Or, more simply and nonclassically:

> If ever two were one, then surely we,
> If ever man were loved by wife, then thee;
> If ever wife was happy in a man,
> Compare with me, ye women, if you can.

Anne Bradstreet's father, Governor Thomas Dudley, is lamented in some fine heroic couplets:

> One of thy Founders, him New England know,
> Who staid thy feeble sides when thou wast low,
> Who spent his state, his strength and years with care
> That after-comers in them might have a share.

The country about Andover and Ipswich delighted her. In her "Contemplations" she comments on the beauty of nature as opposed to the weaknesses of man:

> Under the cooling shadow of a stately elm
> Close sat I by a stately River's side,
> Where gliding streams the rocks did overwhelm —
> A lonely place, with pleasures dignified.

Even here, however, the river is "Neptune's glassie hall," gliding down to "Thetis' house" (the ocean).

The poetess' real self is portrayed in the "Contemplations":

> When I behold the heavens as in their prime,
> And then the earth (though old) still clad in green,
> The stones and trees insensible of time,
> Nor age nor wrinkle on their front are seen;
> If winter comes and greenness then do fade,
> A spring returns, and they more youthful made.
> But man grows old, lies down, remains where once he's laid.

Although we must qualify the contemporary praise which greeted the poetry of the "Tenth Muse," the reader of today will find much to justify her high position in the spiritual and literary life of New England.

Of all the colonial poets, Edward Taylor is the most difficult to categorize. He has been called "a Hellenistic Puritan" or a modernizer of the morality play. The majority of critics describe him as a metaphysical symbolist in the style of Herbert, Vaughn, and Crashaw. A native of Leicestershire, not far from Coventry, after a brief experience as schoolmaster, Taylor emigrated to Boston in 1668 and was promptly admitted to Harvard by President Chauncy, rooming with Samuel Sewall in the class of 1671. Chauncy kept up his friendship with Taylor, and at his death was lamented by his alumnus in a Latin elegy and an English tribute which opened with the usual phraseology and the "baroque" quaintness characteristic of the writer:

> Peace, sobbing Muse, come sum thy loss.
> Rare learning's gone, a Polyglotta
> Extract of Greek and Hebrew.

Taylor, who was held in high regard in the Puritan community, accepted a call to a church in Westfield, Massachusetts, where he spent the rest of his life. He left a library of two hundred and twenty volumes, besides poems in manuscript, journals, and sermons which descended to his grandson Ezra Stiles, president of Yale. The recent publication of this material has opened new vistas in the field of colonial poetry.

The books in Taylor's library[10] reveal a careful study of what we might call the architecture of poetry. It is clear that he made use of the *Prosodia* of Smetius, an English-Latin phrasebook, Farnaby's *Index Rhetoricus*, Pelgrom's *Synonymorum Sylva*, and various florilegia of the type used by college undergraduates. Among many classical authors we find the *Idylls* of Theocritus and Winterton's *Poetae Minores Graeci*. The results of such reading are embedded in his poems, without mention of the sources; and it must be granted at the start that, while he is often pedantic and overornate, he rises to a high level of quality in his spontaneous and mystical interpretation of Christian grace. There are lines of haunting beauty in his "Preparatory Meditations," such as:

> The Morning Star doth rise, Dews gracious fall;
> And spiritual Herbs, and sweet Celestiall flowers
> Sprinkled therewith most frequently do call
> The Day Star up, with golden Curls, and Towers
> Put back the Curtains of the azure skies
> And gild the aire while that the Sun doth rise.

He runs the gamut of vocabulary from the humblest image of a country barnyard (often expressed in the dialect of his native Leicestershire) to exalted descriptions of the coach which carries the saints to glory.

Taylor is a coiner of words rather than a mere imitator. Besides the well-known *Palma Christi*, he hunts out a *Plastrum Gratiae Dei, Unguentum Apostolorum*, and *Herba Trinitatis*. His classical references are incidental and offhand. An early poem indicates his literary independence: "What though my Muse be not adorned so rare/ As Ovid's golden verses do declare." The Golden Mean is one remedy in the struggle against "Satan's Sophistries." Certain proverbs betray their origin: "Rare as a black swan"; "A musty cask doth marre rich Malmsey wine." Justice catches the wrongdoer: "Me leaden-heel'd with iron bands they'll call." And on the avoidance of rashness: "Who'll with a leaking old crack't hull assay/ To brave the raging waves of Adria?" [11]

Seneca was a favorite of Taylor's. He has in mind the scientific observation in the *Naturales quaestiones:* "Strait wands appear/ Crook'd in and out, in running water clear," describing objects which seem curved and distorted under water. It may be that he was thinking of Seneca's tragedy *Hercules Oetaeus* when he wrote, "We humbly beg, O Lord, to know our crime,/ That we thus tortured are before our time." [12] Much of this is a holdover from student days. Taylor becomes more symbolic and scriptural with the advancing years.

An excellent example of his selective use of history is a borrowing from the Roman poet Martial, in proof of the doctrine that Christ's blessings surpass the inventions of man:

> Art, nature's Ape, hath many brave things done:
> As the Pyramids, the lake of Meris vast,

The Pensile Orchards built in Babylon,
Psammitch's Labyrinth (arts cramping task),
Archimedes his Engins made for war,
Rome's Golden House, Titus his Theater . . .
Nature doth better work than art, yet Thine
Out vie both works of nature and of art.[13]

The reader of Martial will remember a similar list of the world's wonders, culminating in the Coliseum. It is entirely possible that this description may have been transmitted through Nathaniel Crouch's *Surprising Miracles of Nature and Art*, published in London in 1685.

A passage in "God's Determinations" has started some speculation about whether it may not have a classical source:

Peace, Peace, my Hony, do not cry!
My little Darling, wipe thine eye.
O Cheer, Cheer up, come see.
Is anything too deare, my Dove,
Is anything too good, my Love.
To get or give for thee?

Here is Christ speaking to the discouraged soul, in terms of affection similar to those which the Emperor Hadrian used in his *animula vagula blandula*. Weathers, the advocate of a Greek origin, recalling the presence on Taylor's bookshelves of a Theocritus and Winterton's *Anthology*, compares the soul to Eros who, in the Hellenistic pastoral, *The Honey-Stealer*, flies to his mother Aphrodite after being stung by a bee.[14] He is consoled and assured by her that his own power is far greater than that of the bee. The dove is the bird of Aphrodite, symbolic of the soul from early Greek vase painting to Maeterlinck's *Blue-Bird*. In the same poem Satan is God's "Sheep-Dog," "Whose barking is to make thee cling/ Close underneath thy Savior's wing." Satan pursues the soul as the Nemean Lion attacked Heracles. The rescue of a cicada from the wiles of a spider is the parable of God's aid to the struggling spirit. These, and others less likely, are reminiscent of the Theocritus (or pseudo-Theocritus) whom Taylor knew well and of the Alexandrian pastoral where sheep and shepherd harmonize with Christian figures of speech and thought.

Other traces of the ancient tradition occur. Personification is of course frequent. The unhappy sinner is described as having "for Companions Fear, Heartache, Grief" — the occupants of the entrance to Hades, as Aeneas saw them. Taylor experiments with some almost Horatian meters when he "wears Sapphic slippers to welcome the sweet and glorious Grace." But all these references are incidental when one reads the lines in which Mercy addresses the Soul:

> Thou simple, learn of mee; I will you teach
> True wisdom for your Soul's Felicity,
> Wisdom extending to the Endless reach
> And blissful end of all Eternity,
> Wisdom that doth all else transcend as far
> As Sol's bright Glory doth a painted Star.

His canticles, hidden for several generations, add a new grace to the Puritan tradition.

Philip Freneau was of French Huguenot stock, a native of northern New Jersey, and a member of a brilliant group of Princeton undergraduates which included James Madison, Brackenridge, Bradford, Aaron Burr, and "Light-Horse Harry" Lee. He began early as an apprentice of the verse-writing "mystery." Voluminous reading of the classics under the guidance of President Witherspoon, sample translations of Greek and Latin authors, debates in which he maintained that ancient poetry excelled the modern — all these experiments developed in him a mastery of poetic technique. Much of it was imitative and sophomoric; but his "Power of Fancy" and his "Pyramids of Egypt" prophesied more than the usual juvenilia of would-be poets. At the commencement of 1771, he and Brackenridge collaborated in a rhapsodic epic, "The Rising Glory of America," extolling British imperial unity and prefixing as motto the passage from Seneca's *Medea* that had charmed the Virginia Argonauts. They foretold the earthly paradise of the brave new world:

Where the Mississippi stream,
By forests shaded, now runs weeping on,
Nations shall grow, and states not less in fame
Than Greece and Rome of old! We too shall boast
Our Scipios, Solons, Catos, sages, chiefs.

His "Pictures of Columbus" idealized a golden age and future Miltons or Homers who would devote their heroics to the land of opportunity.

By 1775, however, this idyllic stage was over. A call to American freedom canceled the imperial idea of British supremacy. As the "Tyrtaeus of the American Revolution," Freneau was commended by Washington for his inspirational support of the colonial cause. The *Massachusetts Centinel* hailed him as a patriot, "a genuine son of Neptune and Clio." The *New York Journal* advertised his "Ciceronian Eloquence" in the poem "American Liberty," and his reputation as a champion of freedom was made. The piece began with a paraphrase of Vergil, where Allecto sounds her war cry to stir the Trojans and the Latins. Uneven, like much of Freneau's work, there are impressive passages:

Virtue disdains to own tyrannic laws,
Takes part with Freedom, and assumes its cause.
She stood with Romans while their hearts were true,
And so she shall, Americans, with you!

Satire followed satire. The Stygian conference of General Gage and Lord Percy, curses on the head of Benedict Arnold (from an epode of Horace), an elegy on the beloved Montgomery, and rebukes to Sir Henry Clinton and the publisher Rivington are among the good and inferior contributions to the Cause. The hapless André, with his attempt at bribery, recalled to his mind the time when the Greek city-states were at odds, and

The Prince of Macedon declared
That those strong gates his javelin could not pierce
Were open still to gold.

Freneau's ship, the *Aurora*, "offspring of the Sun," was captured on the way to St. Eustatia by the British frigate *Isis*.

In the prison hulks, where the poet was for a time in captivity, and whence hapless prisoners were carried off for burial in Wallabout Bay, there were tragic cases:

> Here wastes away. Autolycus the brave,
> Here young Orestes finds a watery grave.
> Here young Alcander, gay, alas, no more
> Dies far sequestered from his native shore.

In his lament for these unfortunates, he applied the Vergilian tribute to the young Marcellus which brought tears to the eyes of his mother Octavia: "What funeral train, O Tiber, shalt thou see, as thou flowest by the new-built tomb!" [15] But his dirge for the soldiers who fell in the battle of Eutaw Springs, devoid of classical ornamentation, is a classic in itself:

> If in this wreck of ruin, they
> Can yet be thought to claim a tear,
> O smite thy gentle breast and say
> "The friends of freedom slumber here."

These revolutionary poems, many in number and uneven in quality, run the gamut from mere abuse to sublimity, redolent of Roman denunciation and current satire. But they served their purpose. The signing of peace was celebrated by "Mr. Peale's Exhibition, with its Ionic pillars in the style of architecture used by the Romans," and an apostrophe by "Tyrtaeus" wherein he hails "the closing of Janus's doors" and greets Washington as "a Roman chief." The establishment of the United States was heralded by a Latin poem on "The Pyramid of the Fifteen American States," adapted from Martial's poem on the wonders of Old Rome.[16] At this point in his career Freneau was at the height of his reputation as a spokesman for democracy.

Now came the hour of decision. Should the eloquent herald of colonial freedom develop his gift for lyric poetry, or should he become a political controversialist in the new nation? He had often complained of the public inattention to his quest for beauty:

> On these bleak climes by Fortune thrown,
> Where lovely fancy has no sway,
> Tell me, what has the Muse to do?

With his excessive enthusiasm for the French Revolution, his denunciation of all Federalist policies, and his unsuccessful editorships, he became involved in bitter partisan warfare.[17] Courageous but melancholic and insecure, the poet was lost in the rough and tumble of politics. We may therefore turn to the few imaginative lyrics which reveal the soul of Philip Freneau.

His avocation as sea captain was his romance. In "Minerva's Advice" he pictures himself in the symbolic role as leader of an Argonautic expedition:

> Ah, Jason, why those sighs and tears,
> Why is that nervous heart unstrung?
> To honour best true courage steers
> When thickest dangers round her throng.
> Sighs ne'er will hush the world to peace,
> Nor gain for you the GOLDEN FLEECE.

The Argo metaphor is frequent in his verses. He kept his records of voyages between 1770 and 1804 on the blank pages of his books, and the third volume of his Ovid is crowded with sea memoranda. He was perhaps happiest on his cruises. "No bard," he declared, "from Hesiod to Peter Pindar has ever commanded such a ship as mine." His New Jersey farm was also a refuge, where he was able *Inter silvas academi quaerere verum.* Two years of employment with Captain Hanson, on the island where nature was lovely but man was cruel, resulted in his long poem, "The Beauties of Santa Cruz" (1776). As an observer of life in the West Indies, he denounced the slave trade, satirizing a certain planter, a "Stygian" creator of "pictures of Hell like those that Vergil's pencil drew": "Here surly Charons make their annual trip,/ And ghosts arrive in every Grecian ship."

Freneau's restless mind touched superficially on Platonic philosophy; and he seems to have been attracted to deism. Like Hopkinson and Trumbull, he wrote verses pleading for a broader and more comparative view of the classics as literature. But what a relief it is to turn to his "Brook of the Valley" ("emblem of restless man") or to "The House of Night," a dream of the death of Death, as eerie as anything in Coleridge or Poe. "The Wild Honeysuckle," Lewis Leary rightly declares, "placed Freneau at the head of America's procession of poets." It loses nothing by comparison with the flora of Wordsworth and Emerson:

> From morning suns and evening dews
> At first thy little being came —
> If nothing once — you nothing lose,
> For when you die you are the same —
> The space between is but an hour,
> The empty image of a flower.

Essentially American was his "The Indian Burying Ground":

> By midnight moons, o'er moistening dews,
> In habit for the chase arrayed,
> The hunter still the deer pursues,
> The hunter and the deer, a shade.

The disappointed old man, who at the age of eighty lost his way in a blizzard and died by the roadside, represents the end of an era, a time before the romantic and the classical had blended in a new combination.

IX

JONATHAN BOUCHER, TORYISSIMUS

THERE were other clergymen of British sympathies who outrank Jonathan Boucher in historical importance. Jonathan Odell, the broadside satirist, and Samuel Seabury, author of the *West Chester Farmer Letters* which roused the pen of Alexander Hamilton, were more in the public eye. Boucher was parochial, and yet the reader of his correspondence with George Washington and his thirteen sermons on pre-Revolutionary issues, feels the force of a driving personality. The man himself was an excellent sounding board for those exciting days. He held out until he was forced to leave America; and he ended his life as a vicar at Epsom in Surrey, publishing his *Discourses* in 1797 and occupying himself with the historical and linguistic studies for which his classical knowledge qualified him well.

Born in Cumberland in 1738, Boucher had no college education, but, after study and some apprentice teaching at Wigton and St. Bee's, he emigrated to Virginia in 1759 in the capacity of a private tutor. Returning to England in 1762, he was ordained and then held several positions in Virginia, finally settling at St. Anne's in Annapolis. This church was familiarly known as *Gradus ad Parnassum* — "a step toward Heaven," described by himself as *ne plus ultra*. Here he was happy, a friend of the governor's and an articulate member of the Homony Club, where literature was a hobby. Over these years he was involved in many current affairs: agricultural improvements, the first Stamp Act discussions, the "Parson's Cause" in connection with clergymen's wages, and the economic problems of the province. He was by no means a shy person, though at times naive. An instance of the first trait was his free advice to the stock-holders of the Potomac Navigation Company. The second was the questionable taste of his letter to a Mr. Addison, whose niece he wished to marry, comparing the lady to "a little unoccupied plantation" which would richly repay cultivation and fortifying his remarks by quotations from two passages of his favorite Vergil, calling to mind "the skilled old Corycian gardener" and repeating the offer of Juno to find a wife for Aeolus, God of the Winds.[1]

We may briefly consider Boucher as a classical educator before we concentrate on him as a pugnacious, politically minded churchman. He kept a school for boys, but his particular attention was given to Jacky Custis, the stepson of George Washington. At the age of fourteen the boy had already been reading intensively in the classics, with a certain amount of passive resistance. In July 1768 the schoolmaster asked the patient and busy planter to "look into his books for Cicero's *De Officiis*, or his Familiar Epistles, and a Livy," to be dispatched as soon as possible. The lad's future college was discussed with care. President Witherspoon of Princeton had criticized Boucher because his pupil was not "put into Greek"; but the latter maintained that an all-round education was more important, "*things* were superior to *books*." William and Mary was too near. Princeton and the College of Philadelphia were "the nurseries of all that frivolous and mischievous kind of knowledge that passed for learning in America . . . they are smatterers in Rhetoric and the belles-lettres."[2] The friendly debate ended in a term under Myles Cooper at King's College (Columbia), with good-sized bills from both tutor and president, and the young student's marriage to Nelly Calvert. The general had been patient and courteous, Boucher honest but expensive. Inevitable circumstances brought this relationship to an end. The rift came on August 6, 1775.

Washington received, presumably at his headquarters in Cambridge, a farewell letter: "I know many Whigs who are not tyrants. In this number it is but doing common justice to place you." But the tone grows more severe: Washington should not have "looked on while he [Boucher] was vilified." The letter closes with a renunciation somewhat like the famous note of Franklin to his friend, the printer Strahan: "You are my enemy, and I am yours." After the peace he wrote to Washington from England in May 1784, not apologizing but sending out a feeler toward renewed friendliness, wishing health and happiness to the Washingtons at Mount Vernon, though still objecting to the new American "Equality of Religious Establishments."

Boucher's main work is his *A View of the Causes and Consequences of the American Revolution*. The volume was dedicated to Washington; and the presentation copy, acknowledged by the recipient, was included in the inventory of Mount Vernon submitted by Thomson Mason, Tobias Lear, and others in 1810. It is a collection of sermons delivered in America before the war, doubtless somewhat altered from their original form. It is generously documented with footnotes and heaped with classical allusions and illustrations. A motto on the title page is taken from William Bellenden's *De Statu Prisci Orbis*, urging the immediate facing of coming problems: *Cum a strepitu tumultuque aures nostrae paululum conquieverint, quid tandem causae est, cur de re publica quid sentiamus taciturnitate diuturniore celemus?* (Since our ears have been for a brief while rested from the din and confusion [of war], is there any reason why we should hide our feelings about the State by further silence?). A lengthy preface congratulates Washington on the wisdom of having established a "mixed government" like that of Britain. It expresses the hope that the modern Cincinnatus, interested in peace, may have followed the Vergilian advice and brought about a regime of peace and order.[8] "The turbulent spirit of Republicanism" must be avoided; for government is *not* founded on the consent of the people. Will the republic endure if, like the earth-men of Cadmus, demagogues spring up and mob spirit prevail as it did during the French Revolution? Many American governors were, as

Phaedrus fabled, chosen only to be King Logs, insulted by the troublemaking frogs. American merchants had been in debt to the British: hence came trouble like that which Cicero and Sallust had predicted as the result of *aes alienum* (debt), an uprising under Catiline.[4] While the rebellion against Tarquin was not a parallel, there was a condition resembling the quarrel between Corinth and Corcyra, where the former claimed the "natural rights" of a mother country and the latter complained of harsh treatment.[5]

The thought always on Boucher's mind is illustrated by his *Quaeres Addressed to the People of Maryland:*

> I. Do not the popular meetings bear a very near resemblance to the tribunitial assemblies of the people in the earlier periods of the Roman history? II. Do not the resolves entered into at such popular meetings resemble also the *Plebiscite or Ordinances* which in after times were as valid and obligatory as the *Senatus-Consulta?* III. By encouraging these, do we not in fact encourage that *Dominatio Plebis,* so much desecrated by the best writers on Government? [6]

Historians would smile at Boucher's comparison of the ineffective Sackville (Lord George Germain) with the Athenian Aristides. They might also be amused at the friendly hint that the father of his country should have refused to take up arms against a tyrant without an order from the Senate, as Verginius Rufus did, declining also to become emperor.[7] There was good reason for the British government to strike hard in 1775, as there was also for the Roman republic to act promptly against its rebellious colonies. In spite of all this, however, the American republic may become "a great Empire under a monarch like Augustus," after a few disturbances and the establishment of a central organization. Church and State must go hand in hand. Perhaps some day the two nations might unite to form a world power, matching the glory of Old Rome, as Anchises prophesied to Aeneas. Polybius had some inkling of the ultimate decline of mighty realms;[8] but the Tory refugee congratulates his friend on a noble career and wishes the young republic

well, in spite of some left-handed criticism and evidence of
the scars of what the writer felt to be an error and an injury.

The first Discourse was a sermon preached in 1763, celebrating the close of the Seven Years' War and welcoming
the opportunity of an extensive agrarian policy on the Virginia Plan, to go hand in hand with the prospect of eternal
peace. Credit is given to the pagan Augustus, who had closed
the temple of Janus and had issued an edict that all the world
should be taxed. This was "a propitious circumstance to the
propagation of the Gospel," reversing the process lamented
by Vergil and Ovid, when pruning hooks were beaten into
spears. The same simile of Janus and world peace under Augustus as an opening for the preaching of the Word is found
in the works of Jonathan Edwards,[9] copies of whose writings are well represented in the 1806 catalogue of Boucher's
library. "War," declared the Tory parson, "is a relic of bar-
barism," as Eusebius and Tertullian had testified. *Latro*
(highwayman) is synonymous with *soldier*. As John Dickinson did, he paired the conquest policies of Rome and Carthage with those of France and England. He revealed his inner convictions when he maintained that Julius Caesar makes
bad company in the presence of Socrates or Fénelon or William Penn. The Discourse ends with a prayer for harmony
and a peaceful rural existence, where "the fields will be yel-
low with ripe grain," and Ceres, "who first taught mortal
men to till the soil with the plow," may come into her own
again.

The second and third Discourses deal mainly with ecclesiastical matters, "On Schisms and Sects" and "The American
Episcopate." Thanks to the Romans, who were lenient in
allowing conquered peoples to retain their own religion, and
to the Greeks, who never tried to convert anyone, the way
was prepared for the Savior to gather believers together
from a variety of creeds. So far, this was sound doctrine —
a united church. But toleration, as Nathaniel Ward had also
maintained a century and a half previously, was to Boucher
a fallacy. Separation into different sects meant the loss of

effectiveness: the ancient Britons, as Tacitus declared in his *Agricola,* could not unite because *in commune non consulunt.* The Virginia clergymen who voted against an American bishopric did not understand that bishops succeeded apostles and that such a succession was "just as proper as the succession of Roman emperors or British kings." There should be one church, a "tower of strength," like the protector whom Medea sought after she had overthrown the house of Jason.

As a conservative educator, Boucher let himself go in the fourth Discourse; it was preached in a region where the well-to-do had tutors while the mass of the population was neglected. Here he was at one with Jefferson, though starting from a different basis. Cicero and Juvenal support his argument: "What better gift can we present to the State," said the former, "than an educated citizenry?" Juvenal's *ut patriae sit idoneus* (ready to serve one's country) should be taken to heart.[10] The ancients, even if their experience of human nature was more limited, and consequently their stock of knowledge less extensive, were superior to the moderns in that they made better use of what they *did* know. Xenophon "was as much a legislator as Lycurgus" — his idea of learning was that it should be "an apprenticeship to the business of life." The Jews took their education much more seriously than did the Greeks and Romans, with special emphasis on their religious code. Boucher's advocacy of learning is backed by the well-known passage on liberal studies in Cicero's *Archias.* Even the Dissenters are insistent on good schooling, and Episcopalians should profit by their example: *Fas est et ab hoste doceri* (Learn a lesson even from your enemy), a proverb popular throughout colonial history.[11] An agricultural society is especially favorable to learning because, according to Aristotle, "the citizens occupy themselves with statecraft, having people to work for them, and they are able to have leisure." Plutarch adds testimony from his essay "On the Education of Children," and for good measure Boucher records the words of Diogenes to the Megarians: "Better to be one of their swine than one of their children!" [12]

The Discourse of 1774 continues this plea for an ultimate union of Churchmen, Catholics, and Dissenters. It was preached in St. Anne's, "On the Toleration of Papists," and may have been intended as a token of agreement with the Quebec Act for Canada, which was finally passed by Parliament in the same year. Furthermore, the writer may have given some thought to the Maryland toleration act, which for a time provided freedom of worship, Catholics included. Persuasion is better than compulsion: *Quis tulerit Gracchos de seditione querentes?* (Who could endure to listen to the Gracchi on the subject of rebellion?).[13] There should be no gospel of hatred, no curse on future generations like that of Dido on the descendants of Aeneas: *Genus omne futurum exercete odiis! Nullus amor populis, nec foedera sunto* (Train all the after-born to hate! Let there be no friendship, no treaties, between the two nations).[14] Catholics should be fairly treated and allowed to educate their children in their own way, instead of having to go elsewhere. On this point, Pliny the Younger was sound: *Educentur hic qui hic nascuntur, statimque ab infantia natale solum amare et frequentare consuescant* (Let those who are born here be schooled here; from infancy onward let them become accustomed to love and to inhabit their home region.)[15] As for the current deism, it should be outlawed: "Some modern writers have extolled the mild spirit of heathenism, as though it had been peculiarly indulgent to persons of different religious creeds." Here the Episcopalian is as emphatic as the Presbyterian Witherspoon — both classical scholars of no mean attainment.

The seventh Discourse continues the plea for unity. "The first criterion," says Aristotle, "is a care for religion." Epaminondas, on being praised by his people for governing well, replied, "You obey well!" Dissenting chatter indicates civic decline. Petronius, a rather shaky witness, lamented the current fashionable *ventosa et enormis loquacitas*. Tacitus in his *Dialogus* bears the same testimony: *Est magna et notabilis eloquentia alumna licentiae* (Heavy and conspicuous flow of talk is the foster-mother of loose morals). Unchecked and disloyal attitudes toward the Establishment are the beginning of deep-seated trouble. But the Word of God is like a rock, to which the unbending King Latinus is compared: *Ille velut pelagi rupes immota resistit/ Ut pelagi rupes magno veniente fragore* (Like a cliff by the sea that stands unshaken, yea, like a cliff by the sea when the surf comes heavily crashing).[16]

The year 1774 was a critical one. Three more sermons were preached within that period, recalling the quarrel between Abraham and Lot and the famous Absalom and Achitophel episode. All three were allegorical of the political situation, reflecting the problem of taxation without representation. There is still hope for the olive branch and a solution similar to the reconciliation of Aristippus and Aeschines.[17] "Our English Livy" (Lord Clarendon) had written with eloquence on the evils resulting from civil war. Boucher's language is akin to that of John Winthrop on civil liberty, stressing acquiescence in "some fixed and steady principles of conduct."[18] The mutual advantages of a loyal colony are as obvious today, he says, as they were to Sallust: *Vobis vero nulla opportunior amicitia nostra* (No friendly alliance could be more beneficial to you than ours).[19] But the tragedy of the situation was obvious, and the misplaced ambitions of would-be tyrants must be checked. There is no place for any Alexanders: *Unus Pellaeo iuveni non sufficit orbis;/ Aestuat infelix angusto limite mundi* (One world is not enough for the young Macedonian, and the hapless one chafes at the narrow limits of his universe).[20]

At this point Boucher's classical comparisons begin to be abusive. Catiline is dragged out from the pages of Sallust, with his mob of *flagitiosi* and *facinorosi;* and Dionysius of Halicarnassus furnishes a parallel, that the loyalists are the patricians and the rebels the plebeians.[21] Hesitation would be fatal — King David was too softhearted, and Tiberius waited too long in the case of the Gallic rebellion of A.D. 21: *Consultus super eo Tiberius aspernatus est iudicium, aluitque dubitatione bellum* (When Tiberius was consulted on this matter, he refused to make a decision, and thus by his wavering he encouraged the war).[22] To the Committees of Correspondence and the many provincial assemblies the preacher cried: "Come, then, ye perturbed spirits, shew me, if you can, in what your conduct differs from that faithless incendiary whose history we have just been reviewing!" Worse yet, the likeness of Benjamin Franklin to Dryden's Achitophel and to Catiline is clearly indicated, and many of his hearers thought that Absalom meant Washington.

By 1775 the attitude of Boucher had become known to a wide circle. His eleventh and twelfth Discourses are direct answers to attacks on the mother country by Dr. William Smith, provost of the College of Philadelphia, and by Jacob Duché, who offered the first prayer before the Continental Congress (he was compromised later). These addresses are also a blend of the classical and Biblical, alluding to rebellious tribes who mistakenly move away and build altars elsewhere, proving Plutarch's contention that "there is in every people, naturally, something of a malignant and peevish temper against those who govern them." [23] The only remedy is firm treatment, as stated in Sallust's Catiline: *Si quid ab Senatu petere vellent, ab armis discedant* (If they wish to petition the Senate, they should first disarm). An appendix to the eleventh sermon repeats at some length the speech of Spurius Servilius, "a patrician maliciously persecuted by the tribunes," taken from the ninth book of Dionysius of Halicarnassus.[24]

In this fateful year the clergyman is absorbed into the politician: "I stand sufficiently vindicated as a preacher of politics." Fortified by Paul's advice, and harking back to the divine right of kings as outlined by Robert Filmer in his *Patriarcha*, Boucher preaches a doctrine of obedience to the constituted powers. For this purpose he ransacks many pagan writers, church authorities, as well as Blackstone, Burke,

Clarendon, and Robertson. The "General Governor," whose very name Samuel Adams abhorred, would have suited Boucher, if the position had been created with parliamentary authority and royal approval. Plato, the "oracle of heathen wisdom," was right in regarding law as the creation of God himself. Locke was wrong in holding that "a right of resistance still exists in the governed" and that the majority have the right to rule.

The Maryland clergyman elevates the authority of the church to a position no less prominent than the Old Testament supremacy of the Puritan John Cotton. Individual opinion takes second place to the law, although the Cicero whom he quotes for the purpose implies a more democratic system of justice; Cicero's law exists *ut liberi esse possimus*. Passive obedience and nonresistance are delusions. Boucher admits that years ago he took part in protests against the Stamp Act. But, like that man in the third book of Xenophon's *Cyropaedia*, who "bowed at the altar of Liberty, hoping to leave liberty to his children," he regards it as a mere thing of the past. If it is incompatible to obey both the Lord and the temporal magistrate, obey the Lord; for Christ himself refused to assume temporal power. His argument is sometimes difficult to follow, but his meaning is clear. If government is to be considered as "by nature absolute and irresistible," and if one's parishioners are ordered to "submit to the ordinances of God rather than to the Commandments of men," where do we find ourselves? One asks "which government?" and "which men?" Or even, in view of the many religious denominations, "whose God?" But to Boucher church and state are one; and if America goes to war, it will be not only against established legislative and executive officers, but against Divine authority. The unbending Tory borrows some classical mythology to make his point: "The Greeks described Eleutheria as a daughter of Jupiter; the Romans drew her with a praetor's wand." But there is in these opinions little advance upon the concepts of Winthrop. In fact, the Puritan desired independence from

England, with all his strictness of internal government, while Boucher the monarchist believed in both colonial status and strict local control.

We have allowed Jonathan Boucher to speak for himself; and we may also allow him to say his own farewell, before sailing into exile or returning "home" in 1775, after preaching his last sermon with a pair of pistols lying on his lectern. Like Nehemiah, he would not take refuge in the Temple. In spite of those who, in the words of Pliny, *fictis mentitisque terroribus vera pericula augerent* (increased the real danger by false and misleading panic), he would not surrender.[25] He declared, with the warrior Turnus, *Terga dabo? Et Turnum fugientem haec terra videbit? Usque adeone mori miserum est?* (Retreat? Never! Shall this land behold Turnus a coward? After all, is it so wretched a fate to die?).[26] He would continue to pray for the King, to withstand the Committees of Correspondence, and to uphold in his own corner the authority of the church (which meant the state also). Even at the end, however, Boucher was hoping that some understanding might still be reached, as in the Roman crisis when Appius Claudius and the tribunes were at each others' throats and Manius Valerius in his capacity as dictator delivered his speech of reconciliation.[27]

After settling in his peaceful village and vicarage of Epsom, in contrast to his hectic career in the colonies, Boucher, always a collector, became a noted bibliophile. Following his death in 1804, a sale of his library was held at Leigh and Sotheby's in London. Augustine Birrell, husband of his great-granddaughter, described the auction in his *Character-Sketch of Frederic Locker-Lampson* (a grandson of Boucher, author of *London Lyrics*, and editor of *Lyra Elegantiarum*): "A collection of books so large that when it was sold in 1806 the auction continued for thirty-six days and disposed of 8562 lots." [28] Along with theological and historical works, there were many sets of Greek and Latin classics. In the catalogue there were three pages of Cicero, two of Horace, two of Vergil, and several copies each of even the most obscure ancient authors. The catalogue of the second sale in 1809 recorded the names of the purchasers. Among them were Sir Frederick Eden, son of Boucher's friend (the governor of Maryland), the Duke of Norfolk, Jeremy Bentham, Richard Heber, Sir Samuel Romilly, and some others whose identities are unsure. "Malone" was perhaps the Shakespearean scholar, and "Dibdin" possibly T. F. Dibdin, the bibliographer. This library was larger than any provincial American collection — even that of Jefferson.

Boucher's death notice in the *Gentleman's Magazine* for June 1804 was written by Sir Frederick Eden. So also was a humorous macaronic poem ("The Vision"), in which the old parson was twitted genially on the study of etymologies and dialect forms — "glosses of ancient and provincial words." The faded leaves of the auctioneer's catalogue throw light on the picturesque industry of Boucher's last nineteen years and the impressive literary and historical attainments of one who, without university training, took all antiquarianism to be his province. During that final period he did not need to preach with a pair of pistols on his lectern.

X

THE CLASSICAL ANCESTRY
OF THE CONSTITUTION

The outstanding feature of the American colonial period, in which practice always went hand in hand with theory, was its vigorous political activity. In no field were Greek and Roman sources more often invoked; and at no time were they more frequently cited than during the preliminary discussions and debates on the Constitution, at the ratifying conventions, in the Federalist Papers, and in such publications as John Dickinson's "Fabius" letters. The framers of the document did not merely echo or imitate the ancient materials: they applied them to the task at hand and transmuted them into workable form. By the middle of the eighteenth century, public affairs were largely the province of lawyers, and there were wide-open opportunities for debate. Themes from antiquity supplied arguments for all sides. It is solely with this great experiment and its relation to the classics that we are here concerned. There will be no attempt to settle certain problems of colonial history or to compare Greco-Roman ideas and influences with those of the modern political scientists whom the colonial theorists also knew so well.

Perhaps a remark of Alfred North Whitehead's may shed some light: "I know of only two occasions when the people in power did what needed to be done about as well as you can imagine its being possible. One was the framing of your Constitution. They were able statesmen; they had access to a body of good ideas; they incorporated these principles into the instrument without trying to particularize too explicitly how they should be put into effect; and they were men of immense practical experience themselves.[1] The other was in Rome, when Augustus called in the 'new men' of new ideas." [2]

These delegates of 1787 were praised by Pitt, by Otto the French attaché, by Chastellux, and by Lord Camden. Jefferson, perhaps with tongue in cheek, called them "demigods." [3] Many had set themselves tasks of extensive reading and study in the classical literature of political science. From Paris Jefferson shipped copies of Polybius and sets of ancient authors to Madison, a former graduate student of John Witherspoon's at Princeton, and to George Wythe, a finished Greek and Latin scholar who "could hardly refrain from giving a line from Horace the force of an act of Assembly." Popularized digests were accessible, such as the younger Gronovius' *Thesaurus Antiquitatum Graecarum*, or the *Opus Chronologicum* and *Vetus Graecia Illustrata* of the Dutch historian Ubbo Emmius. Vattel, Montesquieu, and the standard works were at hand in collections loaned for the use of delegates. Franklin was self-taught in Latin; and noncollegians made up for lost time by systematic reading. Most of the Convention delegates were at home in Latin and in some cases Greek.[4] It is impossible to take seriously the remarks of certain scholars that the colonial leaders were ignorant of the ancient sources in the original languages, that Madison and Wilson had to fall back on translations, or that Adams and Jefferson relied on secondhand material.[5] The speeches of James Otis would alone be proof of such familiarity.

The delegates to the Constitutional Convention assembled at a time when the influence of the classics was at its height. They were not interested in mere window dressing or in popular slogans filched from history books. They dealt with fundamental ideas and considered them in the light of their applicability. Familiar quotations circulated. Plenty of hidden references struck home, as in James Wilson's phrase describing Shays's Rebellion and its perils: "We walked on ashes concealing fire beneath our feet," which every reader of Horace remembered. So much of this atmosphere was habitual that Abbot of North Carolina, at the state ratifying meeting, asked his colleagues, with grim humor, "By whom are we to swear, since no religious tests are required, whether by Jupiter, Juno, Minerva, Proserpina, or Pluto?" [6] The heroics had to run their course. But we may cite the more earnest statement of Jonathan Mayhew in a sermon on the repeal of the Stamp Act, for it made a deep impression on the colonists: "Having been initiated in youth into the doctrines of civil liberty as they were taught by such men as Plato, Demosthenes, and Cicero among the ancients, and such as Sidney, Milton, Locke, and Hoadley among the moderns, — I liked them: they seemed rational." [7] In the reading lists of Jefferson, Adams, Madison, and others we note almost every legal and political scientist from Bracton to Blackstone and every Greek or Latin author of any importance.

The debates before, during, and after the Convention of 1787 can be better understood if the doctrines of three ancient authorities — Aristotle, Cicero, and Polybius — are first clarified in relation to the establishment of the federal government. Their testimony underlies all the suggested patterns for the new republic.

No eighteenth-century statesman could escape the fine Hellenic hand of Aristotle, the student of politics rather than the metaphysician who puzzled undergraduates in the early colleges. His *Politics* is as relevant today as it was when he defined and discussed over one hundred constitutions. His formula was not the first, but it is the best and clearest:

Our customary designation for a monarchy that aims at the common advantage is "kingship"; for the government of more than one, yet only a few, "aristocracy" (either because the best men rule or because they rule with a view to what is best for the state); while when the multitude govern the state with a view to the common advantage, it is called by the name common to all the forms of constitution, "constitutional government" [*politeia*, a republic]. Deviations [*parecbaseis*, perversions] from the constitution mentioned are tyranny from kingship, oligarchy from aristocracy, and democracy from constitutional government. For tyranny is monarchy ruling in the interests of the monarch, oligarchy government in the interest of the rich, democracy government in the interest of the poor; and no single one of these forms governs with regard to the profit of the community." [8]

This is the outline according to which all types of political theory may be examined and identified. It appears almost uniformly in many later writings — in Francis Quarles, the "bestseller" of the seventeenth century; in James Logan's political philosophy; in the "text" which Wilson elaborated for the Convention delegates; and in a statement by Charles Pinckney of South Carolina, who, unlike Wilson, acknowledged his debt to William Paley, "a deacon of Carlisle." The most casual reading, for example, of James Wilson's speeches and the *Esprit des lois* of Montesquieu will reveal the indebtedness of these experts to Dante's "Maestro di color che sanno." It is easy to generalize, but John Corbin reached the root of the matter when he wrote: "The theory of our Constitution derives from Aristotle, and was put into successful practice in ancient Rome, in eighteenth-century England, and in our early state constitutions, before it was given its most perfect embodiment by the Convention of 1787." [9]

We shall see that much of Aristotle's sense of balance appealed to the delegates. The tyrant and the mob were equally dangerous. "The judgment of the many is usually better than the judgment of the one." "The middle group is the best." "The State is a partnership." "Democracies are safer than oligarchies." Both Madison and John Adams emphasized the recommendation of the Greek savant that "the more perfect the mixture of the political elements, the more lasting will be the state." [10]

Cicero's ideas on this subject run like a stream underground through colonial writings. He defines the best state in similar terms: "I consider the most effective constitution to be that which is a reasonably blended combination of the three forms, — kingship, aristocracy, and democracy." [11] His "perversions" are the transformations of *reges* into *tyranni, optimates* into *factio, libertas* into *licentia.* The mob, when it gets out of hand, is *immanius belua,* "more dangerous than a wild beast," as the poet Horace and numerous colonial leaders believed, including the Puritan Winthrop and the conservative Alexander Hamilton. Cicero's *Potestas in populo, auctoritas in senatu* was a sound doctrine, not always observed in the history of his country. Perhaps the most frequent of ancient traditions, from the seventeenth-century Jonathan Mitchell to the Declaration of Independence, was Cicero's version of the "Law coeval with mankind." [12]

Polybius was of special interest to the framers of the Constitution. They studied him intently as the leading authority on the Greek city-states.[13] He is the ancient counterpart of historians like Spengler and Toynbee who analyze the cycles of progress and decay of nations. He has high praise for the Roman system at its best: "the nearest to perfection at the time of the Hannibalic War," when there was a complete balance of consuls, senate, and populace. "The mixture," he declared, "was so effective that it was impossible even for a native to pronounce whether the procedure was aristocratic (senate), democratic (people), or monarchical (consuls)." It is clear that not only was there a system of checks and balances but a separation of powers. Colonials credited Bolingbroke with the doctrine of checks and balances, and Montesquieu with the separation of powers. But Polybius, praising the program of Lycurgus and still more that of Rome in the heyday of the republic, when consuls, senate, and people worked well together, leaves no doubt of his meaning: "When one part, having grown out of proportion to the others, aims at supremacy and tends to become too dominant . . . none of the three is absolute . . . The purpose of the one can be counter-worked and thwarted by the others; none of them will excessively outgrow the others or treat them with contempt . . . any aggressive impulse is sure to be checked." This makes, he believed, for "an equilibrium like a well-trimmed boat." Here are both balance and separation, in a historical setting with which the majority of the delegates were familiar.

Polybius puts his finger accurately on the weaknesses of great nations. Sparta appealed to him; but the wisdom of Lycurgus was ruined by "Spartan aggression towards the rest of the Greeks" and by Sparta's extreme militarism. Thebes failed because she depended on two great men, Epaminondas and Pelopidas, rather than on the law. Athens was handicapped because the populace "resembled a ship without a commander." Crete suffered through an oligarchy seeking little besides wealth. Carthage ultimately allowed the "multitude to have the main voice in deliberations," and her military resources were mainly mercenary. The Roman regime, best of all at the high point of the republic, would ultimately follow the inevitable cycle of greatness and decline.[14] No encomium is more eloquent than that found years later by the traveler Pausanias: "A tablet in a temple of Artemis was inscribed with these words, 'Greece would never have fallen at all if she had obeyed Polybius; and when she met disaster, her only help came from *him*.' "[15]

These three authorities — Aristotle, Cicero, Polybius — are given special emphasis here because of their underlying and essential relationship to the American Constitution. There were many others, some of them even more frequently appealed to, who were discussed during the 1787 debates. One finds Plutarch, Demosthenes, Thucydides, Sallust, Xenophon, Tacitus, Livy, Dio Cassius, and the *Roman Antiquities* of Dionysius of Halicarnassus referred to in various connections. There were scattered single-speech sources, to be found in the libraries of squires, lawyers, merchants, and officials; farmers and working men borrowed classical material at second hand. One question naturally arises: "Why was Plato almost entirely absent from these debates on the Constitution?" The answer is that he was consulted by the colonists as a spiritual adviser rather than as a political scientist.[16] Divines like Samuel Johnson of Connecticut, Jonathan Edwards, the Mathers, Mayhew, and Witherspoon rate him as the first among non-Christian writers. Although worshiped by Cicero as a philosopher, and much used by Milton and the "classical republicans" in England, he rarely appeared in colonial America as an authority on governmental matters. Jefferson and Adams agreed that he was too visionary for practical purposes. "Plato," said Elbridge Gerry solemnly, "was not a Republican." Polybius, as usual, sums up the situation: "It is not fair to introduce Plato's *Republic*, which is belauded by some philosophers. For just as we do not admit to athletic contests artists or athletes who have not been in training, so we have no right to admit this constitution for the prize of merit, unless it first give an exhibition of its actual working." Governor Hutchinson of Massachusetts, one of the best colonial historians, held that Plato's was an ideal creation, but that his characters were not found in real life.

Throughout the colonial period, preference was expressed for the Greek concept of a colony, with its freedom from the domination of the mother city, in contrast to the tightly centralized Roman system. As provincial interrelationships increased, the history of the Greek city-states became a debate topic for the type of government desired by the founders of the new republic. Arguments pro or con culminated in the question of whether the Articles of Confederation were sufficient for national purposes or whether a completely new document should take their place. This was the most frequently invoked topic before, during, and after the Convention of 1787.

The time-hallowed Amphictyonic tribal centers of religious worship, which supervised the sacrifices, the periodic games, the guardianship of the temple treasure, sacred wars and sacred truces, and financial requisitions — these go back into the dawn of history. Their headquarters were at Thermopylae, Delphi, and other shrines, with local delegates attending a general council. Other such associations, less religious, were the Achaean, Lycian, Aetolian, and similar leagues, federated on a more political basis and in many cases representative.[17]

During the decade before the American Revolution, these ancient models had been hunted out and, for the most part, praised as samples of republican polity. Benjamin Church (later a turncoat), Joseph Warren, General Stephen, the Reverend Phillips Payson, Joseph Hawley, and George Mason were all attracted by the Amphictyonic idea. Mason, later an opponent of the Constitution, spoke with approval of "the little cluster of Grecian republics which resisted and almost constantly defeated the Persian monarchy."

John Dickinson characteristically weighed both sides of the argument. Many years before, when he was urging colonial unity against arbitrary taxation and the nonrecognition of provincial assemblies, he remarked: "Why were the states of Greece broken down into the tamest submission by Philip of Macedon and afterwards by the Romans? Because they contended for freedom *separately*." This was a fundamental criticism, which appears often later, notably in the eighteenth Federalist Paper. The Achaean League particularly appealed to Dickinson: "The wit of man never invented such an antidote against monarchical and aristocratical projects." But the "Pennsylvania Farmer," who refused to sign the Declaration, urged the ratification of the Constitution: "We should not suppose that we, in the Argo lately constructed by us, have already reached the *Ultima Thule*."

Alexander Hamilton, with downright definiteness, had made up his mind early on this controversial subject.[18] As "Publius," in an essay of 1778, he declared that "the leagues among the old Grecian republics were continually at war with each other, and *for want of union* fell a prey to their neighbors." In his "Continentalist" paper of 1781 he struck the same note: "The commonwealths of Greece were a constant scene of the alternate tyranny of one part of the people over the other, or of a few usurping demagogues over the whole." In the memoranda he prepared for use at the Convention, we find the same recurring theme. A mixed government should be planned; for, like Winthrop and others, he disapproved of a "state within a state" and regarded the Articles of Confederation as no less unstable than these Greek leagues. The Amphictyons "had ample powers for general purposes, to use force against delinquent members; but their decrees were mere signals of war." The ancient democracies resulted in tyrannies, and democracy was a delusion.

By May 1787 this topic became a favorite debate subject for the delegates. Madison "pointed out all the beauties and defects of the ancient republics." [19] He drew up a commentary on the Lycian confederacy, interpreting it with minute care to the members, citing Polybius and Strabo as firsthand sources and Montesquieu as the modern advocate. In this republic there were twenty-three towns. The largest had three votes in the common council, those of average size two, and the smallest one. Their assessments were proportioned to the number of votes. There was a "Lysiarch" as presiding officer, and special courts were designated. Their council, somewhat resembling the Amphictyons, dealt with wars, peace, treaties, finances, and administration, leaving local matters to the separate towns. La Boulaye, in his introduction to Montesquieu's *Esprit des lois*, states that an abstract of this plan was found among the papers of George Washington. James Wilson, a classical scholar who began his American career as a Latin instructor at the College of Philadelphia, "traced the causes and effects of every revolution from the earliest stages of the Greek commonwealths down to the present time." [20]

In the end, however, Wilson acknowledged that "all these confederacies were formed in the infancy of political science." Madison, after his exhaustive researches, admitted that the Amphictyonic League resembled the Articles of Confederation "only in its nominal power." [21] "Foreign aid resulted in the demolition of their confederacy." Madison warned his friend Jefferson in a letter of March 1786 of the danger "of having the same game played on our Confederacy by which Philip of Macedon managed that of the Grecians, by gaining over a few of the leading men in the smaller members."

One of the most vocal opponents of a "consolidated" government, and consequently a defender of the Articles of Confederation, was Luther Martin of Maryland. In a lengthy address to the Convention, he fell back on the theory previously advanced by Samuel Adams, that the separation of the thirteen colonies from Britain placed them in a "state of nature," where each could frame its own code with a minimum of central control. As a delegate from a smaller state, he deemed it essential that all should have the same number of senators: "In the Amphictyonic confederation of the Grecian cities each, however different in wealth and strength, sent the same number of deputies, with an equal voice in everything that related to the common concerns of Greece." [22] Any change would be a mere transfer, in Aesop fashion, from King Log to King Stork. It was not any internal fault in the system that ruined this respectable council, but rather the ambition and the power of the three largest states: Athens, Sparta, and Thebes (and ultimately Macedon), with modern parallels in Massachusetts, Pennsylvania, and Virginia. Madison also had his doubts on this point, citing Plutarch's *Themistocles*: "The Lacedaemonians insisted on excluding certain smaller nations, in order that they might tyrannize over them." [23]

James Monroe of Virginia maintained that the Amphictyons and the city-state leagues were good models, but collapsed for the same reason that Martin had mentioned. Monroe quoted Polybius[24] and declared that "one could not find a political system and principle so favorable to equality and freedom of speech as that of the Achaean League. For by reserving no special privilege for original members, and by putting all new adherents on the same footing, it soon attained the aim it had set for itself, being aided by two very powerful coadjutors, equality and humanity." Madison also had praise for this league in a letter of 1787 to Jefferson. But

Martin and Monroe, with others who regarded the Articles of Confederation as adequate for a national government, merely served to make ratification a closer contest. Hamilton, who was defeated in his wish for life tenure in the case of the executive and the senate, and who also failed in his effort to reduce the states to "subordinate jurisdictions," had the last word on the Greek city-states. Some rough notes of his read: "Experience corresponds . . . Grecian republics . . . Demosthenes says Athens 73 years, Lacedaemon 27, Thebes, after Leuctra . . . Philip." [25] He stuck to his belief that the British system was the soundest, and he jotted down "Aristotle, Cicero, Montesquieu, Neckar." William R. Davie of North Carolina gave these republics a respectable burial, with the words: "Such was the fate of the Achaean League, the Amphictyonic Council, and the ancient confederacies." [26] Light-Horse Harry Lee felt likewise, and Hamilton had previously summed up the whole problem: "We are laboring hard to establish in this country principles more national and free from all foreign ingredients, so that we may be neither Greeks nor Trojans, but truly American." Impatient at the lapse of time before the Articles of Confederation were signed, he had argued that it was "as ridiculous to seek for models in the small ages of Greece as it would be to go in quest of them among the Hottentots and Laplanders." [27] Delegate Barrell of Massachusetts grew satirical over the current worship of Cicero and Demosthenes. One finds little comedy in these deliberations, but Randall of the Bay State must have lightened the proceedings when he remarked that "the quoting of ancient history was no more to the point than to tell how our forefathers dug clams at Plymouth."

These classical experiments in government did not convince the delegates of 1787, but they did serve to promote intelligent discussion. Franklin's advice ultimately prevailed — that it was irrelevant to follow the example of "those ancient republics which contained the seeds of their own dissolution." There must have been a haunting charm to them, for Calhoun used them as illustrations for his states'-

rights theory, and, much later, Senator John Sharp Williams of Mississippi suggested at the start of the First World War "a court or association of nations and an Amphictyonic Council of the civilized world." [28]

Next in amount to the citations of the Greek leagues was the almost universal feeling that the power of any individual should be strictly limited; and history was ransacked for warnings and examples of such abuse.[29] It was conceded that certain great pioneers in statecraft should be regarded with respect and honor. Madison in the thirty-eighth Federalist Paper made his bow to Minos of Crete, Zaleucus the Locrian, Lycurgus of Sparta, and Romulus at Rome. He said that credit should be given to Aratus, the stabilizer of the Achaean League, and that Solon's reforms lasted down into the Athens of Demosthenes. But these wise men were displaced by tyrants or democrats whose activities were based on aggrandizement. The value of the new constitution, with its collective security, lay in its prevention of such individual domination. In the fourteenth Federalist Paper Madison pointed out the error of confusing a representative republic with "the turbulent democracies of Greece." The "Superior Man" whom Aristotle often mentions as a leader should be defined in terms of character, integrity, and ability. James Wilson's correlation of ancient and modern ideas on this subject was most acceptable to the delegates.[30] He commented critically on cases in history where mere prominence or force enabled the ruler to do what he pleased. The *vae victis* of the Gallic Brennus and the sarcastic proverb of Thucydides ("You may rule over anyone whom you can dominate") were to him illustrations of violation of the Law of Nature and Cicero's *consensus iuris*.

Hamilton devoted his first Federalist Paper to cautioning his readers against "men who have over-turned the liberties of republics, commencing as demagogues and ending as tyrants." In the sixth. he disapproved the action of the supposedly democratic Pericles, who attacked Samos and Megara, ultimately bringing on the Peloponnesian War. To the leeway which the Articles of Confederation granted to the separate states he compared the danger that Persia risked when the satraps of various provinces assumed too much power.[31] Roman army leaders made it clear that the civil authority should be supreme. Hamilton, whose ambitions had been distinctly military, went on record emphatically: "Neither the manners nor the genius of Rome are suited to the republic or to the age we live in. All her maxims and habits were military: her government was constituted for war. We should not attempt a display of unprofitable heroism."[32] Wilson, in the earlier days of the Convention, held that a too centralized control, with the states subservient, would produce "a General Government as despotic as even that of the Roman emperors."[33] George Mason of Virginia, whose views were more democratic than those of most planter-squires, was apprehensive about the domination of an army commander. Such a person could "surround the senate with 30,000 troops. It brings to my mind the remarkable trial of Milo at Rome."[34] This was a reference to the riots in the Forum between the hired gangs of Clodius and Milo, when Cicero, losing his nerve and failing to speak his oration on Milo's behalf, was the cause of Milo's going into exile. Thacher of Massachusetts was equally sensational: "Are we not in danger? Will not some Sylla drench the land in blood, or some Cromwell or Caesar lay our liberties prostrate at his feet?" The Thirty Tyrants, the Gracchi, Catiline, Caesar, and the names of other troublemakers were on the lips of many delegates.

At the Convention there was an almost automatic reaction to the suggestion of a triple-executive regime. Wilson argued that this would be as perilous as a Roman triumvirate, with three officials contending until one alone became master: "first Caesar and then Augustus are witnesses of this truth. So are the kings of Sparta and the consuls of Rome. So also were the Thirty Tyrants and the Decemvirs."[35] Standing armies were called "nurseries of vice and the bane of liberty."

Two preventives against despotic behavior appeared in

three of the first state constitutions; but they were omitted in the national document. The Pennsylvania constitution of 1776 arranged for a group of "censors," to oversee the legality of all proceedings and the conduct of officials. This Roman position was abandoned as unsatisfactory in 1790. The states of Virginia and Delaware, as Madison noted in his thirty-ninth Federalist Paper, provided for the impeachment of the chief magistrate if malfeasance were proved within eighteen months after retirement, though both agreed that the subject was "not impeachable until out of office." This would seem to be a Roman loan, like the censorship, and a clear imitation of the law *De Repetundis*, aimed at extortion and misgovernment in the provinces, or the *Euthyna* — an accounting which Athenian officials had to render when their terms expired. Another suggestion, in the Greek tradition, was that of James Wilson, who would have the presidential electors chosen by lot. This idea soon died a natural death.[36]

Much of the discussion about a possible "Man on Horseback" was mere apprehensiveness. But on three occasions[37] there was talk of a dictatorship, touched off by the hard times of the Revolution and mentioned in the eighth, twenty-fifth, and seventieth Federalist Papers. "Offering the crown to Caesar" was at once rejected by Washington, and the Cincinnati were criticized as near the borderline of monarchy. In 1776, with Patrick Henry possibly the person in mind, the speaker of the Virginia Assembly, Colonel Archibald Cary, had threatened "tyrannicide" to anyone so chosen. In 1781 the motion to create a dictator failed, and the members were satisfied to appoint a military leader for defensive purposes. The motion was lost by only six votes; and Henry, if Jefferson's account can be believed, had seconded it. "Sic semper tyrannis," in accordance with the state seal of Virginia. At the state convention of 1788 Henry dwelt on the Roman heroes who saved the state in certain crises, but the unanimous choice of Washington cleared the atmosphere. The delegates solved the military problem with a state-chosen militia under congressional control. Hamilton tossed another idea into the proceedings by citing the Spartan law which forbade the post of admiral to be conferred twice on the same person, and he noted Lysander's trick of continuing as vice-admiral with full admiral's powers.[38]

Foreign influence and its dangers prompted John Jay, in the fourth Federalist Paper, to mention the weakness of the Articles of Confederation: like the Greek states, which could not or would not combine to resist attack, America would be helpless in the face of such an offensive. The small cities in the neighborhood of Rome and Athens illustrated this principle. Pinckney quoted evidence to suggest a time limit before newcomers were eligible for the franchise, bringing up the Athenian law "which made it death for any stranger to intrude his voice into their legislative assembly." [39] "Foreign influence," declared Hamilton, "is truly the Grecian Horse to a republic" — a phrase worn threadbare by the end of the colonial period.[40] A remark of Gunning Bedford, a Delaware delegate, caused heated disapproval by Rufus King of Massachusetts. Bedford accused the three large states of self-interest, with a possibility of "the sword and the horrors of war." [41] The small states would need to confederate: "Sooner than be ruined, there are foreign powers who will take us by the hand." France's assistance of the previous decade was evidently another matter.

Whether or not the name "senate" was a consciously classical touch, as were undoubtedly the censors in the Pennsylvania state constitution, there seems to have been little hesitation in establishing the second chamber. When the great compromise, of two senators and proportional representation in the House, was achieved, and when a few delegates, including Franklin, abandoned their pleas for a single legislative body, the debates centered on its functional importance in the threefold grouping of offices. Ruler, Lords, and Commons had had their counterpart in colonial governor, council, and assembly. The upper houses of Rome, Carthage, Athens, and Sparta were regarded with approval; and Randolph's

Virginia Plan, modified to suit the new conditions, fitted into the combination.

John Dickinson, in his fifth "Fabius" letter, had stressed the importance of a strong senate: he ascribed the subversion of liberty in Carthage and Rome to popular encroachment on its authority.[42] Wilson, who had received his legal training in Dickinson's office, spoke several times to the same effect. Hamilton cited Sparta, Rome, and Carthage as satisfactory samples of aristocratic representation. Madison in the sixty-third Federalist Paper devoted himself to the importance of the second chamber: "There was no long-lived republic that did not have a senate: Sparta, Rome, and Carthage thus protected themselves against 'popular fluctuations.' " In another paper (number fifty-five) he criticized what he regarded as unwise democracy in Athens — "Had every Athenian citizen been a Socrates, every Athenian assembly would still have been a mob." The Spartan ephors and the Roman tribunes caused much discussion both pro and con: one group held that they weakened the government and encouraged "faction" (an ill-omened word in those days); others hailed them as protectors of freedom. The majority felt that the tribunes and ephors, as well as special officials such as triumvirs and decemvirs, contributed to the enfeebling of the senate and should be no part of the American system.[43] Madison suggested a small but authoritative upper chamber, on the order of the Athenian Areopagus. Dickinson, however, believed that a reasonably large number brought better results and reached more of the citizens. Wilson concluded that two legislative branches would avoid such errors as those made by the city-states and leagues.[44]

Much of the debate centered round this point of whether an upper house, in close alliance with a strong executive, would not weaken the principle of democratic freedom. Richard Henry Lee expressed the opinion that extreme federalism would "render the state governments as feeble and contemptible as was the senatorial authority under the Roman emperors: the *name* existed, but the *thing* was gone." [45] Elbridge Gerry, who refused to sign the final document, declared that "the Constitutionalists were sailing down the Pactolean [rich man's] channel." [46] Noah Webster answered the radicals, who feared collusion, with a statement that "the American senate was more of a people's affair than the House of Lords or the Roman Senate." But many speakers contrasted this supposed weakness with the heyday of Roman senatorial authority in the middle of the second century B.C., with Polybius as the source of their information.[47]

One of the last hurdles that had to be cleared before the signing of the document was an objection emphasized by Patrick Henry. Hamilton had stated, in the thirty-fourth Federalist Paper, that Rome was at its zenith when the *comitia centuriata* and the *comitia tributa* were working in balanced harmony. But Henry saw in this a dangerous parallel — a rich Senate and a subordinate popular House.[48] In Rome, the former body voted according to a property classification, weighted in favor of well-to-do citizens, while the larger assembly was more indefinite in its powers, dependent on the initiative of a magistrate, subject to senatorial veto. Charles Pinckney pointed out that America did not classify citizens according to wealth, as Solon did: hence the comparison was vain.[49] Henry seemed to be making the most of the contrast between rich and poor, illustrated by the activities of ephors and tribunes. The final opinion was that such special officials were not necessary, that the conflict of patricians and plebeians should be avoided. Even the conservative Gouverneur Morris regarded the ephors as a hindrance; they simply "encroached on the popular branch of the government."

This chapter has been purposely limited to the classical ideas which the framers of the Constitution and their critics applied to the making of a new nation, in the discussions of 1787 and 1788. Not only the story of the Greek city-states, but an extensive amount of Hellenic and Roman material, served the delegates for their illustrations. These ancient ideas were debated from a contemporary point of view, in the language of the colonists themselves, and they were live issues rather than mere theory. However important the training of these men was in local and provincial *Realpolitik*, there is no doubt that the Greco-Roman tradition was a basic source of the Constitution.

XI

EPILOGUE: ADAMS AND JEFFERSON

THE essays in this book, in which the colonial mind has expressed itself through various personalities and episodes, can be summarized by the testimony of the two statesmen whose old-age correspondence offers a retrospective and panoramic view of the years when a colony was being converted into a nation. John Adams and Thomas Jefferson, though absent from the Constitutional Convention on diplomatic service, have added yet another classic to American history and literature. Their exchange of letters, after their reconciliation through Benjamin Rush in 1811, reviews most of the issues and events of the time, "in calm of mind, all passion spent." These two writers fit the Emersonian definition of "Man Thinking." The most profound student of political science exchanges ideas with the most versatile contributor to the theory and practice of democracy and human relations. Intellectual without being pedantic, they touch on all phases of colonial culture; and they are artists in their application of the classical tradition.

Adams the Stoic and Jefferson the Epicurean, each preserving loyalty to a nonliturgical Christianity, reviewed the events of the colonial period. Jefferson, in his last letter to Adams (March 1826), spoke of the "Argonauts of a Heroic Age." They weighed its virtues and its foibles, speaking out with the frankness of two former presidents whose opinions were built on historical knowledge and practical experience. Adams' inclinations were for aristocracy and moral philosophy. The two Greek ladies, Aristocratia and Democratia, would never, he believed, be reconciled. Justice for everyone is the only answer. There must be protection against mob movements: "Checks and Balances, Jefferson, however you and your party may have reconciled them, are our only security." Turgot and Franklin, in the opinion of Adams, were risking mob rule in desiring a single legislative chamber. Jefferson, on the other hand, leaned toward democracy and science. His plans for public education, religious freedom, and agricultural improvements were only a few of his projects.

Their voluminous reading in history, especially Tacitus, who was the prime favorite of both men, undoubtedly led them to a fundamental problem stated in the *Annals* of the Roman: "A mixed government, composed of three simple forms, is a thing rather to be wished than expected." [1] Adams had upheld from youth to old age the Aristotelian canon of executive, council, and popular assembly, in his draft of the Massachusetts state constitution, his *Thoughts on Government*, and his voluminous *Defence of the Constitutions of Government of the United States*. But the Virginian answered in the affirmative to Adams' question: "Can a popular government preserve itself? If it can, there is reason to hope for all the equality, all the liberty and every other good fruit of an Athenian democracy, without any of its ingratitude, levity, convulsions, or factions." In the end, they settled for the *Politeia* of Aristotle, Jefferson having some doubts about the judiciary and some fear of a too powerful senate.

They were agreed on the harm done to the science of government since the days of Aristotle and Cicero by "ecclesiastical and imperial despotism." They equally abhorred tyrants like Sulla and Caesar, Cleon and the Gracchi. They concluded that the Romans, however great, never possessed real liberty: there was pride, strength, and courage in their leaders but no fundamental harmony because of the gap between rich and poor. They were both skeptical of Augustus' one-man rule. They regarded Solon's reforms as unsatisfactory because of their emphasis on property and gradation according to wealth. The Articles of Confederation were inadequate: "If the thirteen states were put into a league like the Achaean or the Aetolian, each an independent entity, the result would be chaos." But both of them would have sympathized with the opinion of a later scholar, E. L. Godkin, who cited with approval "the composition of the Roman Senate, which consisted of notables who had in some manner rendered the state marked service." [2]

These two elder statesmen reveal a mastery of the classics and a practical application of ancient ideas to modern situations. They were at home in Latin, and Jefferson's Greek was actively kept up. "Classics," said Adams, "in spight of our friend Rush, I must think indispensable." Jefferson had thanked his father for insisting upon such training: "I would not exchange this attainment for anything which I could then have acquired and have since acquired." He put this theory into practice with his daughter's efforts to "conquer her Livy," as did also Aaron Burr with his highly cultivated Theodosia. For admission to the University of Virginia, he prescribed a stiff amount of the same diet.

Throughout this correspondence we note the casual use of classical phrases aphoristically quoted (not always accurately) from memory. *Nil Americanum alienum*, wrote Adams, with the Terentian proverb in mind. Jefferson, who had "given up newspapers for Tacitus and Thucydides, Newton and Euclid," bade his friend beware "Pickerings, Wolcotts, *et id genus omne*" (evoking Horace). Both cite Hesiod, using the Greek text on man's duty to honor the gods. They exchange humorous comments on the Bacchanalian antics of Merry-Mount Morton, ending with the Vergilian *paulo maiora canamus*, from the fourth *Eclogue*. Out-of-the-way writers like Silius Italicus and the astronomer Manilius are familiar to them. Sallust and Seneca on civic harmony, the golden rule of Pythagoras, the elder Pliny on pirates — all these are suggested by some modern instance. Both regret the loss of the Sibylline Books and the gaps in the histories of Livy and Tacitus. An especially lamentable lacuna is

Cicero's *De republica* (existing before 1820 only in small fragments), "a loss as much to be regretted as that of any Production of Antiquity."

They corresponded on linguistic neologisms, which Jefferson approved and illustrated by the various forms built up from one root word — such as those from *adelphos* and *fraternal*. Pitch and quantity in Greek verse, the Italian method of scanning hexameters, and all the techniques of ancient poetry and prose drew their attention. When Adams asked whether the word *gloriola* was used in classical Latin, Jefferson went to his numerous lexicons and found it as "a little bit of glory" in a letter of Cicero. When Adams confessed to having read the fifteen-volumed *Correspondence* of Baron Grimm, he warned the Virginian: "*Digito compesce labellum,* — Don't give me away!"[3] There is much occasional badinage, when "The Duke of Braintree" speaks of his "Senectutal Loquacity," or "The Man of the Mountain" (Monticello) confesses his "Senile Garrulity."

They seem at home in all fields of history. Adams deflates "the great work of a Scotchman on the Court of Augustus, in which he undertook to prove that 'had Brutus and Cassius been conquerors, they would have restored virtue and liberty to Rome.' But I don't believe it!" And yet both men admired the humanity of Cicero who, with Brutus and Seneca, left indelible marks of conscience and religion. In any case, remarked Jefferson, what good could even Cicero, Cato, or Brutus have done with a broken-down Roman republic? The will of the people was lacking. On the question of states or nation legislating on slavery, he asked: "Are we to see Athenian and Lacedaemonian confederacies? Wage another Peloponnesian War? Or merely a servile war?" These were questions that had been in circulation among the leaders in many of the colonies.

Jefferson, confused by "the forest of opinions, discussions and contentions which have occurred in our day," writes out for Adams, in Greek, the passage from Theocritus, where the woodcutter on Mount Ida, gazing at the thousands of trees, wonders where to begin.[4] Adams reacts with: "Lord, Lord, what can I do with so much Greek? . . . I am in the same situation as the wood-cutter on Ida . . . Some years ago I felt a kind of affection for one of the flames of my youth, and again paid my addresses to Isocrates and Dionisius [sic] Halicarnassensis. I collected all my Lexicons and Grammars and sat down to the latter's volume *Peri Syntheseos Onomaton*" (On the Treatment of Words). He complains because words escape him so easily in his wrestling with what we should call linguistics or semantics.

I have noted in a previous chapter that both these political philosophers were allergic to Plato. Jefferson criticized his "foggy mind," wondering how Cicero could have elevated him to such a degree of worship. Adams seems to have made a special effort to understand him, writing his friend that in 1784 he went through Plato's works, using Latin and French versions and comparing them with the Greek. He complained that the *Republic* and the *Laws* were "a bitter satyre upon all republican government."

A lengthy discussion back and forth took place over the famous Hymn of the Stoic Cleanthes. They wrote out much of it in the Greek. Adams welcomed it as a sample of "the divine simplicity which constitutes the charm of Grecian eloquence in prose and verse." Adams copied and sent parts of the hymn in Latin, French, and Italian versions. He maintained that "the Shadow of God with the intelligence and moral qualities of man is as clearly asserted by Cleanthes as by Moses." Both men read and pondered Priestley's *Socrates and Jesus Compared*. Priestley, they agreed, should have shown more appreciation of ancient pioneers like Zaleucus of Locri, Charondas of Catana, and others who had a deep understanding of the universe. Adams called himself a unitarian, "trusting the Ruler with his skies"; and Jefferson explained his well-known excerpts of the sayings of Jesus from the New Testament, discussing the daemon of Socrates and concluding that the Hymn of Cleanthes is second only to the best of the Psalmist. Jefferson scours his library for renderings in classical languages of Sternhold and Hopkins' Psalms, concluding that Buchanan's and Johnston's translations into Latin were fairly good, but that Duport's Greek version of the eighteenth Psalm is really worthy of quotation. In Jefferson's eightieth year, he communicated to Adams an impressive piece of research, reviewing the New Testament, Origen, and Tertullian on the saying of Christ that "God is a Spirit." Adams complained of the inaccurate accounts of the saints in the writings of Christian authors; he agreed with the French critic, Armand Gaston Camus, who regretted that Diogenes Laertius wrote lives of the philosophers with more industry and exactness than those who produced biographies of saints and martyrs.

First they differ and finally almost agree on the definition of the superior citizens, the best men, the *aristoi*. Adams believes that there is an aristocracy of birth, copying out the text and supplying a Latin translation of the Greek Theognis, who declared that nobility is to be found not only among human beings but also in the breeding of horses or sheep or asses. Who are these *aristoi?* asks Adams. Xenophon is cited as supporting the theory of the "well-born"; and in popular parlance these *aristoi* are too apt to be, not the wise and good, but the rich, beautiful, and powerful. Thus what chance has raw talent?

But Jefferson seems to have the last word. Checking again with Theognis, he concludes that "there is a natural aristocracy among men. The grounds of this are virtue and talents." "Good men," said Theognis, "have never harmed any city." Hence he disagrees with Adams, who had suggested putting the "pseudo-aristoi" into a second chamber or senate, as a buffer against the mob but limited in their powers of legislation.

So runs the spontaneous flow of the *iucunda senectus*. They philosophically await the close of life and comment peacefully on the history they helped to make. Jefferson craves quiet and retirement, according to Horace's *Solve senescentem mature sanus equum* (Be sensible and turn out the old horse to pasture). "You and I, my dear sir, should not, like Priam of old, gird on again the *arma desueta trementibus aevo humeris.*" Weighing the good and the evil in Jupiter's two urns,[5] they agree that life has been worth living. Death does not terrify them. Each believes in some sort of immortality, defining himself, in the words of Martial, as one who *summum nec metuit diem nec optat* (neither fears nor craves the close of life).[6] These two great statesmen made the past their own possession, interpreting it with charm, originality, and relevance. Those who believe that literature and scholarship should go hand in hand will agree that this interchange of letters constitutes an American masterpiece. It also represents the high-water mark of the classical tradition in colonial writings. Bacon's happy description of the uses of learning — "Studies serve for delight, for ornament, and for ability" — was never more convincingly exemplified.

REFERENCE MATTER

INDEX

REFERENCE MATTER

1. The Classical Background of the Colonial Mind

BIBLIOGRAPHY

For British and European backgrounds, see Gilbert Highet, *The Classical Tradition* (Oxford, 1957); J. A. K. Thomson, *The Classical Background of English Literature* (London, 1948); Moses Hadas, *Ancilla to Classical Reading* (New York, 1954).

Gummere, R. M., "The Heritage of the Classics in Colonial North America," *Proceedings of the American Philosophical Society*, 99:68–78 (April 1955).

—— "The Classical Element in New England Almanacs," *Harvard Library Bulletin*, 9:181–196 (1955).

Briggs, Samuel, *The Essays, Humor, and Poems of Nathaniel Ames, Father and Son, of Dedham, Massachusetts, from Their Almanacs, 1726–1775* (Cleveland, 1891).

John Saffin, His Book, ed. Caroline Hazard (New York, 1928).

Kimball, Fiske, *The Domestic Architecture of the American Colonies and of the Early Republic* (New York, 1927).

McIlwain, C. H., *The Growth of Political Thought in the West* (New York, 1932).

Morison, S. E., *The Intellectual Life of Colonial New England* (New York, 1956).

Tolles, F. B., "A Literary Quaker, John Smith of Burlington and Philadelphia," *Pennsylvania Magazine of History and Biography*, 65:300–333 (1941).

Wertenbaker, T. J., *The Golden Age of Colonial Culture* (New York, 1942).

Wright, Louis B., *The Cultural Life of the American Colonies, 1607–1763* (New York, 1957).

—— "The Classical Tradition in Early Virginia," *Papers of the Bibliographical Society of America*, 33:85–97 (1939).

NOTES

1. S. P. Sherman, *The Genius of America* (New York, 1923), p. 200. See also G. Chinard, *Letters of Lafayette and Jefferson* (Baltimore, 1929), p. 84.

2. I.11.27: *Caelum, non animum mutant qui trans mare currunt.*
K. M. Rowland, *The Life of George Mason* (New York, 1892),
I, 384.

3. K. Duncan and D. F. Nickols, *Mentor Graham* (Chicago,
1944), pp. 10, 13, 52. The seminary soon became the classical
Transylvania College.

4. H. R. Shurtleff, *The Log Cabin Myth* (Cambridge, Mass.,
1939), p. 198.

5. Kenneth B. Murdock, *Literature and Theology in Colonial
New England* (Cambridge, Mass., 1949), p. 35; also pp. 44 and 49.

6. R. H. Barry, *Mr. Rutledge of South Carolina* (New York,
1942), p. 97.

7. Perry Miller, *The New England Mind: The Seventeenth
Century* (Cambridge, Mass., 1954), p. 86.

8. Ovid, *Metamorphoses*, I.84–86 (trans. F. J. Miller, Loeb
Classical Library). Also, Cicero, *De legibus*, I.26, and Lactantius,
Divine Institutes, II.1.

9. *Georgics*, II.458.

10. Horace, *Odes*, III.6.45–48.

11. See *Virginia Magazine of History and Biography*, 25:39
(January 1917); also T. J. Wertenbaker, *Virginia under the
Stuarts, 1607–1688* (Princeton, 1914), p. 73. The poppy story is
told in Herodotus, V.92; Aristotle, *Politics*, 1284a; Livy, I.54.

12. Martha W. Hiden, "Latin in Colonial Virginia," *Classical
Weekly*, 22:41–45 (November 1928).

13. G. Chinard, *Thomas Jefferson, the Apostle of Americanism*
(Boston, 1939), p. 175.

14. W. H. Foote, ed., *Sketches of Virginia* (Philadelphia, 1850),
I, 279.

15. Increase Mather, *Early History of New England*, ed.
S. G. Drake (Boston, 1864), contains many such words, now out
of use.

16. That is, "Enriching the Treasury," a term found in Con-
dorcet's *State of France* and discussed by Adams in a marginal
note in his copy of that work.

17. Gouverneur Morris, *A Diary of the French Revolution*
(Boston, 1939), II, 389.

18. For typology, especially as applicable to religious literature,
see Chapter III.

19. *De l'esprit des lois*, Pt. I, Bk. 4, Chap. 6.

20. *Oeuvres complètes* (Paris, 1824), I, 117.

21. *Diary and Letters of Gouverneur Morris*, ed. Anne C.
Morris (New York, 1888), I, 114.

22. Rowland, *Mason*, I, 264–266. For the final motto, see Vergil, *Eclogues*, 1.6.

23. *Letters of Members of the Continental Congress*, ed. E. C. Burnett (Washington, 1923), II, 49–50. See also Xenophon, *Memorabilia*, II.1.21.

24. Horace, *Odes*, I.7.27; W. B. O. Peabody, *James Oglethorpe* (New York, 1905), p. 89, in The Makers of American History series. For the same motto, recommended by Whitefield to Sir William Pepperell for the Louisburg expedition, see J. G. Palfrey, *History of New England* (Boston, 1890), V, 66.

25. Curtis P. Nettels, *George Washington and American Independence, 1732–1775* (Boston, 1951), p. 68; Paul van Dyke, *Washington, the Son of His Country* (New York, 1931), p. 221; *Inventory of the Contents of Mount Vernon*, ed. W. C. Ford (Cambridge, Mass., 1909).

26. R. W. Moore, in *Virginia Magazine of History and Biography*, 41:2 (January 1933).

27. W. O. Stevens, *Washington, the Cinderella City* (New York, 1943), p. 12.

28. For these sources, in order, see: Lucan, *Pharsalia*, II.657, 383; Cicero, *De officiis*, I.77; Manilius, *Astronomica*, III.39; Livy, 28.44; Phaedrus, I.15.9.

29. I. B. Cohen, *Benjamin Franklin* (Indianapolis, 1953), pp. 182–184. The Latin couplet, not identified, was perhaps made up by Franklin or one of his friends. See also *The Papers of Benjamin Franklin*, ed. L. W. Labaree (New Haven, 1961), IV, 147, 150; Cicero, *Pro Ligario*, 38.

II. The Virginia Argonauts

BIBLIOGRAPHY

Gummere, R. M., "The Classics in a Brave New World," *Harvard Studies in Classical Philology*, 62:119–139 (1957).

Brown, Alexander, *The Genesis of the United States* (Boston, 1890).

Cawley, R. R., *Unpathed Waters* (Princeton, 1940).

Davis, R. B., *George Sandys, Poet-Adventurer* (London, 1955).

Jones, Howard M., "The Colonial Impulse," *Proceedings of the American Philosophical Society*, 90:131–161 (May 1946).

———— "The Literature of Virginia in the Seventeenth Century," in *Memoirs of the American Academy of Arts and Sciences*, vol. 19, no. 2 (Boston, 1946).

Porter, Harry C., "Alexander Whitaker, Cambridge Apostle to

Virginia," *William and Mary Quarterly*, Series 3, 14:317–343 (July 1957).

Smith, Bradford, *Captain John Smith: His Life and Legend* (Philadelphia, 1953).

Stith, William, *History of the First Discovery and Settlement of Virginia* [1747]: no. 6 of Joseph Sabin's *Reprints* (New York, 1865).

Strachey, William, *Historie of Travell into Virginia Britannia*, ed. Louis B. Wright and Virginia Freund (London, 1953).

The Travels and Works of Captain John Smith, ed. E. Arber and A. G. Bradley (Edinburgh, 1910).

Tyler, L. G., *Narratives of Early Virginia, 1606–1625* (New York, 1907).

NOTES

1. Alexander Brown, I, 276: a report concerning "New Britain," addressed to "The chief Treasurer of the Virginia, Muscovite, and East India Companies."

2. From Plutarch's essay "On the Fortune of the Romans" (trans. F. C. Babbitt, Loeb Classical Library), *Moralia*, IV.331. Alexander Brown, I, 275.

3. Trans. B. Perrin (Loeb Classical Library), I, 3. After the completion of this chapter, I noticed a similar application of the Plutarch passage in Edwin Björkman's "Atlantis: Protean and Immortal," *South Atlantic Quarterly*, 37:184 (April 1938).

4. *Medea*, lines 375–379.

5. Sixth edition (Boston, 1855), p. 191. For a skeptical view of all these guesses, see *The Writings of Thomas Jefferson*, ed. A. E. Bergh (Washington, 1903), XIII, 246.

6. The best ancient account of the Argonauts can be found in Diodorus Siculus, IV.40–56 (trans. C. H. Oldfather, Loeb Classical Library). Also the epic of Apollonius Rhodius, *Argonautica* (trans. R. C. Seaton, Loeb Classical Library).

7. From Latin *sinus*, "bay" or "inlet."

8. Dio Cassius, *Roman History*, XLIII.46 (trans. E. Cary, Loeb Classical Library). Also, Plutarch, *Julius Caesar*, 58.

9. The seventh edition (1678) of Sandys is extensively annotated with classical references and comment on native customs and Indian anthropology. For this couplet, see Book IX, lines 147–148; the Medea passage is Book VII, lines 53–61.

10. Inscription composed by F. J. Miller, who has translated the *Metamorphoses* in the Loeb Classical Library. See Martha W. Hiden, "Education and the Classics in the Life of Colonial

Virginia," *Virginia Magazine of History and Biography*, 49:21-22 (January 1941).

11. For interesting details of this sort, see Howard M. Jones, "The Literature of Virginia in the Seventeenth Century."

12. *Epistles*, II.1.250-253.

13. *Odes*, III.27.18-24.

14. Plutarch, *Themistocles*, 3 — a frequent epigram on disappointed ambition. For Caesar's jealousy, see Dio Cassius, XXXVII.52; Suetonius, *Div. Jul.*, 7; Plutarch, *Caesar*, 11. For the Numa story, see Plutarch, *Numa*, 15.

15. *A Discourse and View of Virginia* [1663], reprinted by W. H. Smith, Jr. (Norwalk, Conn., 1914), p. 3.

16. Ecclesiastes, 11:1; *Aeneid*, VIII.364-365.

17. Polybius, *Histories*, X.45-47 (trans. W. R. Paton, Loeb Classical Library).

18. Somewhat garbled, from the account of the elder Pliny, *Natural History*, 35.85, wherein Apelles retorts to the criticism with the words *Ne supra crepidam sutor* (Shoemaker, stick to your last).

19. Dio Cassius, XXXVIII.37; also Caesar's *Gallic War*, I.39-40. The Smith quotations are from his *Travels*, I, 179-180.

20. *Hippolytus*, lines 177-180.

21. Lucretius, *De rerum natura*, V.1211, IV.483-485.

22. Claudian, *Poems* (trans. M. Platnauer, Loeb Classical Library), I, 307; from the poem "On the Fourth Consulship of Honorius," quoted in the piece *On Loving-Kindness*. If not by Smith, the verses were written under his direction. For the same idea, the harmony of nature, see Ovid, *Metamorphoses*, I.5-31.

23. Donne's sermon is found in *The Sermons of John Donne*, ed. G. R. Potter and E. M. Simpson (Berkeley, 1959), IV, 264. For the opinion that Donne *did* write a tribute to Smith, see Edmund Gosse, *The Life and Letters of John Donne* (New York, 1899), II, 163.

III. Novanglia: Church, State, and the Classics

BIBLIOGRAPHY

Gummere, R. M., "Church, State, and Classics: The Cotton-Williams Debate," *Classical Journal*, 54:175-183 (January 1959).

Brockunier, S. H., *The Irrepressible Democrat Roger Williams* (New York, 1940).

Morison, S. E., *Builders of the Bay Colony* (Boston, 1930), esp. the chapters on Winthrop, Sr., and Ward.

Narragansett Club Publications, 6 vols. (Providence, 1866–1874).
The Puritans, ed. Perry Miller and T. H. Johnson (New York, 1938).
Selections from Cotton Mather, ed. K. B. Murdock (New York, 1926).
Walker, G. L., *Thomas Hooker, Preacher, Founder, Democrat* (New York, 1891).
Ward, Nathaniel, *The Simple Cobler of Aggawam in America*, ed. L. C. Wroth, facsimile ed. (New York, 1937).
"The Writings of John Cotton," J. H. Tuttle, in *Bibliographical Essays: A Tribute to Wilburforce Eames* (Cambridge, Mass., 1924), pp. 363–380.

NOTES

1. *The Winthrop Papers*, IV, 382–383 (Massachusetts Historical Society, Boston, 1944): from Winthrop's *Defence of the Negative Vote* (1643). For Hooker's view, see *ibid.*, p. 82.

2. For a modern edition of the Johnson work, see W. F. Poole, ed. (Andover, Mass., 1867).

3. For a theory that the aristocratic type of government in ancient states stemmed primarily from Pythagoras, see A. De-Latte, *La Constitution des Etats-Unis d'Amérique et les Pythagoriciens*, Bulletin of the Académie Royale de Belgique, 5th series (1948), pp. 383ff.

4. *Satires*, II.73–74 (trans. G. G. Ramsay, Loeb Classical Library).

5. Published by the Prince Society (Boston, 1865).

6. Claudian, *Carmina minora*, XX, "The Old Man of Verona" (trans. M. Platnauer, Loeb Classical Library).

7. *The New English Canaan*, ed. C. F. Adams, for the Prince Society (Boston, 1883).

8. From *De officiis*, I.22: "We are not born for ourselves alone."

9. *Epistles*, I.8.17 (to Celsus).

10. See K. B. Murdock, "Clio in the Wilderness: History and Biography in Puritan New England," *Church History*, 24:221 (September 1955).

11. Ovid, *Tristia*, V.6.13.

12. Polybius, *Histories*, VI.44.

13. For these sources, see Song of Solomon, 1:15; Ovid, *Tristia*, I.9.7; Pliny, *Epistles*, X.96; Pliny, *Natural History*, X.104.

14. For several such by-the-way allusions, see Cotton's *Way of the Congregational Churches Cleared* (London, 1648).

15. Pliny, *Epistles*, VI.16.

16. *Aeneid*, IV.188.

17. Polybius, *Histories*, VI.5–7; Aristotle, *Politics*, 1252a and b (from Williams' *Christenings Make not Christians*, pub. by Sidney S. Rider, in *Rhode Island Historical Tracts*, vol. 14 [Providence, 1881]).

18. For a discussion of this edict, see E. E. Bryant, *The Reign of Antoninus Pius* (Cambridge, Eng., 1895), pp. 194–196; E. G. Hardy, *Christianity and the Roman Government* (London, 1894), pp. 132–138, 145; for Constantine, see *Narragansett Club Publications*, III, 184, and IV, 441, 344.

19. *Of Plymouth Plantation*, by William Bradford, ed. S. E. Morison (New York, 1952), p. 4.

20. Vergil, *Aeneid*, I.150; Horace, *Epistles*, I.2.62. For Jerome's frequently quoted phrase, see his *In Jeremiam*, in Migne's *Patrologia*, vol. 24: *S. Hieronymi Opera*, vol. 4.

21. G. R. Potter, "Roger Williams and John Milton," *Rhode Island Historical Collections*, 13:113–129 (October 1920); A. S. P. Woodhouse, *Puritanism and Liberty* (London, 1938), *passim*.

22. Acts, 18:12–16.

23. *Satires*, XIII.180.

24. *Epistles*, 94.46.

25. From Williams' *Experiments of Spiritual Life and Health*. Seneca, *Epistles*, 99.19, 12.8, 120.14; also the *Consolatio ad Marciam*, 21.

IV. Colonial Reactions to a Classical Education

BIBLIOGRAPHY

Gummere, R. M., "Some Classical Side Lights on Colonial Education," *Classical Journal*, 55:223–232 (February 1960).

———— "A Scottish Classicist in America," *Publications of the Colonial Society of Massachusetts*, 35:146–161 (April 1944).

Broome, E. C., *A Historical and Critical Discussion of College Admission Requirements* (New York, 1902).

Collins, V. L., *President Witherspoon, a Biography*, 2 vols. (Princeton, 1925), esp. II, 229ff.

Cubberley, E. P., *Readings in the History of Education* (Boston, 1920).

Dexter, E. G., *History of Education in the United States* (New York, 1904).

Farish, H. D., ed., *Journal and Letters of Philip Vickers Fithian, 1773–1774* (Williamsburg, Virginia, 1945).

Gould, Elizabeth P., *Ezekiel Cheever, Schoolmaster* (Boston, 1904).

Latimer, J. F., and K. B. Murdock, "The 'Author' of Cheever's Accidence," *Classical Journal*, 46:391–397 (May 1951).

Lovejoy, A. O., *The Great Chain of Being* (Cambridge, Mass., 1936).

Morison, S. E., *Harvard College in the Seventeenth Century* (Cambridge, Mass., 1936).

Norton, A. O., "Seventeenth Century Harvard Text-Books," *Transactions of the Colonial Society of Massachusetts*, 28:361–438 (April 1933).

Seybolt, R. F., *The Private Schools of Colonial Boston* (Cambridge, Mass., 1935).

—— *The Public Schools of Colonial Boston* (Cambridge, Mass., 1935).

Tyler, L. G., "Education in Colonial Virginia," *William and Mary Quarterly*, 5, 6, 7 (April, July, October 1897; January, July, October 1898).

Walsh, J. J., *Education of the Founding Fathers of the Republic* (New York, 1935).

Witherspoon, John, *Lectures on Moral Philosophy*, ed. V. L. Collins (Princeton, 1912).

—— *Works*, 5 vols. (Philadelphia, 1802–1803).

Young, E. J., "Subjects for Masters' Degrees in Harvard College, 1655–1791," *Proceedings of the Massachusetts Historical Society*, 18:119–151 (1880–1881).

NOTES

1. Ezra Stiles, *Itineraries*, ed. F. B. Dexter (New Haven, 1916), p. 400.

2. *Letters on the American Revolution*, ed. F. R. Kirkland (New York, 1952), II, 13.

3. D. D. Wallace, *Life of Henry Laurens* (New York, 1915), pp. 182, 190, 434.

4. Ezra Stiles, *Literary Diary*, ed. F. B. Dexter (New York, 1901), III, 102–103.

5. For this and similar experiments, see *Virginia Magazine of History and Biography*, 3:9 (1895) and 6:70 (1898–1899).

6. K. M. Rowland, *Life of George Mason* (New York, 1892), II, 77.

7. *Virginia Magazine of History and Biography*, 11:117 (1903).

8. E. A. Stackpole, *The Sea-Hunters* (Philadelphia, 1953), pp. 35–39.

9. H. H. Brinton, in *Pennsylvania History*, 25:234–235 (1958).

10. Stiles, *Itineraries*, pp. 530–531.

11. S. E. Morison, *Builders of the Bay Colony* (Boston, 1930); V. L. Parrington, *The Colonial Mind* (New York, 1927).

12. Willard Connely, "Colonial Americans in Oxford and Cambridge," in *The American Oxonian*, 29:6–17, 75–78 (1942).

13. Stiles, *Itineraries*, p. 202.

14. *The Churches' Quarrel Espoused* [1717] (Boston, 1860), p. 173.

15. *Satires*, III.164, adapted by Samuel Johnson as "Slow rises worth, by poverty depressed."

16. Lloyd Lewis, *Sherman, Fighting Prophet* (New York, 1932), p. 4.

17. Stiles, *Itineraries*, p. 41.

18. In a letter to Benjamin Rush: *Old Family Letters*, ed. A. Biddle (Philadelphia, 1892), p. 456. Adams is mimicking Witherspoon's Scotch accent.

19. Epictetus, *Discourses*, 2.14.14.

V. William Byrd and Samuel Sewall: Two Diarists in the Ancient Tradition

BIBLIOGRAPHY

BYRD

Another Secret Diary (1739–1741), ed. Maude H. Woodfin and Marion Tinling (Richmond, 1942); further letters on pp. 191–475.

"Letters of William Byrd, II," in *Virginia Magazine of History and Biography*, 9 (October 1901–January 1902).

The London Diary (*1717–1721*), ed. L. B. Wright and Marion Tinling (Oxford, 1958).

The Natural History of Virginia, or The Newly Discovered Eden (Berne, 1737), ed. and trans. R. C. Beatty and W. J. Mulloy (Richmond, 1940).

The Secret Diary of William Byrd of Westover (*1709–1712*), ed. L. B. Wright and Marion Tinling (Richmond, 1941).

The History of the Dividing Line, ed. W. K. Boyd (Raleigh, 1929).

The Writings of Colonel William Byrd, ed. J. S. Bassett (New York, 1901), including a biography, *The History of the Dividing Line, Journey to the Land of Eden*, and *Progress to the Mines*.

SEWALL

Diary of Samuel Sewall, 3 vols., 1674–1729, Massachusetts Historical Society Collections, Series 5, V–VII (Boston, 1878–1882).

Samuel Sewall's Diary (selections), ed. Mark van Doren (New York, 1927).

Letter-Books of Samuel Sewall, 2 vols., 1685–1729, Massachusetts Historical Society Collections, Series 6, I–II (Boston, 1886–1888).

For other writings of Sewall, see J. L. Sibley, *Biographical Sketches of Graduates of Harvard University* (Cambridge, Mass., 1881), II, 345–364.

NOTES

1. Ovid, *Metamorphoses*, II.235–236.

2. For these charitable acts of Sewall, see his *Diary*, II.143; III.251; II.369.

3. Ovid, *Tristia*, II.279–280 (trans. A. L. Wheeler, Loeb Classical Library); Sewall's *Letter-Books*, II.29–30.

4. *Diary*, III.379.

5. Dated "VI Kal. Mart., 1671" (aged 18), *Letter-Books*, I.17–18. See Ovid, *Tristia*, I.1–2.

6. *Diary*, III.31.

7. Jane Sewall Gerrish, born in England, died in 1716. *Letter-Books*, II.84.

8. *Diary*, II.244, III.258.

9. *Letter-Books*, I.198.

10. *Metamorphoses*, XV.158–159 (trans. F. J. Miller, Loeb Classical Library); *Letter-Books*, I.372.

11. *Diary*, III.330.

12. *Another Secret Diary*, p. 276.

13. Byrd, *Secret Diary*, pp. 171, 410, 414. For Sewall, see his *Diary*, II.42, 55.

14. *Diary*, II.191; Vergil, *Eclogues*, III.111.

15. For a catalogue of Byrd's library, see J. S. Bassett, *Writings*, pp. 413–444.

16. Livy, 41.21; Thucydides, II.48–53; Lucretius, VI.1138–1286.

17. *Secret Diary*, for March 26: "I read Italian and some of my own to the ladies."

18. *Virginia Magazine of History and Biography*, 37:101 (April 1929).

19. *Another Secret Diary*, p. 386 (trans. W. A. Harris, Professor of Greek at the University of Richmond).

20. Martial, *Epigrams*, I.16.

21. Pliny, *Natural History*, X.43.

22. Philostratus, *Life of Apollonius of Tyana*, I.20 (trans. F. C. Conybeare, Loeb Classical Library).

23. *Diary*, II.111 ("The Deplorable State of New England").

24. See *The Three Dreaming Travellers*, in Sir Roger L'Estrange, *Fables of Aesop and other Eminent Mythologists* (London, 1708), p. 522.

25. Pliny, *Natural History*, 32.13.1; Juvenal, *Satires*, 12.34–36; *Fabulae Aesopicae*, ed. John Hudson (Oxford, 1718), p. 25.

26. See Lucian, *On the Syrian Goddess*, 8; also Strabo, *Geography*, 755.

27. See Athenaeus, *Deipnosophists* ("Banqueters in Wisdom"), IX.410c: "Scythisti Cheiromaktron Ekkekarmenos" (with head shorn in Scythian fashion to make a towel); trans. C. B. Gulick, Loeb Classical Library. Also Pliny, *Natural History*, 7.2.12.

28. *William and Mary Quarterly*, Series 2, 10:269–274 (1930).

29. M. C. Tyler, *History of American Literature* (New York, 1878), II, 66.

30. Ovid, *Metamorphoses*, XI.706–707 (trans. F. J. Miller); Sewall, *Letter-Books*, II.74.

31. Ovid, *Tristia*, I.7.31, V.2.71.

32. *Letter-Books*, I.387.

33. Horace, *Satires*, I.5.87 — "a town which cannot be fitted into my verse."

34. *Diary*, III.321.

35. *Letter-Books*, II.193.

36. *Diary*, II.137; *Revelations*, 15, 16 — the mark of the Beast and the pouring out of the Vials.

37. *Diary*, III.241.

38. *Letter-Books*, I.293.

39. For other instances where Sewall assisted young persons wrestling with Latin versification, see *Diary*, III.49, III.245–246.

40. *Letter-Books*, II.104.

41. *Diary*, II.22. October 5, 1714: Anne died on August 1 of that year.

42. *Letter-Books*, I.245.

43. *Letter-Books*, II.178. For Judge Quincy (Harvard Class of 1699), see W. S. Pattee, *History of Old Braintree* (Quincy, Mass., 1878). *Montem* is doubtless Mount Wollaston.

VI. Colonies, Ancient and Modern
BIBLIOGRAPHY

Gummere, R. M., "John Dickinson: The Classical Penman of the Revolution," *Classical Journal*, 52:81–88 (November 1956).

―――― "Thomas Hutchinson and Samuel Adams, a Controversy in the Classical Tradition," *Boston Public Library Quarterly*, July and October 1958, pp. 3–24.

―――― "John Wise, a Classical Controversialist," *Essex Institute Historical Collections*, 92:265–278 (July 1956).

Cook, G. A., *John Wise, Early American Democrat* (New York, 1952).

Hutchinson, Thomas, *The History of Massachusetts Bay*, ed. L. S. Mayo, 3 vols. (Cambridge, Mass., 1936).

LeBoutillier, C. G., *American Democracy and the Natural Law* (New York, 1950).

Miller, John C., *Sam Adams* (Boston, 1936).

Mullett, C. F., "Some Political Writings of James Otis," *University of Missouri Studies*, 4.3–4 (1929).

Sherwin-White, A. N., *The Roman Citizenship* (Oxford, 1939).

NOTES

1. Thucydides, I.34 (trans. C. F. Smith, Loeb Classical Library).

2. Lactantius, *Divine Institutes*, VI.8.6–9, from Cicero, *De republica*, III.33 (trans. C. W. Keyes, Loeb Classical Library).

3. *The Works of James Wilson*, ed. James DeWitt Andrews (Chicago, 1896), I, 91–93, 118; Cicero, *De legibus*, I.23–24.

4. Horace, *Odes*, III.4.20. For the subsequent enlargement by Adams of the notes taken at the trial, see *The Adams Papers*, ed. L. H. Butterfield (Cambridge, Mass., 1961), I, 211, n. 6.

5. Cicero, *De oratore*, I.55.

6. Vergil, *Aeneid*, XI.320–322 (trans. H. R. Fairclough, Loeb Classical Library); also *Aeneid*, XII.503–504, 190–191.

7. See Pliny, *Natural History*, III.3, for a list of towns in the province of Baetica, varying from complete self-government to a tributary status.

8. *Roman Antiquities*, III.11. It was King Tullus Hostilius who disagreed with the Alban Fufetius.

9. Juvenal, *Satires*, VI.223 (trans. G. G. Ramsay, Loeb Classical Library) — an often recurring provincial refrain.

10. Otis possibly reconstructed this from memory, recollecting Hanno's efforts with the Carthaginians. See Silius Italicus, *Punica*, XVI.32: "They lacked not skill, nor vigilance in war, nor the strong right arm" (from Otis' *Letter to a Noble Lord*, 1765).

11. J. C. Miller, *Origins of the American Revolution* (Boston, 1943), p. 231.

12. C. H. McIlwain, *The American Revolution: A Constitu-

tional Interpretation (New York, 1923), pp. 9, 11, 15, 135–136.

13. *Aeneid*, III.639–640.

14. Daniel Dulany, Sr., *The Right of the Inhabitants of Maryland to the Benefit of the English Laws* (Annapolis, 1728). See A. C. Land, *The Dulanys of Maryland* (Baltimore, 1955); also *Maryland Historical Magazine*, vols. 6 and 7 (1911 and 1912).

15. *Satires*, V.28–29 (trans. G. G. Ramsay), reading as above instead of *haud totum*.

16. Horace, *Epistles*, I.1.14. Also, Aristotle, *Politics*, 1255a.

17. Persius, *Satires*, V.100–101; Seneca, *Hercules furens*, 164–166.

18. Phaedrus, I.12.13–15.

19. *Aeneid*, I.199.

20. Published at Williamsburg in 1766 (ed. Earl G. Swem, Richmond, 1922). For Lactantius, see his *Divine Institutes*, II.8, trans. W. Fletcher (Edinburgh, 1871), I, 96.

21. *Germania*, 11.

22. See O. C. Kuntzleman, "Joseph Galloway, Loyalist" (Philadelphia, 1941).

23. S. G. Fisher, *The Evolution of the Constitution of the United States* (Philadelphia, 1910), p. 236.

24. Joseph Galloway, *Political Reflections on the Late Colonial Governments* (London, 1783).

25. For some of these sources, see Sallust, *Jugurtha*, 31.6; Vergil, *Eclogues*, IV.49, on the Golden Age; Cicero, *De officiis*, I.22.

26. *Agricola*, 12.

27. For these monopolies and restrictions, see Tacitus, *Annals*, XIII.31; Polybius, *Histories*, I.72; *The Writings of Benjamin Franklin*, ed. A. H. Smyth (New York, 1906), V, 161.

28. Vergil, *Aeneid*, VI.726–727; Sophocles, *Antigone*, 453–457 (trans. Thomas Francklin, London, 1759). For the same thought, see Chapter VII, note 36.

29. *De officiis*, II.44.

30. *The Writings of Samuel Adams*, ed. H. A. Cushing (Boston, 1904–1908), II, 262.

31. Hamilton, *Works*, ed. H. C. Lodge (New York, 1904), I, 87.

32. Two frequently used phrases in colonial days, borrowed from Plutarch, Cicero, Petronius, and Marcus Aurelius; see George Wythe in *Journals of the Continental Congress* (Washington, D.C., 1906), VI (1776), 1071.

33. Cicero, *De oratore*, III.2. Hutchinson, *History*, III, 326–327.

34. Miller, *Sam Adams*, p. 19.

VII. Logan, Franklin, Bartram: Humanist, Pragmatist, Platonist

BIBLIOGRAPHY

LOGAN

Hindle, Brooke, *The Pursuit of Science in Revolutionary America* (Chapel Hill, 1956).
Johnson, Joseph E., "A Statesman of Colonial Pennsylvania — James Logan" (unpub. diss., Harvard University, 1943).
Tolles, F. B., *James Logan and the Culture of Provincial America* (Boston, 1957).

FRANKLIN

Gummere, R. M., "Socrates at the Printing Press," *Classical Weekly*, 26:57–59 (December 1932).
Franklin, W. T., ed., *The Private Correspondence of Benjamin Franklin* (London, 1817).
Labaree, L. W., ed., *The Papers of Benjamin Franklin* (New Haven, 1959—).
Smyth, A. H., ed., *The Writings of Benjamin Franklin*, 10 vols. (New York, 1905–1907).
Van Doren, Carl, *Benjamin Franklin* (New York, 1952).

BARTRAM

Gummere, R. M., "William Bartram, a Classical Scientist," *Classical Journal*, 50:167–170 (January 1955).
Earnest, E., *John and William Bartram* (Philadelphia, 1940).
Fagin, N. B., *William Bartram, Interpreter of the American Landscape* (Baltimore, 1933).
Fairchild, H. N., *The Noble Savage* (New York, 1928).
The Travels of William Bartram, ed. Mark van Doren (New York, 1928); with introduction by John L. Lowes (New York, 1940); ed. F. Harper (New Haven, 1958).

NOTES

1. *The Writings of Thomas Jefferson*, ed. A. E. Bergh (Washington, D.C., 1905), II, 94–96.

2. S. E. Morison, *Builders of the Bay Colony* (Boston, 1930), pp. 269–288.

3. Hindle, *The Pursuit of Science in Revolutionary America*, p. 191.

4. W. J. Bell and R. L. Ketcham, "A Tribute to John Bartram," *Pennsylvania Magazine of History and Biography*, 83:446–451 (October 1959).

5. *American Bibliography*, vol. 1, items 2625 and 3160 (New York, 1941). See also *Papers of Benjamin Franklin*, I, 113, n. 2.

6. *The Diary of the Reverend Ebenezer Parkman*, ed. Harriette M. Forbes (Westborough, Mass., 1899), pp. 128, 260.

7. Johnson, "Statesman of Colonial Pennsylvania — James Logan," pp. 492–493.

8. Bernard Faÿ, *Franklin, the Apostle of Modern Times* (Boston, 1929), pp. 140, 38, 149.

9. See I. B. Cohen, *Benjamin Franklin* (Indianapolis, 1953), pp. 273–274.

10. Pliny the Younger, *Panegyric* (to Trajan), 68.6.

11. Tacitus, *Histories*, I.1.

12. Ovid, *Tristia*, II.563 (trans. A. L. Wheeler, Loeb Classical Library). See also *Papers of Benjamin Franklin*, I, 48–51.

13. *Satires*, I.61–62 (trans. G. G. Ramsay, Loeb Classical Library).

14. *Aeneid*, III.56–57.

15. Horace, *Epistles*, I.7.46–95.

16. Cicero, *Tusculan Disputations*, V.5.

17. See above, p. 100.

18. Pliny, *Natural History*, II.106; Plutarch, "Natural Questions," XII, from his *Moralia* (ed. W. W. Goodwin, Boston, 1898), III, 503. See also Smyth, *Writings of Benjamin Franklin*, I, 63.

19. Vergil, *Aeneid*, VIII.485–488.

20. Smyth, *Writings of Benjamin Franklin*, I, 47–48, 197–198. Manilius, *Astronomica*, I.104.

21. See *The Private Correspondence of Benjamin Franklin*.

22. Vergil, *Aeneid*, I.291.

23. *Georgics*, IV.237–238 (trans. Theodore C. Williams).

24. Horace, *Odes*, I.15.32.

25. This section is an outgrowth of some early thoughts on Bartram — see R. M. Gummere, "Apollo on Locust Street," *Pennsylvania Magazine of History and Biography*, 56:86–87 (January 1932).

26. References are to the first edition of Bartram's *Travels* (van Doren–Macy–Masius ed.).

27. John L. Lowes, *The Road to Xanadu* (Boston, 1927).

28. We possess two travel journals of the elder Bartram, to Lake Ontario in 1751 and to East Florida several years later.

29. Horace, *Satires*, I.5.41–42.

30. Arber and Bradley, *Travels and Works of Captain John Smith* (Edinburgh, 1910), II, 564.

31. *Travels*, p. 26. For Byrd's view, see *The Writings of Colonel William Byrd*, ed. J. S. Bassett (New York, 1901), pp. 8–10, 21, 100–102.

32. See *Travels*, pp. 313, 315, 357ff, 388ff.

33. See A. O. Lovejoy and G. Boas, *Primitivism and Related Ideas in Antiquity* (Baltimore, 1935). For Bartram's "primitive state of man, peaceable, contented, and sociable," see *Travels*, p. 110.

34. *Folia sensibilia, insecta incarcerantia*, pp. 19, 373–374.

35. *Travels*, p. 159.

36. *Mens agitat molem* — a near translation of Vergil, *Aeneid*, VI.726–727.

37. R. M. Gummere, "Classical Precedents in the Writings of James Wilson," *Transactions of the Colonial Society of Massachusetts*, April 1937, pp. 534–535.

38. Pliny, *Natural History*, X.52; *Travels*, p. 35.

39. E. Greenlaw, "Modern English Romanticism," *Studies in Philology*, 22:538 (October 1925).

40. See J. Notopoulos, "The Symbolism of the Sun and Light in Plato's *Republic*," *Classical Philology*, 39:163–172, 223–240 (July and October 1944).

41. Pliny, *Epistles*, IV.30, describing a spring which pours into the "Larian Lake [Como], ebbing and flowing by regular amounts three times a day." *Travels*, p. 196, commenting on the "ebullition" and recession of the Manate Spring.

42. *Travels*, p. 220.

43. Jared Sparks, *Life of Alexander Wilson* (Boston, 1834), p. 61; Pliny, *Natural History*, X.34, 49; Aristotle, *Historia animalium*, VIII.16 (600a); *Travels*, p. 234. See *Papers of Benjamin Franklin*, III, 116, for Peter Collinson's disagreement with this hibernation theory.

VIII. The Transatlantic Muse

BIBLIOGRAPHY

BRADSTREET

Campbell, Helen, *Anne Bradstreet and Her Time* (Boston, 1891).

Ellis, John Harvard, ed., *The Works of Anne Bradstreet* (New York, 1932).

Norton, Charles Eliot, ed., *The Poems and Prose of Anne Bradstreet* (New York, 1897).

FRENEAU

Leary, Lewis, *That Rascal Freneau* (New Brunswick, 1941).
Pattee, Fred L., ed., *The Poems of Philip Freneau* (Princeton, 1902, 1903, 1907).

HOPKINSON

Hastings, G. E., *The Life and Works of Francis Hopkinson* (Chicago, 1926).
Sonneck, O. G. T., *Francis Hopkinson, the First American Poet-Composer* (Washington, D.C., 1905).

LIVINGSTON

Sedgwick, Theodore, Jr., *A Memoir of the Life of William Livingston* (New York, 1833).

TAYLOR

Johnson, T. H., ed., *The Poetical Works of Edward Taylor* (Princeton, 1943).
Stanford, D. E., ed., *The Poems of Edward Taylor* (New Haven, 1960).

TOMPSON

Fussell, E. S., "Benjamin Tompson, Public Poet," *New England Quarterly*, 26:494–511 (December 1953).
Hall, H. J., ed., *Benjamin Tompson's Poems* (Boston, 1924).

TRUMBULL

Cowie, Alexander, *John Trumbull, Connecticut Wit* (Chapel Hill, 1936).
The Poetical Works of John Trumbull, 2 vols. (Hartford, 1820).

NOTES

1. T. S. Eliot, *The Sacred Wood, Essays on Poetry and Criticism* (London, 1920), p. 43.

2. See, for example, H. S. Jantz, *The First Century of New England Verse*, American Antiquarian Society (Worcester, Mass., 1944).

3. Seneca, *Epistles*, 82.3, and Vergil, *Eclogues*, 2.62.

4. Tibullus, I.1.4, I.10.45.

5. Perhaps a version from memory of Cicero, *Philippics*, X.10.

6. That is, "harmonize."

7. Turnus, the Rutulian leader. For Nisus and Euryalus, see *Aeneid*, 9.176–449.

8. A reference to the First Continental Congress.

9. From the "Second Day" of the *Divine Weeks.*
10. See pp. 204–220 in T. H. Johnson's edition of Taylor's *Poetical Works.*
11. Juvenal, *Satires,* VI.165. Horace, *Epistles,* I.2.69; *Odes,* III.2.31, II.14.14.
12. Line 1259: "Permit me at least to know for what crime I am to die."
13. Martial, *De spectaculis,* I.
14. These passages, mostly ascribed to Theocritus, are discussed by W. T. Weathers, "Edward Taylor, Hellenistic Puritan," *American Literature,* 18.1:18–26 (1946). See also *The Greek Anthology* (trans. W. R. Paton, Loeb Classical Library), V.263, IX.372; *The Greek Bucolic Poets* (trans. J. M. Edmonds, Loeb Classical Library), pp. 234, 316ff, 112, 348.
15. *Aeneid,* VI.873–874.
16. *De spectaculis,* I.
17. See V. L. Parrington, *The Colonial Mind, 1620–1800* (New York, 1927), pp. 368–381.

IX. *Jonathan Boucher, Toryissimus*

BIBLIOGRAPHY

Gummere, R. M., "Jonathan Boucher, Toryissimus," *Maryland Historical Magazine,* 55:138–145 (June 1960). For other letters and memoranda, including correspondence with George Washington, see p. 138, note 1, of this article. The adjective "Toryissimus" was used by M. C. Tyler, the historian, to describe the Tory balladist, Jonathan Odell, and by Sir Walter Scott as a humorous name both for himself and for his friend, the Bishop of Llandaff. See Tyler's *Literary History of the American Revolution* (New York, 1897), II, 99.

Boucher, Jonathan, *Reminiscences of an American Loyalist, 1738–1789,* ed. Jonathan Bouchier [a grandson] (Boston, 1925).

—— *A View of the Causes and Consequences of the American Revolution, in Thirteen Discourses Preached in North America between the Years 1763 and 1775* (London, 1797).

Letters from Jonathan Boucher, ed. W. C. Ford (Brooklyn, 1899).

Parrington, V. L., *The Colonial Mind, 1620–1800* (New York, 1927), pp. 214–218.

NOTES

1. *Georgics,* IV.127; *Aeneid,* I.73–75.
2. Boucher, *Reminiscences,* p. 101.

3. *Aeneid*, VI.852ff — the prophecy of Rome's greatness.
4. Cicero, *Catiline*, I.25, II.20; Sallust, *Catiline*, 14, 40.
5. Thucydides, Book I.
6. *Reminiscences*, p. 128.
7. Pliny, *Epistles*, VI.10.
8. Polybius, *Histories*, VI.57.
9. Ovid, *Fasti*, I.639; Vergil, *Georgics*, I.508; Jonathan Edwards, *Works* (ed. of 1844), I, 386.
. 10. Cicero, *De divinatione*, II.2; Juvenal, *Satires*, XIV.71.
11. Ovid, *Metamorphoses*, IV.428.
12. Diogenes Laertius, *Vitae philosophorum*, VI.41. (In this version it was a ram, not a pig.)
13. Juvenal, *Satires*, II.24.
14. *Aeneid*, IV.622.
15. Pliny, *Epistles*, IV.13.
16. *Aeneid*, VII.586.
17. Diogenes, II.82–83.
18. S. E. Morison, *Builders of the Bay Colony* (Boston, 1930), p. 103.
19. Sallust, *Jugurtha*, CII.7.
20. Juvenal, *Satires*, X.168.
21. Dionysius, *Antiquitates Romanae*, VII.1 (trans. E. Spelman, London, 1758).
22. Tacitus, *Annals*, III.41.
23. From Plutarch's *Praecepta gerendae reipublicae*, 16.
24. *Antiquitates Romanae*, IX.28–33.
25. Pliny, *Epistles*, VI.20.
26. *Aeneid*, XII.645.
27. Dionysius, *Antiquitates Romanae*, VI.38–41, VII.54.
28. *Character-Sketch* (London, 1920), pp. 21ff.

X. *The Classical Ancestry of the Constitution*

BIBLIOGRAPHY

Gummere, R. M., "The Classical Ancestry of the United States Constitution," *American Quarterly*, 14:3–18 (Spring 1962).
Barker, Ernest, *The Political Thought of Plato and Aristotle* (London, 1906).
Beck, James M., *The Constitution of the United States*, revised by J. T. Adams (New York, 1941).
Chinard, G., "Polybius and the American Constitution," *Journal of the History of Ideas*, 1:38–58 (January 1940).
Elliot, Jonathan, ed., *Debates on the Constitution*, 5 vols. (Washington, D.C., 1836–1845).

Farrand, Max, ed., *The Records of the Federal Convention of 1787*, 4 vols. (New Haven, 1911–1937).

The Federalist Papers, ed. Clinton Rossiter (New York, 1961). The following numbers contain references to or reflections from classical authorities: 1, 4, 6, 8, 9, 14, 16, 18, 21, 25, 34, 38, 39, 41, 43, 45, 49, 52, 55, 58, 63, 70, 75.

Ford, P. L., ed., *Essays on the Constitution of the United States* (Brooklyn, 1892).

—— *Pamphlets on the Constitution of the United States* (Brooklyn, 1888).

McIlwain, C. H., *The Growth of Political Thought in the West* (New York, 1932).

Walsh, C. M., *The Political Science of John Adams* (New York, 1915).

The Writings of James Madison, ed. Gaillard Hunt, vols. 1–4 (New York, 1900–1910).

NOTES

1. "Men of experience in popular assemblies as well as theorists." See Zoltán Haraszti, *John Adams and the Prophets of Progress* (Cambridge, Mass., 1952), p. 220.

2. Lucien Price, *Dialogues of Alfred North Whitehead* (Boston, 1954), pp. 161, 203.

3. Farrand, *Records of the Federal Convention of 1787*, III, 15, 76, and *The Papers of Thomas Jefferson*, ed. J. P. Boyd (Princeton, 1950—), XI, 286.

4. For this view (undoubtedly the correct one), see G. Chinard, "Polybius and the American Constitution," *Journal of the History of Ideas*, 1:40 (1940); Haraszti, *John Adams*, pp. 15–16, 24; John Fiske, *The Critical Period of American History* (Boston, 1899), pp. 224ff.

5. For example, see E. A. Freeman, *History of Federal Government in Greece and Italy* (London, 1893), p. 249; T. R. Glover, *Democracy in the Ancient World* (Cambridge, Eng., 1927), p. 135.

6. Elliot, *Debates on the Constitution*, IV, 192.

7. *The Snare Broken* (Boston and London, 1766).

8. *Politics*, 1279a, b (trans. H. Rackham, Loeb Classical Library). For Solon's compromise, see 1273b.

9. *Saturday Review of Literature*, December 20, 1930.

10. For these various statements, a few selected out of many, see Aristotle, *Politics*, 1288a, 1286a, 1295b, 1252a, 1302a, 1297a.

11. Cicero, *De republica*, II.41 (quoted by Nonius), and *De legibus*, III.28.

12. *De republica*, III.33 (quoted from Lactantius, *Divine Institutes*, VI.8.6–9). Also, *De legibus*, II.8, I.18. For this law as applied to colonial problems, see Chapter VI above. For a general discussion of Stoicism and statecraft, see R. M. Wenley, *Stoicism and Its Influence* (Boston, 1924), pp. 31–37.

13. Polybius, *Histories*, VI, esp. chaps. 18, 11, 2–5, 9–10, 43–51 (trans. W. R. Paton, Loeb Classical Library); Chinard, "Polybius"; Kurt von Fritz, *The Theory of the Mixed Constitution in Antiquity* (New York, 1954); F. W. Walbank, *A Historical Commentary on Polybius* (Oxford, 1957).

14. All these cases, at various times, were discussed in connection with the Constitution.

15. Pausanias, *Description of Greece*, VIII.30, 37 (trans. W. H. S. Jones and H. A. Ormerod, Loeb Classical Library).

16. Polybius, VI.47.7–9; Aristotle, *Politics*, 1261a, 1264b; J. K. Hosmer, *Life of Thomas Hutchinson* (Boston, 1896), p. 88; John Adams, *Works*, ed. C. F. Adams (Boston, 1856), X, 18, 102; Thomas Jefferson, *Writings*, ed. P. L. Ford (New York, 1905), XI, 396, and XII, 141; W. C. Greene, "Platonism and Its Critics," *Harvard Studies in Classical Philology*, 61:63–64 (1953).

17. The principle of representation was known to the Greeks and Romans: the founding fathers erred in calling it a purely modern one. See J. A. O. Larsen, *Representative Government in Greek and Roman History* (Berkeley, 1955), esp. pp. 18, 31, 41, 69, 83, 105, 111, 120; A. H. J. Greenidge, *Handbook of Greek Constitutional History* (London, 1920), pp. 223, 233; Sir Ernest Barker, *Greek Political Theory* (London, 1925), pp. 34–35.

18. *The Works of Alexander Hamilton*, ed. H. C. Lodge (New York, 1904), I, 217, 246; Elliot, II, 235.

19. *Writings of James Madison*, published by Congress (Philadelphia, 1865), I, 293ff; Strabo, *Geography*, XIV.3.3; Farrand, I, 110.

20. Farrand, III, 92.

21. Elliot, V, 219; III, 129–130.

22. Farrand, III, 153, 184.

23. Farrand, I, 441; Elliot, V, 252; Plutarch, *Themistocles*, 20.

24. *Histories*, II.38; Elliot, III, 209–211.

25. Farrand, I, 307: from the Third Philippic of Demosthenes. See *Federalist*, No. 18.

26. Elliot, IV, 59.

27. From "The Continentalist," 1782.

28. G. C. Osborn, *John Sharp Williams* (Baton Rouge, 1943), pp. 294, 330.

29. Exemplified by the overworked complaint against tyranny,

from Juvenal, VI.223: *Hoc volo, sic iubeo; sit pro ratione voluntas.*

30. Aristotle, *Ethics*, 1102a and 1235b, describes "the man of superior qualities." The subject is discussed at length in R. M. Gummere, "Classical Precedents in the Writings of James Wilson," *Transactions of the Colonial Society of Massachusetts*, 32:534 (1937).

31. Farrand, I, 323.

32. R. B. Morris, *Alexander Hamilton* (New York, 1957), p. 114.

33. Farrand, I, 157.

34. Elliot, III, 494; II, 146.

35. Farrand, I, 74, 254, 261.

36. John Fiske, *The Critical Period of American History* (Boston, 1899), p. 281; Farrand, II, 103.

37. The circumstances of this episode are not entirely clear. See *The Writings of Thomas Jefferson*, memorial edition (Washington, D.C., 1903), II, 173ff, and XIV, 170–171; W. C. Rives, *The Life and Times of James Madison* (Boston, 1859), I, 284; Elliot, III, 160; Farrand, I, 329.

38. Plutarch, *Lysander*, 7; *Federalist*, Nos. 25, 41.

39. Elliot, V, 398.

40. Morris, *Hamilton*, pp. 378, 537.

41. Farrand, I, 490–493; I, 310.

42. Ford, *Pamphlets on the Constitution*, pp. 189–190.

43. Aristotle had noticed this problem in *Politics*, 1265b, 1270b; *Federalist*, No. 75.

44. Elliot, V, 167; Farrand, I, 151, 153.

45. *Letters of Richard Henry Lee*, ed. J. C. Ballagh (New York, 1911–1914), II, 472.

46. For similar comments, see Ford, *Pamphlets on the Constitution*, I, 7, 42.

47. *Histories*, VI.11.1.

48. Elliot, III, 175–176.

49. *Ibid.*, I, 443; III, 568.

XI. Epilogue: Adams and Jefferson

BIBLIOGRAPHY

Gummere, R. M., "The Classical Politics of John Adams," *Boston Public Library Quarterly*, 9.4:167–182 (October 1957).

Boyd, Julian P., ed., *The Papers of Thomas Jefferson* (Princeton, 1950 —).

Butterfield, Lyman H., ed., *The Adams Papers* (Cambridge, Mass., 1961 —).

Cappon, Lester J., *The Adams-Jefferson Letters*, 2 vols. (Chapel Hill, 1959).

Commager, Henry S., "Leadership in Eighteenth-Century America and Today," *Daedalus*, Fall 1961, pp. 652–673.

Haraszti, Zoltán, *John Adams and the Prophets of Progress* (Cambridge, Mass., 1952).

Lehmann, Karl, *Jefferson, American Humanist* (New York, 1947).

Way, A. S., trans., *Hymns of Callimachus and Cleanthes* (London, 1934), pp. 35–36.

NOTES

1. Tacitus, *Annals*, IV.33.
2. E. L. Godkin, *Unforeseen Tendencies of Democracy* (London, 1898), p. 35.
3. Literally, "put your finger on your lips," Juvenal, *Satires*, I.160.
4. Theocritus, *Idylls*, 17.9.
5. Homer, *Iliad*, 24.527.
6. Martial, *Epigrams*, 10.47: "On the Happy Life," quoted in full and translated by Franklin in *Poor Richard's Almanack* for 1750.

INDEX